THE CHAIN

SIR BRADLEY WIGGINS

WITH JOHN WOODHOUSE

THE CHAIN

HarperCollins*Publishers*

NOTE
Some readers may find the descriptions of sexual abuse
and drug use in this book distressing.

HarperCollins*Publishers*
1 London Bridge Street
London SE1 9GF

www.harpercollins.co.uk

HarperCollins*Publishers*
Macken House, 39/40 Mayor Street Upper
Dublin 1, D01 C9W8, Ireland

First published by HarperCollins*Publishers* 2025

1 3 5 7 9 10 8 6 4 2

A catalogue record of this book is
available from the British Library

HB ISBN 978-0-00-876773-0
PB ISBN 978-0-00-876774-7

All images are from the author's personal collection, with the exception of:
p4 top left, p5 bottom right, p6 top right, p6 bottom right: PA Images/Alamy
Stock Photo; p4 top right, p4 bottom: Doug Pensinger/Getty Images; p5 bottom
left: John Berry/Getty Images; p6 top left: Mark Large/ANL/Shutterstock;
p6 bottom left: WENN Rights Ltd/Alamy Stock Photo; p8 bottom left:
Karwai Tang/WireImage/Getty Images

Printed and bound in the UK using 100%
renewable electricity at CPI Group (UK) Ltd

To Ben, Bella and Ava.
And to Courtney.

CONTENTS

Quietly I turn the handle and enter my walk-in wardrobe. Flicking the light on, I look along the rails. Sharp suits, parkas, two-tone shoes. The uniform of a monstrous creation. I shut the door behind me and click the lock.

I see the shelf I'm after. On it is my Sports Personality of the Year trophy and my Olympic gold medal from London. I take the medal in my hand. Big, weighty, it represents an incredible high. Hundreds of thousands of people lining the route, shouting, cheering, as I power towards time trial glory at Hampton Court Palace. I even sat on a throne at the finish. The lad from Kilburn was king that day.

There's a cubbyhole. I reach in and take out a small tightly folded piece of paper. Carefully, hands shaking slightly in anticipation, I unwrap it and look at its contents. Snow white but far from innocent. I lay the medal flat on the shelf and carefully empty the paper onto its surface. Nike, the goddess of victory, vanishes. On the engraved metal it's hard to tidy the powder into a line. I do my best and then roll-up a £20 note. Bending my head slightly, I snort the cocaine.

'What a fall from grace!' I laugh.

I use the words deliberately. I'm well aware there's a huge element of self-sabotage in what I'm doing. This might look like 'Wiggo', the cheeky chappy from 2012, saying, 'Look how funny I am, doing coke off my London Olympic medal!' but there's so much more to it than that. There's a layer of anger, a layer of self-hatred. What was the point? In any of it? What was the point?

I'm disrespecting this medal, this particular medal, because I blame it for the person I've ended up. It's the ultimate manifestation of my wish, right now, that none of it, the Tour de France win, the Olympics, none of it, had happened. The ultimate desecration of what I've achieved.

I wish I'd crashed, I tell myself.

PROLOGUE

For a long time I never knew who I was.

When the cameras captured that famous picture of me sat on the throne, both hands raised in a Churchillian victory 'V', I'd just won gold in my home Olympics, ten days after becoming the first Briton to win the Tour de France. In that moment I'm a man with the world at my feet. Sporting hero. People's champion. Legend. Everyone knows who Bradley Wiggins is. Everyone, that is, but me.

The only skin I ever felt comfortable in was that of a cyclist. I believed in myself as that person. I could execute Olympic finals perfectly. I could win the biggest bike race in the world. But off the bike I was a shadow man. Distant memories of abandonment and abuse left me feeling totally exposed. For years, each and every pedal stroke put distance between me and those echoes. But when finally I stopped cycling they grew louder and louder until eventually I was overwhelmed by their presence, a mental collapse which took me to depths I never knew existed.

The years after winning the Tour de France and London Olympics would be an infinitely greater test than anything I'd ever faced on the bike. And that left me weighed down with a single overriding question – *Was it all worth it?* It felt like my descent only happened because I was Sir Bradley Wiggins who achieved what he did. But then I started going back through my life. Slowly I began to piece together a tangled past of deep torment and hurt. I saw the relationship I formed in my head with an absent father, this mythical figure racing a bike, and I saw the desire it created in me to be like him. I saw the abuse I suffered at the hands of my childhood coach, and I saw my isolation, the complete absence of help. I saw how I achieved something incredible and then hid inside the shell of a character so people wouldn't see the real me, with my shattered self-esteem. I saw how I conquered the world for people I looked on as big brothers and father figures, only to feel they abandoned me too. And I saw the bleak reality of the witch-hunt that followed. In the end, I saw that I'd abandoned myself. The consequence was years of self-sabotage.

Tunnelling deeper and deeper into my life opened the door on who I am in a way I'd never previously understood. Parts of that process were incredibly difficult. There are things in my past that shouldn't happen to anyone. But in analysing each and every episode and incident, I finally see the links that hold them together. The links that make me the person I am. I see *The Chain*.

Sharing my chain in this book means revealing my true self, my inner soul, in a way I've never thought imaginable.

Every last shield, every last deflection mechanism, has gone. The result is there are elements that will shock. But full disclosure is vital, because by talking about my chain, frankly and honestly, I hope I can help others to come to terms with theirs. Not that long ago, I'd have found the idea that I could help anyone navigate a route through their issues totally laughable. How on earth could someone who'd crashed so spectacularly be the one at the wheel? But this person who so resolutely kept everything locked away has come to see that the way to recovery is sharing. If we don't talk about our problems we condemn ourselves, and others, to keep travelling the same dark pathways. I want people to understand they're not alone in their battles; that no matter how tightly shackled they might feel, the key to freedom is not to pull against their chain, it is to understand it. There are, I promise, those out there who will help you do so. In my case, they were my children. Ultimately, when I stared into the abyss, they were the ones who pulled me back from the brink. You are my lifesavers. I will never know how to thank you.

Today, 13 years after the summer that defined me, I have finally defined who I am. The disguises have gone. I've made peace with myself. Recently I put some photographs out in my new home. In one of them a toddler, held in the arms of his dad, feeds the ducks in the park. I look at that little boy and for the first time in my life I comprehend who he is and what happened to him.

It's the final link. *The Chain*, I realise, has gone full circle.

CHAPTER 1

IDENTITY

*'So many contradictions. So many
things that don't add up.'*

If I try really hard I can summon up a memory of being happy as a child. I'm lying in a single bed being spooned by my mum. She's listening to a Lionel Richie cassette. It's her favourite, and she plays it over and over again, the two of us just lying there with it going round and round in our heads. It's restful, soothing. I feel secure and safe. Me and my mum in our little one-bed flat.

I'm overwhelmed by feelings of abandonment. When I say there've been periods in my life where I've wondered who I am, I mean it quite literally. The most basic facts that everyone else takes for granted are missing. Identity issues? I might as well have put out a welcome mat.

I'm told there was once talk of naming a maternity ward after me in Ghent, where I entered this world (they like me in Belgium – I might be the first British winner of the Tour de France, but I'm also the last Belgian winner of the Tour de France), but I don't actually have a birth certificate. All I have is a certificate of citizenship granted to me when I was ten by the Australian embassy. And a dual British/Australian passport. Although I qualify for an Irish one. As of now, the best way I can describe myself is as a Belgian-born dual citizen of Britain and Australia with Irish heritage. I say 'as of now' because day by day I'm looking for jigsaw pieces in the hope of making the picture just that little bit clearer. All too often, however, the relevant piece is missing and once again I'm left scrabbling around on the floor.

The Australia bit comes from my dad, Gary Wiggins, a bike racer who met my mum Linda when he came over to London to cement his name in the sport. Together they moved to Ghent so he could ride on the lucrative 'Sixes' circuit, a relentlessly tough series of lung-bursting indoor races which shifted from city to city across Europe. Mum told me I had a Belgian passport as a kid but she changed my nationality when I was six because otherwise I'd have had to do national service when I turned 18. It made a certain amount of sense. I was born in Belgium, that much is an undeniable fact. But then a few years ago I googled 'national service in Belgium' and found it was abolished in 1972. When I put this to my mum the story changed. Now I was on my dad's Australian passport until I was six. After Dad left Mum and me when I was a toddler, depositing us back in London before disappearing back to mainland Europe, she was scared he could up and off with me to Australia any time he wanted. Subsequently, she told me, she wrote to the Home Secretary to get my citizenship changed to British.

I was used to confusion. When it came to information about my dad, I'd grown up in a wasteland. I expect Mum felt she was protecting me, but actually I was left with a big empty hole which bit by bit I tried to fill myself. It was like trying to plug a mineshaft with a teaspoon. In the end, I've concluded that being Australian until I was six is the most likely version of events. It fits with Dad travelling to England with me and Mum when they split up. Being on his passport, if he hadn't been with us I wouldn't have got into the country. But there's no certainty in any of this. I've questioned my own sanity at times trying to work it all out. The only certainty is that, in my mid-40s, it's crazy I don't know who I am. The more I've thought about it, the more I've realised just how damaging it's been to be denied a basic understanding of my past, and how significant an impact that feeling of being cast adrift had, not only on my childhood, but on the person I became.

Gaps are everywhere. I've no idea, for instance, how long Mum and Dad had been together by the time I was born in 1980. All I know is he was already married, with a daughter, my half-sister Shannon, who's eight years older than me, when they met at the cycling track at Paddington Recreation Ground. Right on the doorstep of the flats in Kilburn where she grew up, Mum would go down and watch the racing. I imagine Gary, with his jet-black hair and athletic physique, was a pretty imposing sight. In his early twenties, he was also a few years older than her. Whatever the attraction, I've been told very little about my mum and dad's life together, just as it was never explained to me why he left. Instead, I just got a certain version of events, told in a very confusing way.

Obviously, I remember nothing of what happened in the short time I was in Belgium. All I know is what Mum said, that when I was one and a half, Dad left us and never came back. But even then I find myself doubting the timeline. Was that really it, as far as me and my dad were concerned? There are pictures of me with him when I'd say I'm clearly older, more like three. I also remember sitting on a couch in Belgium eating Jaffa Cakes with this large gentleman with black hair. One of the few things my mum told me about my dad was that he loved Jaffa Cakes so much he used to eat a packet a day. Could I have remembered that aged one and a half? Or is that more likely to be a memory from four or five? I must have spent time around him as an infant for that to sink in. It took me years to work out that surely I saw him more than I was told, but it makes total sense. He was racing in Europe right up until 1987 before, as far as I can tell, his visa ran out and he had to go back to Australia, so why wouldn't I have seen him on and off? It's hardly out of the realms of possibility that we went over to the continent to see him or he came the opposite way.

Then there were the stories. Several times Mum told me, light-heartedly, how one day when Dad was washing his bike in the basement of our Ghent apartment I went down the stairs to find him and he threw a bucket of water over me. I came back up to her soaking wet. Looking back now, that confuses me. Could I walk down a flight of stairs on my own at one and a half? And if I did make it down to the basement and he threw a bucket of water over me, an 18-month-old toddler, that's not playfulness, it's child abuse. Mixed messaging was a speciality. Mum laughed when she told me Dad pushed her through a glass door when he was drunk. I expect she was disguising her own painful memories of life with Gary by recalling horrific incidents in a jovial manner – I've done it myself – but as a child it was incredibly confusing to hear bad things being told in a jokey way. It seemed to me that unpleasant, dangerous or reckless behaviour was being dressed up as something silly or insignificant.

Another time Mum told me that Dad, who, like pretty much every 'Sixes' rider, relied on amphetamines to get him through the endless days of racing, would hide his drugs in my nappy when we crossed international borders. But I look at that drugs story now and wonder, *Can that tale actually be true?* Surely nobody would be so stupid as to take a risk like that. So many contradictions. So many things that don't add up. But as a child you accept what you're told. It's only as I've got older that I've stopped in my tracks thinking, *Surely that can't be true.* Sadly, the likelihood is that we're way too far down the line for the veracity of any of these stories ever to be established.

While Mum was telling me these tales about Dad, she was also glorifying him as a cyclist. The message I got was clear – as a dad he was useless, but on the bike he was an absolute beast. Unsurprising, then, that bikes were part of my life from as young as I can remember. My nan always reminds me of what happened when I got my first bike aged two, a little red one with a basket on the back. I took one look at the stabilisers and blurted, 'I don't want them bloody things on it!' I'm not sure what the bigger part of that story's meant to be. The fact I could ride straight off without stabilisers or the fact I was swearing at the age of two.

After three years without Dad in our lives, a gap which maybe confirmed in Mum's mind that he wasn't coming back, a stranger moved into our flat. 'This is your new dad,' Mum told me. Straightaway, she left me to sleep on my own and instead shared a sofa bed with this man, Brendan, in the living room. I never regained that same relationship with my mum. The way I saw it, I'd now been abandoned by my parents. At the age of five, I'd lost them both. It took a while to flourish, but the day Brendan moved in a seed was sown. In my head, I began to form a makeshift relationship with my real father – *OK, he might not be here, but I'm going to be like my dad. I can do what he did, go where he went. I can be his mirror image.* From the word go, my relationship with my dad was tied up in the most complicated of knots. To this day, it's never been undone.

A year later, for my sixth birthday, my grandad George got me something more akin to a proper bike. That was it then. There was a big oval path in the courtyard between the blocks of flats where we lived. In my head it was only one thing – a track. As my nan says, I used to go round, and round, and round. Meanwhile, back at home, Brendan was being imposed on me as Gary's replacement. He'd come in at night and read me books. 'Why don't you call me dad?' he'd ask. I didn't. A couple of years later, his own son, Ryan, came along, and I felt that was the spark for Brendan's attitude to me changing dramatically.

For a while as a kid there was a bit of me that wanted to be a footballer. Mum wasn't impressed. 'You're a cyclist,' she'd tell me. 'It's in your genes.' It was a message she never tired of drumming into me. When I was eight, she even took me to watch the Ghent Six Day. Sitting in the stands, I was overwhelmed by this amazing spectacle. Brightly clad riders hurtled round a tiny wooden track at ridiculous speeds while hundreds of passionate fans hollered their lungs out, their shouts amplified by a roof so low it felt like it was falling in. I fell in love with the Ghent Six Day there and then. It was so exciting. Heart beating out of your chest exciting.

It wasn't just Mum. I heard how I was fated for success from others too. After I won the Tour de France, a documentary was screened, *A Year in Yellow*, following me during that period. I watched it again recently, amused to see my nan pop up. She's not one for a lot of fuss and on *A Year in Yellow* only agreed to be interviewed so long as she had the back of her head to camera. When I watched filmmaker John Dower ask her, 'Why do you think he's so good at cycling?', her reply really stuck with me. 'It's in his genes, isn't it?' That was so much the narrative that I had growing up. And it's true. I still put my whole cycling career down to the DNA I inherited from my dad.

I didn't actually need those constant reminders of my absent dad's sporting heritage. The fact he was a cyclist certainly wasn't lost on me, and while there wasn't much cycling on TV back then I did my best to follow it, a particularly vivid memory being the end of the 1989 Tour de France. Watching at my nan's house, I was swept up in the drama of the final stage, a time trial in Paris, as the American Greg LeMond beat bespectacled French hero Laurent Fignon to win the race by eight seconds, the narrowest margin ever.

But the moment that changed everything came on 29 July 1992. I was messing around outside with some mates when my mum called me in. The track cycling was on at the Barcelona Olympics. Chris Boardman was about to go in the final of the men's individual pursuit. I sat in front of the TV and watched him set up on the track. Even now I can picture that futuristic black bike with its yellow Lotus logo. Four and a bit minutes later, Chris had overtaken his German counterpart and become Britain's first Olympic cycling gold medallist in 72 years. I was 12 and knew straightaway I wanted to emulate his feat. Another 12 years later I did just that, with the man himself, my mentor no less, stood trackside, when I won my first Olympic gold.

Chris captivated me for two reasons. He was an extraordinary bike rider and an ordinary bloke. I was aware of other great British cyclists, such as Philippa York (formerly known as Robert Millar) and Sean Yates, who I'd see on TV riding the Tour, but they were somehow distant. Being them felt out of reach. They lived full-time on the continent, part of a tiny smattering of British riders in big European teams. I was this lad from a council flat in Kilburn. How the hell could I ever do that? Chris, on the other hand, was different. He wasn't from a glamorous background. He'd grown up on the Wirral. Yes, he raced all over the world, but he did so from home. Doing what he did seemed achievable. He was a viable role model, not a hero from another world.

The day Chris won gold at Barcelona was the day I became a cyclist. Immediately, Mum wrote to British Cycling and told them she had a son who wanted to take up racing. They wrote back, inviting me to a race meeting on the Hayes bypass in west London. I couldn't have been more excited. The countdown was on to start my journey to Olympic glory. When finally the day arrived, we headed out west to Hayes where the bypass had been closed to allow hundreds of bike racers to blast up and down for a few hours. Straightaway my mum spotted a few old faces from the Archer Road Club, the cycling outfit my dad had once ridden for. It had been more than a decade since she'd gone to events with Dad, but a lot of the same people were still at the club, including the race organiser Stuart Benstead.

'This is Bradley,' she said, 'Gary Wiggins' boy.'

There was no holding him back. 'Wiggo's boy? Really? Does he want to join our club?'

'Wiggo's boy.' Stuart wasn't the only one to say it. A couple of others looked me up and down. 'He's Wiggo's lad!' It was the moment that finally I had a dad. He might not have actually been there, but I had a dad. No one said, 'Oh, isn't his dad around?' It was just, 'That's Gary Wiggins' son!' And when you haven't got a dad, that means a lot. To hear those words was as incredible as it was inspiring.

Joining the Archer Road Club was a done deal. That same day I was introduced to a club coach, Stan Knight, a 72-year-old former military policeman. Immediately he took hold of my wrist. 'I've never felt a pulse like it,' he said. He looked me in the eye – 'You're going to be the greatest cyclist this country has ever produced.' From that moment on, Stan told anyone who'd listen that I was special, that I was destined to be the best. I liked the fact he had belief in me. And there was one thing in particular. Unlike everyone else, Stan didn't tell me I was special because of who my dad was. He told me *I* was special. Me. And right there sits the most awful paradox. The man who gave me belief in myself, who made me feel like my dream was possible, was the man who for the next three years sexually abused me.

CHAPTER 2
STAN

*'The person who abused me is the person
who made me believe in myself.'*

When I'm 13, my mum gives me a load of photos of my dad that she's found. There he is, in his cycling kit, racing. It's a definite 'Wow!' moment, like he's been brought to life in my hands. Those photos become my greatest treasure. Eventually, I'm allowed a little reading lamp. One night, after I've been out on my bike, I look at one of the photos. In the dim light, I turn it over. 'Dear Dad,' I write. 'I've been racing at Herne Hill like you used to do.' It's as if I'm talking to him, writing him a letter. Straightaway I hide the photo from my mum. I have a little tin I use to put coins in. I empty them out, place the photo at the bottom, and put the coins back on top. I would be so embarrassed if she found it.

I understand now that writing that 'letter' was sheer escapism. I wasn't prompted to do it. No one was ever going to see what I'd written. It was just for me. I found solace in the process. It made me feel like there was a way out – I hate being here, hate this life. My dad's out there somewhere, and I want to be like him.

In another life I might have been a snooker player. When I started to find success on the bike, I was interviewed for a Q&A in a magazine. Under 'If you weren't a cyclist, what would you be?', I put 'A professional snooker player in the World Championships', the reason being we had a 'Steve Davis' six-foot table in our living room. My mum would be sitting there trying to watch the telly while me and Ryan would be edging round the sides, cue at 45 degrees to stop banging it into the wall. I'd had a little bit of success on the green baize. When I was 12, we went to Pontins at Camber Sands and I won the kids' pool tournament. Subsequently, Pontins invited me to Rhyl to compete in a 'grand final' against the victors from their other holiday camps. I didn't win, but since we were up in the north-west I was adamant we should head to Ribble Cycles, in Preston. Other manufacturers were available, but Ribble had sponsored the Great Britain Olympic team at Barcelona. No two ways about it, my first bike had to be a Ribble.

It was on that bike that I headed out for my first Sunday ride with Stan. It was dangerous for a kid my age to ride through central London and so Brendan dropped me at his house in Acton. Stan was waiting in some weird old cycling kit – woolly top, loose shorts, the kind of thing you'd have seen on someone in the 1950s as they rode through the countryside on a classic touring bicycle with panniers. As we pedalled the 40 or so miles to Burnham Beeches and back, I expect people thought it rather touching, this old chap riding along with a keen young lad; two very different generations brought together by cycling, a throwback to altogether more innocent times. We made good progress, arriving back at Stan's a couple of hours before Brendan was due to collect me. So, with time to kill, we sat in his kitchen chatting for a while. And then Stan looked at me. 'Do you want a massage?' That would have sounded unusual had massage not always been a big part of cycling, an established way of aiding recovery after a strenuous ride.

Stan took me up to his bedroom and, with my cycling shorts rolled up, I lay on my back on his bed. After a while he asked me to turn over so he could do the back of my legs. Before I could say or do anything, he pulled my shorts down. 'Let's get these off so I can get to your glutes.' I was startled. I felt embarrassed, uncomfortable. *What the hell?* The glutes are essentially the muscles in your buttocks and there wasn't even a towel over me. I felt powerless to say anything. He was the coach, I was just some kid.

He started massaging my glutes. As he did so, his thumbs were going inside my anus. There I was, a boy just turned 13, on the bed of a 72-year-old man. He'd pulled my shorts down and was doing this to me. I lay there, frozen, unable to say a word, a child devoid of the confidence to do anything about what was happening. For his part, Stan was doing his best to make what he was doing appear perfectly normal. 'Don't worry, all the other lads do this.' Eventually, he finished. We went back downstairs and not long afterwards Mum and Brendan arrived. 'We've just had an incident,' I heard him tell them as he answered the door. I've no idea how the rest of that conversation went, but I assume he was smoothing the way, coming up with a scenario that worked for him, so if I said anything I'd be blamed for getting the wrong impression of what this kind old man was doing to help me recover after a long ride. I didn't say anything. My world at this point was cycling. It was all I had. My life in the flat had been getting messier and more unbearable by the day. Speak up and chances were, whether I was believed or otherwise, my only source of escape – cycling – would be taken away. I'd be trapped.

As Ryan got older I felt that Brendan got more combative with me. If Grandad was there, sometimes he'd step in – 'I think he's had enough now' – or occasionally my mum would tell Brendan to stop. They'd argue and he'd storm out. It felt like Brendan could lose it anywhere. One time I went to a parents' evening with him. Mum stayed at home. She said she wasn't going because it would be embarrassing listening to the teachers saying how bad I was doing. As we sat with one teacher, I saw a mate of mine and gave him a bit of a smirk. Immediately I felt intimidated by Brendan staring daggers at me. If looks could kill. He barked at me.

If my stepdad wanted me to be scared of him, then he won. I was definitely scared of him. I also knew he was pathetic. He thought he was tough as old nails, puffing his chest out like a big man. But he wasn't; he was weak, taking his anger out on a child a fraction of his size. I'd behave myself out of fear.

After a harsh reprimand, I'd go off and cry. We were in a two-bed flat now and I shared a bunk bed with Ryan. My life was unbearable, and so, on that top bunk, I disappeared into a different one. I spent hours up there – I had to. Ryan was eight years younger than me but we had the same bedtime. Once he'd gone to bed, I wasn't allowed to sit in the living room, and so there I was, a teenager, lights out at half-seven. It was like being in prison – in more ways than one. The bunk bed had a tubular frame so I'd poke all sorts of stuff down there. If ever I wanted to look at anything I'd get a pen and scoop it back out. That sounds extreme but too often my own private tastes or possessions had been pried into or mocked. When I got an Alanis Morissette cassette, for example, I knew immediately I'd get stick for it. If I had anything with a picture of a woman on it, my stepdad would be straight in there. 'Oh, you fancy her, do you?' In a way that felt mocking. And so, up in my little hideaway I removed the sleeve from the box, flicked the plastic cap off the corner tube, and stuffed it inside.

Sleep, understandably, never came easy. For years I've looked back and thought, *I must have had insomnia*. But of course not only was my metabolism set to a completely different rhythm to my half-brother's, but my general unease in that flat meant relaxation was impossible. Within those walls I was utterly controlled. Even when I was 15 or 16 and off school ill I wasn't allowed to rest in the flat on my own. I'd have to go up to my nan's house. Bedtime offered no respite from the overbearing atmosphere. I was never allowed to shut the bedroom door, and Mum and Brendan never shut theirs. In fact, from my position in the top bunk I could see into their room and hear them arguing.

Occasionally, early in the evening, I'd hear Brendan come into our room. Mum wouldn't let him watch football in the living room with her and so I'd see the flicker of the portable TV light up the walls. He'd have the sound down so he didn't wake Ryan. Meanwhile, if he saw I was trying to sneak a look, he'd bark at me. 'You're not supposed to be up.' I'd have to roll over and face the wall. I mean, Jesus, could I not just watch the football like any other teenager? Headphones and a radio were my lifesaver. Either not tired enough or too scared to sleep I'd tune into DJs like Caesar the Geezer. Other times I'd listen to tapes of Billy Connolly, back to back, over and over. I found comfort in the voices in my ears.

The photos of Dad that my mum gave me changed everything. For that kid on top of the bunk bed in that flat, living in his own head because the everyday world so often let him down, Dad was a saviour. Here was someone who gave me hope, someone I could emulate, someone who differentiated me from everyone else on the estate and got me through the tough times with my stepdad. Add to that the way my mum glorified him as a cyclist, I saw that – as his son, with his attributes, those genes people kept mentioning – I too could be special on a bike. Her narrative helped me see that possibility. Mum would also tell me that Dad not being around was in my favour. 'You'd never have been a cyclist. He'd have knocked it out of you. He'd have been too critical.' That mix of Dad's absence and the way he was spoken about was the only thing in childhood that gave me a drive. My cycling dream was all I had. I wasn't going to give up on it for anything. And Stan was a big part of that.

After that first incident at his house, nothing happened with Stan for a few weeks. I came to understand this was how he operated. His methodology was to act incrementally, going slowly, step by step. Everything would settle back down for a while and then he'd start again, massaging my legs while his hands moved gradually upwards. If I said anything – 'What was that?' – he'd mutter, 'Sorry, just an accident.' Constantly, he was touching me, at the same time presenting himself as just a bit clumsy rather than the calculated paedophile he clearly was. It maybe explains why I was never afraid of him. I knew something wasn't right, and there was an underlying uneasiness in being around him, but I wasn't fearful of him. It wasn't like I was being overpowered or attacked, the kind of things that as a kid you imagine are part and parcel of sexual assault.

But I did feel very alone. This was something that was happening to me. Just me. It wasn't until decades later I learned that was actually far from the case and Stan was abusing other young riders, among them a lad, around 18 months older than me, who I accompanied, with Stan, to a hostel at Litton Cheney in Dorset. There was only the three of us in the place. So two boys, aged 13 and 14, sharing a little dormitory room in a tiny village in the middle of nowhere, with a grown man. Clearly, Stan felt completely empowered in this situation. One time he insisted on showing us how to clean our scrotums. It's important in cycling to maintain hygiene to avoid saddle sores and infections. For him, that provided the perfect excuse to violate us. He made us strip off and get in the shower with him. He then held our scrotums to show us the required method. I avoided having a shower for the rest of the week.

Another time, I was up vomiting half the night. I woke the next morning with no pyjamas on. I had no memory at all of taking them off. As I lay there naked, my mind went back to the previous evening. Stan had wanted us to eat with him, but we didn't like the look of what he was making and instead had made ourselves some noodles. Stan was really angry that we were cooking for ourselves rather than him preparing our meal. All the time we were cooking he was hovering over us and the food. I know somehow, be it through the food or another way, he drugged me. I know that sounds outlandish but there's no other explanation for what subsequently happened – the sickness, the memory loss. All I remember is puking up, and Stan being there, helping me. Afterwards, nothing. I've since heard stories of people who've been drugged with date-rape substances like Rohypnol. My own experience feels horribly similar. It was precisely the way Stan operated, working clinically and deliberately to get what he wanted. By way of explanation, Stan said the next morning he'd taken my pyjamas off while I was asleep because he'd felt my temperature and I was too hot. But I've never been a heavy sleeper, and yet somehow I didn't stir while some bloke was taking my pyjamas off? I don't believe it for one second. It fits totally with him administering some sort of drug.

Next day, I was completely washed out and so he and the other boy went cycling while I stayed behind. I felt desperately uncomfortable and lay miserably on my bed thinking about how I couldn't wait for the week to end. Sadly, there were still a few more days to negotiate. A couple of nights later, fed up with the freezing cold dorm, I added a second duvet to my bed. Again, I woke in the morning and my pyjamas were gone. There was also only one duvet. And there was Stan again with his excuse. He'd checked my temperature in the night, found that I was hot, and so, for the second time that week, he'd taken my pyjamas off. That was it. From that point on, I slept in my cycling shorts. I knew they'd be harder to get off than pyjamas because they had bibs – straps over the shoulders. They were my favourite Z-Peugeot cycling shorts, as worn by Greg LeMond. It's things like that which remind me just how young, innocent and helpless I was when all this was happening.

I will never know what Stan did while I was asleep those two nights. I can speculate, but it's not going to help me going forward. All I can say is that the abuse continued for the next three years, a constant insidious feature of my life right up until I was 16. As I got older, while he'd suggest different things, the pattern stayed pretty much the same. He'd open up a conversation that would present whatever he wanted to do as normal. 'If you want to get erect,' he'd say during a massage, 'feel free to ejaculate. Don't be shy in front of me. Feel free to come on your belly while I'm massaging you.' Often, he'd add, 'Can I do it for you?'

The last time I had to put up with Stan's nonsense was at my nan's caravan at Camber Sands in East Sussex. We'd gone there alone for a week-long training camp. By then Stan was 75 and couldn't stay the pace with me so I'd go out cycling on my own. Back at the caravan, he'd massage me, still coming out with the same old disgusting stuff. I remember that week especially because every night I'd watch the Atlanta Olympics on the telly. That Games is remembered as being a low point for Great Britain as we came back with only one gold medal, won by Matthew Pinsent and Steve Redgrave in the rowing. But it also featured my greatest sporting memory, Michael Johnson's world-record-breaking run in the 200 metres. Sadly, in my mind, Stan and that race will forever be intrinsically linked. Every time I see that footage I'm instantly reminded of him.

By the time we went to Camber Sands, Stan was losing control of me, and he could sense it, becoming more and more spiteful as he realised I was no longer this kid he could take advantage of. Gone was that meek 12-year-old boy whose pulse he'd taken. I was 16, strong, single-minded, ambitious to be up there on the biggest sporting stages, like the one I was seeing right there on the telly. The more self-assured I became as a cyclist, the more I found it easier to cope with Stan. He'd become an irrelevance. Everyone was telling me what a great cyclist I was, how I was turning into a young man with an incredible future, and there he was wanting me to stay a little kid forever and preserve me in aspic. He'd have a go at me for eating toast with Philadelphia cheese on it and stupid stuff like that, but now I had the wherewithal to stand up to him. I could see how f**ked up the whole situation with him was.

'You're a weirdo,' I told him.

'What do you mean, a weirdo?'

'You know what I mean.'

From then on, I vowed to stay as far away from him as possible and was relieved when, at the end of 1996, I was told by my mum and another coach, Sean Bannister, that I was leaving Stan and Sean would coach me instead.

The last time I saw Stan was four years later. I've still got the picture. I'm 20, just back from the Sydney Olympics, standing next to him, proudly displaying my team pursuit bronze medal. As difficult as it is to stomach, the confidence Stan gave me as a cyclist resulted ultimately in that prize. He was the first person ever to make me feel that I had some worth. Straightaway he told me I was going to be the greatest cyclist. The person who abused me is the person who made me believe in myself. He made me who I was. I know how mad that sounds, but that is my truth. I had a dad who wasn't there and I had a stepdad who I felt afraid of. And then I had Stan, who told me I could be anything I wanted to be. Another reason, in hindsight, why I put up with what he was doing. It's easy to see the manipulation. I'm sure Stan knew that telling me what I was so desperate to hear, filling me up with the self-esteem that was so obviously lacking, was a direct pathway to getting what he wanted. But I'm sure also that he did genuinely believe in my ability.

I once saw Mike Tyson talk about the first time legendary boxing trainer Cus D'Amato clapped eyes on him sparring as a 13-year-old in a juvenile detention centre in New York. D'Amato watched him for less than ten minutes and declared right there and then that he was going to be heavyweight champion of the world. 'How did he know I was the one?' wondered Tyson. 'How did he f**king know?' It reminded me so much of my own first meeting with Stan – 'You're going to be the greatest cyclist this country has ever produced.' He didn't just say it once. He'd tell anyone who'd listen, 'This kid's got something special.' I honestly, to this day, think he knew I was destined for greatness. And it happened. I became what he predicted I would. Ultimately, only he knows whether he meant what he said, and he took that to the grave with him. But you have to remember he was a cycling coach as well as a paedophile. He abused me horribly and repeatedly, but at the same time there was the coaching. The fact he was a paedophile doesn't discount everything he knew about the sport. If Stan simply wanted access to children I'm sure there were easier ways he could have gone about it. What I do believe is that the better I was, the more fascinating I was to him from a sexual point of view. I was, of course, also fatherless, and I have read enough news stories to know that one of the biggest things paedophiles look for is a broken home. There's no threatening figure to worry about, plus that child may unwittingly be looking for attachment.

Whatever Stan's motivation, it's a terrible thing that a coach should combine abuse with the giving of belief. How, as a child, are you supposed to reconcile those two things? I never came to terms with that contradiction. Years later it would come back to haunt me. That boy who watched Chris Boardman win the Barcelona Olympics never had a clue what his biggest challenge would be.

CHAPTER 3

ISOLATION

'Self-worth was never given to me in any other way.
Everything in my life depended on the bike.'

It's a weekday afternoon. As usual, I've skipped school and gone out on my bike. Afterwards, I've nipped to the newsagents for some protein drinks. The route home takes me right past the front gate of St George's, the Roman Catholic school which is literally below my bedroom window. It's the end of the school day and everyone's pouring out. I've only one thought – I need to get back as quickly as possible. I'm wearing the uniform of the 'rival' school, St Augustine's. Hanging around isn't a good idea. I'm hurrying along, when I see about 40 pupils coming out the gate. Nothing unusual. But then there's this other group of 10 or 15 others who seem to have come out of nowhere. They're causing a massive commotion and there in the middle of it all is a teacher trying to sort it out. In a flash I see what looks like a lad punching him. The teacher's on the floor. Total hysteria. Kids running in all different directions. It looks like there's going to be a huge ruckus and so I run back to the flat as fast as possible. Not long after, my mum's watching the *Six O'Clock*

News. She calls out to me, 'The headteacher's been stabbed over the road!' I can't believe what I'm hearing. The head, Philip Lawrence, has been murdered trying to protect a pupil. I look down out of the window and there are blue lights everywhere. I stay quiet. I don't tell Mum I was there when it happened. I don't want to be interviewed as a witness. I'm scared what might happen to me if the gang who've done it find out.

Next afternoon, I'm out again on my bike. I head out past Wormwood Scrubs, to Acton, Hanger Lane and on outwards across west London. I'm just riding down the hill into Perivale when I see a load of television crews outside a big detached house. I know instantly what's going on. It's where Philip Lawrence lives. Or lived. I feel sick to the pit of my stomach.

One reason why Stan was able to do what he did for so long was because I lived in isolation. I don't just mean in my flat. I mean generally. Isolation.

Before I found cycling, and for a little while afterwards, I had mates like everyone else. I used to go to White Hart Lane to watch Spurs when Gazza and Gary Lineker were playing. I'd stand on the terraces with my mates among all these blokes shouting and screaming, a tribal mentality which actually made me feel really protected. I wasn't a Spurs fan, but I was a fan of Gazza and Lineker because of what they'd done at Italia 90. Funnily enough, though, it was an opposition player who had the biggest influence on me.

Ryan Giggs was 17, just six years older than me, when I saw him turn out for Manchester United. As I watched his brilliance I had only one thought. *I want to be like that one day.* I didn't mean as a footballer. I was never going to be good enough. But I knew, if I put my mind to it, I could be exceptional at something.

The same thing happened two years later when I was gripped by the sight on TV of a soaked-to-the-skin Lance Armstrong winning the World Championship road race in the pouring rain in Oslo. I was awestruck. This bloke was just eight years my senior. Next day I had a race myself. It was chucking it down and so, with Lance's antics in Norway fresh in my mind, I pretended I was him. Naturally, I get stick for saying Lance was a hero of mine. You get held over a barrel for saying something like that. But I'm not going to lie. I was a kid searching for inspiration and he handed it to me in spades, same as he did for thousands of other young riders. To say otherwise is just erasing history. Seeing people realise their dreams makes your own dreams seem real, and that day I saw Lance realise his.

I needed something to aim at, because life, inside and outside the flat, was grim. Needles from drug addicts littered the estate. Adults told us not to touch them, but that didn't stop some kids picking them up and pretend-stabbing each other. The dangers don't bear thinking about, but it just shows how normalised we all were to that environment, just as we were to the dealers blithely walking around. We knew what they were up to without anyone ever actually telling us.

I guess it's what people mean when they describe kids as being 'streetwise'.

This was our playground. We'd kick a ball around and then after a while ballgames were banned and so we'd just hang around doing nothing. The older lads would be looking in car windows. Nicking car stereos was the thing in those days. I was having none of that. I knew the difference between right and wrong – Grandad had instilled that in me – and I was terrified of being involved in something criminal. School was the same. Every day kids would be going down the wrong path. At break-time, we'd play football, then peer pressure began to take over. A group of lads started going off for a smoke. One day I went with them. Immediately I wished I hadn't and ran back to school. Thing is, once you resist that peer pressure and turn away from 'the group' you mark yourself out as different. They turn on you. I'd always avoided negative attention by being the class clown, doing impressions of teachers or just generally messing around, but when I got to 12 or 13 and began to ostracise myself out of fear of getting into serious trouble, and also to concentrate on cycling, I became a target.

Then one day a group of lads surrounded me on my way back to the estate. They started making up some nonsense, saying I'd disrespected one of their mums. A few of them held me still, and then another lad produced a broken Lucozade bottle and placed its jagged edge against my throat. I was absolutely terrified. Whether he had any intention of using it or not, I'll never know. Luckily for me a guy in a white van drove past. 'Oi! Leave him alone!' The boys loosened their grip and I managed to wriggle free and run home. From that day on I was always watching my back. At the same time it hit me that I had no one in my life to step in and defend me. A dad or a big brother would have sorted those lads out, warned them off. Me? I felt totally alone.

I lived in my own head and within that solitude cycling became a fantasy world which, time and again, I withdrew into. By then I'd started buying cycling magazines. I'd flick through the pages and see pictures of cyclists racing through the sun-drenched fields and snow-capped mountains of Italy, France and Spain and imagine myself in their position. And then there was Belgium, where I was born. 'If you want to be a professional cyclist,' my mum would tell me, 'you have to move to Belgium, because that's the heartland.' Belgium fascinated me. It was, after all, where my dad had achieved so much of his success. I had posters of Belgian legends such as Johan Museeuw, who won both the Tour of Flanders and Paris–Roubaix cobbled classics three times, and Freddy Maertens, who pocketed Grand Tour stages for fun. I'm pretty sure I was the only kid in Kilburn with pictures of Belgian cycling heroes on his bedroom wall.

It wasn't just magazines and posters. I'd record every race that was on telly. Pedalling away on the turbo trainer in the flat, I'd watch epic stages of the Tour de France, pretending I was climbing the mountains with my heroes. As well as the actual races, I'd watch cycling videos back-to-back. *A Sunday in Hell*, the classic film following the 1976 edition of Paris–

Roubaix, featuring the great Eddy Merckx, was watched so often that even now I can recite it word for word. I'd also hunt down niche documentaries about professional cycling teams and was particularly captivated by Motorola, the giant American outfit Lance Armstrong rode for. Behind-the-scenes footage showed how the team stored all the day-to-day bits and pieces for the riders – gels, towels, energy bars, etc. I set straight about turning my wardrobe into a carbon copy, with nutrition bars, flannels, everything, all set out perfectly. My little bedroom became, in essence, the manifestation of my determination to live the life of my dad.

That investment, that process, gave me a haven to lose myself in while negotiating my way through life with my stepdad. I noticed that his treatment of me seemed to be getting worse and worse. One time when I was 15 we were on the way to a race in Norfolk. Me and Ryan were in the back of the car arguing. I wanted to lie down ahead of the race. He didn't want to give up any space. In the end he started crying. That was it. Brendan turned round and just lost it. I really felt his wrath. My mum was screaming, 'You're going to crash the car!' I was supposed to get on my bike and race after that.

The extended family would sometimes go to Butlin's at Bognor Regis on Christmas Eve and stay until a couple of days before New Year. Of all the kids there, I was by some distance the eldest. Little children would be running around all over the place while the adults were drinking and playing cards. Of course, there'd be accidents and, naturally, it was me who got the blame. One time, Brendan seemed absolutely incensed by me. He put his face right next to mine and screamed something at me. I was desperately trying not to cry in front of everyone. My uncles were letting me have a shandy, play a bit of cards, and I wanted to look like a man. I walked out the room and cried my eyes out.

The non-stop stress of living in those conditions manifested itself physically as well as mentally. For a while I developed a tic, a noise in the back of the throat. I wasn't aware I was doing it but my nan used to say, 'God, you sound like a pigeon!' I also bit my nails relentlessly and walked around with a stoop. A few years ago I came across a video of me aged 16. I'd just won a track competition and was waiting to go up on to the podium. My then wife Cath spotted it first. 'I can't believe your posture!' I was hunched, head down. Cath had never seen me at that age before. I was cowed, because that's how Brendan made me feel. And there he was in the background, clapping. I got off the podium and he stuck his arm round me. No one ever saw it, but I felt firmly under his rule. Very occasionally I'd stand up to him, but it always ended in the same way.

'You're not my f**king real dad,' I told him in one argument.

'Well, go and find your real dad!' he shouted.

There was a stand-off. We squared up to one another. I backed down. I was very nonconfrontational. It just wasn't my way, but underneath I saw him for exactly what he was. My guess is that the better I got at cycling and the more my real dad's prowess as an athlete was mentioned, the more his own manliness felt threatened. Most blokes who like to throw their weight around are insecure.

Whatever the reason for Brendan acting this way, the end result of living with him and my mum was a child who grew up feeling marginalised and vulnerable. Mum was emotionally guarded and then I had to watch the dynamic with my stepdad, the unconditional love he had for his own son while I seemed to receive the opposite. There was never any levelness. I always felt helpless, exposed. Ultimately that comes down to never having a father figure in my life, but I was in no way unusual in that. But this was my normality and, as far as I knew, it was every other kid's normality too. Just part of growing up. When you're young you form a view of life based on what happens within your own four walls. It was only as my own kids got older that I came to realise how twisted a domestic set-up I feel it was. I have never ever come near to treating my children in a remotely similar manner. As far as I was concerned, my upbringing was a normal childhood and I was being cared for. And actually, bearing in mind the area I grew up in, the way I saw it I had it better than most. At least I had a stepfather, whereas lots of kids on our estate didn't have a dad around at all. Not just dads actually. Either parent could disappear overnight.

A friend's mum packed her bags one day and left. I bumped into his cousin in a pub a couple of years ago and asked what had happened to my old mate. It was truly tragic to hear. His dad became an alcoholic, the family imploded, and the happy young lad I remembered had developed deep mental health issues and tried to kill himself. Another schoolfriend was a great footballer, but by Year Nine he'd stopped playing. His brother was a crackhead so there's every chance he started doing the same thing. And then one day he brought a sledgehammer into school and tried to attack someone. Naturally, he was expelled. I never heard from him again until he contacted me about five years ago on Facebook. I was relieved to hear he'd turned his life around. When people talk about kids going off the rails, it's no wonder considering the environment so many grow up in. There's so much trauma for them to deal with. Like I say, my homelife was far from great, and set me up for a whole load of issues in later life, but down the years I've heard some truly dreadful stories about other children's suffering in that area. One day in 2007 my mum showed me the local paper. 'Have you seen this?' The lad who held the broken bottle to my throat, Samuel Duncan, had been jailed, along with his partner, for 22 years for a systematic campaign of child abuse against their four-year-old disabled daughter. I felt sick to my core when I read it.

I'm so grateful, and fortunate, to have had a nan and grandad who did show me love. More than that, they pretty much brought me up. Grandad picked me up from school every day and I'd have my dinner at their place, in the same block of flats, before they'd send me back home at seven. I loved being there as much as I hated going home. Actually, make that feared going home. So often I'd see the clock ticking round to seven and think, *I'd give anything to stay here*. Nan and Grandad were the only stability I had. They weren't physically affectionate, but then no one in my family was. Whatever the generation, no one ever told you they loved you or hugged or kissed. I don't say that as a criticism, it's just the way it was. What Nan and Grandad did do, though, was show affection by acting totally the opposite. So if they said to me, 'Bloody hell, Bradley, you're useless aren't you?', I knew they were really saying how fond they were of me! Sounds mad, but there'll be thousands of people who grew up in families like that who'll know exactly what I'm saying.

Nan and Grandad also provided an incredible amount of light relief from the daily crap at the flat. Nan worked in Tie Rack on Oxford Street and would come home with carrier bags full of ties and handkerchiefs. For years she smoked fifty Silk Cut a day, her fags kept in a novelty cigarette box – open the lid and a duck bobbed down and came back up with a cigarette in its beak. It wasn't the only Del Boy-esque feature. Theirs was a two-bedroom flat in which they'd raised three daughters. In fact, until Mum sorted out her own place, for a short while that two-bed flat was home to me, Mum, Nan, Grandad and my mum's two sisters. When finally all the girls had moved out, Grandad wasted no time turning that spare bedroom into a bar. It was like the British Legion in there – optics on the wall, beer towels on the bar, peanuts, dartboard, TV, slot machine. He even had a bell for last orders. No swearing though. Grandad was a classic bloke of that era, liked a drink, liked a flutter, but knew his manners. He'd never eff and blind in the household because there were women around, although he did develop his own form of cursing, basically removing the 'F'. 'Ucking good goal that, wasn't it?' The walls of that room were covered in pictures of me racing. It was like a little supporters' club. In fact, while Grandad died in 2010, nothing's changed. Nan's still there – she's lived in that flat since 1957 – and everything's the same. Except she doesn't smoke. One day she stopped and that was that. Which goes to show, you can beat addiction.

I have many great memories of Nan and Grandad, but perhaps my favourite was the night in 2000 when, after winning bronze at Sydney, I was invited over to Buckingham Palace for dinner with Princess Anne in her capacity as President of the British Olympic Association. It was an intimate do, with around 20 guests, and afterwards I wandered out the front of the building and left via the main gates. I had to go that way because that was where Nan and Grandad were waiting in their Vauxhall Astra to pick me up. They told me later that, understandably, a policeman had come over while they were sat there.

'Can I help you two?'

'Oh no, we're all right,' Nan replied. 'We're just waiting for our grandson to come out.'

Twenty-five years on and I can still feel their pride in being able to say that. Grandad, an electrician by trade, worked for the London Electricity Board. He was a hard-working man, high up in the union. To see his grandson win an Olympic medal made him incredibly proud. In 2008, after winning my two golds in Beijing, I was made a CBE and invited him along to the medal ceremony at Buckingham Palace as my guest. With the brain I've got I couldn't help thinking of it as like *Charlie and the Chocolate Factory* when Charlie takes his grandad as the plus-one on the golden ticket.

As a union man, Grandad had an anti-authority streak which I always liked. My family was Labour through and through. Even think about voting Conservative and you were cast into the wilderness. Growing up, when the news was on, I'd hear him railing against the Tory government and 'bloody Thatcher'. His outlook was one of the reasons why, in 2012, I was initially resistant to the offer of a knighthood. I told Nan I was going to refuse it, thinking he'd have been proud. I was wrong. 'Your grandad will turn in his grave if you don't take that.'

'Really?'

'He always used to say, "You take what they give you," because they don't give things like that to people like us.'

I duly went along and collected the knighthood. I was very gracious in front of the Queen, did all the right things, said all the right things. Although sadly the get-up I wore, a fancy suit and brogues, had the unfortunate effect of giving me more than a passing resemblance to Nicholas Lyndhurst in the time-travel sitcom *Goodnight Sweetheart*.

Nan knew what she was talking about when it came to 'people like us'. Her mum died when she was eight, leaving her in the hands of her bare-knuckle-boxer dad. It was left to the little girl to bring up her younger brother while looking after an alcoholic father who eventually drank himself to death. By anybody's standards, that's a tough start. Being starved of a mother from so young an age could well explain her own reticence for showing physical affection to loved ones later in life.

Alongside Nan, Mum's sister Debbie was like a second mother to me. It was her who first took me to the outdoor velodrome at Herne Hill, driving me across there on a Thursday night. And then one day she was gone. She died suddenly when I was 18, shortly after giving birth to my cousin Adam. At the funeral I saw my nan crying. You might think that's an odd comment – of course she was crying, she was burying her daughter. But my nan never cried at anything. It was the first time I ever saw it happen. At the graveside, she and Grandad watched as soil was thrown on the coffin. Then everyone walked away. The next day it was as if nothing had happened. I find it so sad that something so emotionally devastating was never discussed, but that's what our family was like. No one ever spoke about their feelings. There's been a lot of death and upset but it was never aired, never disseminated. It was a part of us that was never allowed to breathe. If anything, after Debbie died the family disbanded. Christmas, first at Nan's, and then in later years at Butlin's, stopped being a thing.

When life's tough you can either drown in the past or look to the future. Grandad was the sort of person to choose the second option. He certainly showed belief in me. In 1992, when I was 12, he went down to Ladbrokes and put a bet on that I'd win the Tour de France within the next 20 years. Of course, in 2012, just in the nick of time, I did exactly that. Trouble is, Grandad had gone by then and no one had any idea what he'd done with the betting slip. My nan was forever looking in the back of their carriage clock, a favourite place of Grandad's for tucking away important scraps of paper, but she could never find it. 'He must have put it in the mechanism or something.' I've no idea what kind of windfall she'd have been in for. Knowing him, he'd have bet a tenner, but God only knows what the odds would have been on a random 12-year-old from Kilburn winning the Tour de France.

Grandad was at home among bookmakers. Me and him would go down to the dog tracks at Wimbledon or Wembley on a Saturday night and I loved watching these big characters communicating the odds with the old tic-tac moves. The original Wembley was fantastic. Between the Twin Towers was a ballroom with a bar where all the betting happened. I was mesmerised by what I was seeing – the shouting, the drinking, blokes with big bundles of money. It was amazing to be right there in that famous old stadium with all this life happening around me. Next day we'd be back for Wembley Market. Effectively, my grandad did everything with me that a dad's supposed to do. Brendan could be quite supportive at times, driving me to races, things like that, but sadly the good in him never outweighed his domineering side. I felt the way he imposed himself on me was unforgiveable. Grandad was my true father figure, and, while he never told me, having brought three daughters into the world I'm pretty sure that to him I was the son he never had.

While my grandparents provided welcome respite, no two ways about it my overriding emotion in adolescence was fear. I felt a horrible atmosphere in my home and violence outside of it, and on top of it all, I also had the abuse I was subjected to by Stan. One overriding theme occupied my head, the need for a protector. 'Just someone save me!' More often than not that 'someone' I yearned for was my dad. I so wished he could have been there. *Stan wouldn't be doing what he was doing if Dad was here*, I'd tell myself, *and if he did Dad would kill him.* I knew enough about what a tough character Gary was to know that was true. As I got into my late teens and started doing the same races that he'd done and meeting the people he used to hang around with, I began to hear things. 'Gary? Jesus! I remember once he punched this guy's lights out.' 'Christ! Gary! Catch his eye wrong and you'd had it.' More often than not they'd be laughing as they said it. While some teenagers in my position might have found that a shock, in all honesty, for me, crying out for someone to look out for me, it was empowering. But then, of course, I didn't actually want my dad to kill someone. These conflicting thoughts constantly filled my head.

I did at least have some support at school. I kept my early cycling career under wraps. The last thing I wanted was the headteacher to announce I'd won something in assembly, bringing a whole load of s**t my way from the bullies. But my PE teacher, Mr Hatch, definitely knew how well I was doing. Mum worked in the school office and told him what was happening. From the off, Mr Hatch was really supportive, the only male teacher who'd invest time in me, and one of the few people I felt safe around. It felt like he understood me and, while he could be strict, I did occasionally make him laugh, something that continued long after we'd parted ways. After I won the Tour, I saw him interviewed on breakfast TV. He'd particularly liked it when I climbed on to the podium on the Champs-Élysées and announced, 'We're just going to draw the raffle numbers!' I was delighted to think I'd made Mr Hatch proud. In school he was an incredible male role model, not just to me but to lots of kids. But outside of school he wasn't there. And outside of school was where I spent a fair amount of time. I never played truant in the traditional sense but I would go home for lunch and then go out on my bike for a couple of hours in the afternoon. Mum knew and didn't mind because, as far as she was concerned, it was for a good cause. The teachers, meanwhile, just thought I was lazy and wasn't arsed about my GCSEs. I quite liked them thinking that. *Little do you know I'm actually out training to be Olympic champion!*

By now I was making serious progress as a cyclist. When I was 15, having won the British Juvenile points race title, British Cycling invited me to train with the junior track squad at the velodrome in Manchester. I'd go up there every other weekend and absolutely loved it. Back then the general feeling in cycling was that the further north you looked, the better the talent you found. It was an assumption based on terrain. The north is where all the hills are. I turned that on its head when, in my second year on the squad, I won four titles at the 1996 Junior National Track Championships – the 1 km time trial, 3 km individual pursuit, points race and scratch race – as well as the road series, a season-long competition to identify the most consistent young rider. Only when that success became public knowledge through coverage in the media did I let the school in on the secret of what I'd been doing all that time. Years later, in 2014, a sculpture inspired by my feats in 2012 was unveiled at St Augustine's. Decorated with cogwheels, the aim was to encourage pupils to make their own hopes and dreams come true. Mr Hatch gave a speech at the ceremony. 'How fantastic that all these successes were achieved by a young man brought up just a few hundred yards from where we're standing,' he told the assembled crowd of kids and dignitaries. 'He wasn't too keen on the academic side,' he continued, 'he liked to have a joke in the classroom. He could be a bit of a pain. But he loved sport.'

I might not have been the most committed pupil but there was one assignment I was delighted to get stuck into. For business studies we had to compile a brochure for a travel agent. Mine was selling a trip to Paris. I found a picture of the French capital and started on the blurb – *Every year Paris hosts the final stage of the Tour de France. Head over there and you'll see me riding in it one day!* By then I had actually been to Paris to watch the Tour. My mum took me in 1993 and I found a plum position on the corner of the Place de la Concorde, watching Miguel Induráin in the yellow jersey and on his wheel the rainbow jersey of World Champion Gianni Bugno. Both were huge heroes of my mine. Fast forward 19 years and right there, on that same bit of tarmac, it's me in the yellow jersey with Mark Cavendish behind me in the rainbow jersey as I lead him out to victory on the Champs-Élysées. In the heat of the moment in 2012, I wasn't thinking back to when I was a kid in 1993. There was way too much going on for that to happen. But I was reminded of it more recently when I was covering the stage, doing commentary from a motorbike, for Eurosport. As we entered the Place de la Concorde, I told the viewers, 'I stood on that corner in 1993!' And then I pointed out the spot where I tapped my bum, the signal to Cav that the waiting was over and it was time to buckle up and go full pelt for the win. Two incredible memories which will never leave me. I can actually feel myself light up as I think of them. For a long time, what came after 2012 took that ability to light up away.

Three years after Paris, Mum took me to Belgium to watch the Tour of Flanders. It was incredible for me to see the riders who I idolised in the flesh. But those trips abroad proved rare flashes of delight in a teenage existence that was so weighed down with darkness; where I'd reconcile one bad thing as being bearable because ultimately it was helping me avoid another. Everything was linked. Archer Road Cycling Club was an escape from life in the flat. It was a place where, even in his absence, my dad's name gave me a certain strength. My dad's name, however, couldn't protect me from Stan. But I'd put up with Stan because it was better than having a broken bottle put to my throat round the estate. At least with Stan I was doing what I loved – cycling. So in my head my attitude was set. *If it means I can get away from the estate, and ride my bike, I can put up with a bit of fingering.* I know how horrible that sounds, but that's precisely what I was thinking. As a paedophile, of course, Stan's radar would have been finely tuned to the fact I had every reason not to tell.

Essentially, my loner life meant I missed out on my teenage years. I only left the flat to go cycling, which was risky enough in itself. Most kids round my way wanted to be footballers. They were hanging around in replica kit while I was heading out in cycling gear. That definitely wasn't cool and I was justified in being scared of getting picked on. That self-isolation meant I also had no interaction with girls. Not that I wanted any. I didn't know how to deal with any of that stuff. Being abused had placed a mental block in my head. The idea of touching or being touched being something natural or good had been skewed. Normal sexual behaviour had been tainted to the extent that I never used to masturbate as a teenager. I saw masturbating as something dirty. That lack of a standard cognitive relationship with sex followed me into adulthood. I never had a girlfriend until I was 22. Not only had my mind been messed up but I'd been emasculated by the overbearing presence of my stepdad.

There was another thing about getting a girlfriend. I'd heard it from coaches so many times. 'How good was that lad? And then one day he discovered girls.' Getting a girlfriend was clearly the fast lane to oblivion! When finally it happened and I met Cath, one of the British Cycling coaches did actually say, 'That's it, we've lost him now, he's c**t-struck.' I remember thinking, *What a horrible thing to say.* And actually what happened was completely the opposite to that awful comment. It was after I met Cath that I was most successful because I was happy and confident and she was supportive. In adolescence, however, my fear of sex and girls meant I threw myself even more into cycling.

As much as I found the road fascinating, studying everything about it, the riders, teams, races, history, stats, the track was where I felt I'd find greatness. Dad's record in the velodrome was my ultimate driver. He'd represented Australia at the Track Cycling World Championships, ridden the Six Day circuit for years and been national champion in the 1 km time trial. I didn't have the self-belief that I'd make it on the road, but I felt 100 per cent destined to do what he'd done. Everyone I met who knew Dad told me I could be just as good, or even better, than him, and my lightning-fast progression through the ranks seemed to prove the point. From the age of 15 I was beating men. And because of my Dad's achievements that was absolutely normal to me. *Why wouldn't I beat men? I'm Gary's son.* It occurs to me now more than ever that without that thought process I'd have had nothing. And that's why, despite him not being there, I'm grateful to him.

Of course, it's not every adult who likes being beaten by a kid, but again, because my dad was Gary Wiggins, while occasionally someone might have a go at me, what I generally got was respect. I was also unflinching. I knew how hard my dad was as a cyclist because my mum had always glamorised that side of him, and I'd try to ride in exactly the same way. Forget the real-life me, stripped of assertiveness and certainty, I was a totally different character on the bike. There were occasions where I'd actually try to knock another rider off because I knew it would bring praise from my mum. 'That's just like Gary!' she'd laugh afterwards, and it would make me feel good. She was good at dropping tiny seeds of information about my dad into the conversation and letting them grow. The first time I raced at the hilly Eastway track in east London I got lapped five times. I just couldn't get up the inclines. Afterwards, I realised my wheel was rubbing, slowing me down. I was totally pissed off with the whole thing. 'I really hate climbing,' I told my mum. 'Oh, Gary would have said that,' she laughed. 'He used to say that all the time.' For better or worse, those little seeds would instil in me a real feeling of being just like my dad.

Ironically, being so hyperfixated on the bike meant my world was opening up in ways far beyond the daily existence of my peers in the flats. Great Britain had sent riders to the

Junior Worlds for years and no one had ever done anything. By 1997 they had no money to send a team, but because of the promise I was showing they found just enough funding to pack me off on my own. For a lad who'd barely been further than Bognor Regis it was a massive culture shock. Riding to the velodrome in Cape Town, I'd pass alongside the townships, extreme poverty and desperate inequality staring me in the face. On the track, meanwhile, I just missed out on a medal, finishing fourth in the points race, unheard of for Great Britian at that time. It just showed, when it came to other British cyclists my age, without a doubt the fuel I had to succeed was a lot more potent than theirs. Wanting to be like my dad, and him not being there, delivered a drive that nobody could match. Add in adversity, trauma and zero distractions of friends or girls, and mine was an explosively powerful combination. I wasn't the only youngster out there with a famous cycling dad, but while others fell by the wayside I just got better and better.

Unlike most kids in those mid-to-late-teenage years I had absolute focus. Whenever I got on a bike, one thing was very clear to me, I was going to make it all the way to the top. Every single day that was the motivation. It was never, *I wonder if I might be good at this*. It was always, *I'm going to be the best. I want to win the Six Days of Ghent. I want to be Olympic Champion. I want to wear the yellow jersey in the Tour de France*. I never believed I wouldn't do it, to the extent I actually used to try to work out how much money I'd be earning at different stages of my career! I never realised, but that intensity didn't go unnoticed. My cycling peers say I was different as a kid, that I was like a professional, turning up with an immaculate bike and total unbending purpose. I never got a hint of it at the time, but years later riders on the senior track squad would tell me how they used to see me turn up at races and think, *God, this kid's going to be good!* Looking back now, I can see I was odd in the single-minded cycling-or-nothing way I approached my life. At the time, however, the only reason I thought I was odd was because I'd never had a girlfriend.

Throughout it all, Mum kept on encouraging me, pushing me forward. She kept scrapbooks of every year of my career from a young age and would film me racing and receiving medals and trophies on an old camcorder. She obsessed over me as a cyclist. As a kid I went to ride at the velodrome in Leicester, at the time the only steeply banked track in the country. I'd excelled on the shallower inclines of the concrete Herne Hill, Reading and Welwyn velodromes, and now Mum wanted to see how I'd go on a traditional wooden track. It shouldn't have been a problem, but straightaway I could barely get more than a few inches up the boards without sliding straight back down again. Mum was huffing and puffing, rolling her eyes. 'You've got to ride faster!' But I was going plenty fast enough to stay up there. I felt totally demoralised. No one could understand what was going wrong. Eventually, the coach took a look at my wheels. 'Hang on, what's all this?' Turned out my mum, to make my tyres look blacker and shinier, had buffed them up with boot polish. Once the coach had rubbed it all off with a bit of sandpaper, I was riding round the banking absolutely fine.

Back home after a race, Mum would wash my bike on the balcony and it shared her bedroom, living under a sheet. She really did make it the absolute focal point of my life. The only time she ever let me stay up past my half-brother's bedtime, for instance, was to go on the turbo. Anything else, it was, 'No! Go to bed!' The result was someone whose only source of identity growing up was on the bike. Self-worth was never given to me in any other way. Everything in my life depended on the bike. One time I performed terribly in a race at Welwyn only to arrive at the finish line and find Mum and Brendan had driven home without me. I had to ride all the way back to London down the A41. 'We ain't going to waste petrol money taking you to any more races if you're going to perform like that,' she told me. After that I made sure I won every week. The flipside, if I rode well, was that I'd get taken for something to eat at a Garfunkel's restaurant on the way home. Carrot and stick. Punishment and reward.

And yet the incongruity is that without that approach from my mum I'd never have got to where I am today. Had she not told me who my dad was I'm 100 per cent sure none of what I went on to achieve would have happened. She could have chosen to shield me from that information, never mentioned cycling, and I'd be a completely different person leading a completely different life. So why did she? Was it knowing that she'd hear from him one day? Did she think my own talent would arouse Dad's interest and potentially he'd come back into her life? Did she push me into cycling so one day I'd be better than him? Sometimes she'd say he didn't want me to be a cyclist. So me not only becoming a cyclist, but then being better than him, would be a good way of getting back at him for all the hurt he'd caused her, wouldn't it? Maybe she knew that would wind him up.

What I do know is that, in similar circumstances, most mothers would tell their child, 'Your dad wasn't a very nice person. One day you'll meet him and find out for yourself.' They'd turn their child against the father to some degree. But she didn't do that. She built me in her lost husband's image. She looked at Bradley and always saw Gary. He was never there but always there. A constant presence. His brilliance on the bike exalted. His bad traits romanticised. I'm not blaming her for that. She had her own memories of Gary to deal with; a relationship that I'm sure was far from easy, and took a heavy toll. But in so doing, she inadvertently built a monster. This person who won the Tour de France, who rang the bell at the Olympic Opening Ceremony, who won the gold medal in the time trial, that was the monster. Someone with a superpower but totally unable to deal with everyday life. That has to be the case. Otherwise, I wouldn't be sitting here now writing this book.

The indisputable truth is that had Mum sat me down when I was old enough and told me all about my dad, chances are I'd never have got into cycling. But even then that's not the end of the quandary. I mean, OK, maybe I'd have been all right. Maybe I'd have had a steady job, been a teacher perhaps like my half-brother. But equally there's a big part of me that suspects I'd have been dead in a gutter. I don't know why, but I've always felt that the alternative scenario to champion cyclist would somehow have been bleak for me. Who knows? Either way, it happened. I became a monster, did things on the bike that were beyond anyone's expectations, and changed cycling in this country forever.

The more I reflect, the more I don't think I'll ever have a definitive answer to the big questions about my childhood. I worry sometimes that I bang on about it too much. After all, lots of people have deep-seated issues with their early life. But I do see it as something that's really f**ked me up. One thing I do know is that whatever my mum's motivation, conscious or otherwise, I was obsessed with cycling as a teenager – and I'm glad I was. Cycling saved my life. Within those layers of trauma I was experiencing, it was the one constant I could turn to. I'm not saying I'd have killed myself without cycling, but I really don't know where I'd be today without it.

My dad's absence was the most essential ingredient in that life-saving fascination. And then one day he was back.

CHAPTER 4

DAD

'You're 18 ... don't underestimate the impact that meeting your dad for the first time will have on you.'

The worst is still to come. After I win one night, he approaches me in the centre of the track. As applause rings round, he pulls me close. 'Remember,' he says to me, 'you'll never be as good as your old man.' In that moment he punctures everything I hoped our relationship might be. Him saying that was everything I wasn't interested in.

'There's something you should know, Brad.' I looked at my mum. 'Your dad has rung up your nan's house. He's left his number in Australia. He says he wants to talk to you.' I was 17 years old. For the first time I could remember, I was going to speak to my dad.

I didn't actually make the call from Nan's. Mum wasted no time having a landline put in and made me ring him from the flat. I dialled the number. The phone rang a couple of times. He knew right away it was me. 'Hi, Bradley, it's your father,' he said, in a voice that I half-recognised. That was it, he burst into tears – and never stopped.

I remember that moment like it was yesterday. In the end, I passed Mum the receiver. 'He's crying, what do I do?' She talked to him for 20 minutes and put me back on. Again, though, he couldn't speak properly through the tears. Put simply, he was a complete emotional wreck. In the end, he promised to write me a letter. A few days later, Mum handed it to me. I took it into the bathroom and locked the door. I don't remember the contents other than it being what I expect he'd been trying to say on the phone – that he'd missed me and it was great to be back in touch. I needed to write back but so ill-equipped was I to express my inner feelings that I put down pretty much the same as I'd written on that photo a few years earlier. It was just cycling, cycling, cycling. 'I've been to a race in France, and I'm going to Cuba for the Junior Track World Championships' – all that kind of stuff.

If I couldn't articulate in words the joy I felt about Dad getting in touch, then I definitely could on the bike. It felt like overnight I'd been given an extra gear. Two months later I went to those Junior Track World Championships and won the 3 km individual pursuit. I put it down to him 100 per cent. No longer was he this fantasy figure in a photograph; he was in my life, in my corner. It was obvious I was going to succeed. *My dad's Gary Wiggins, of course I'm going to win!* I actually rang and told him about my success while I was out there. He was delighted for me.

After all the s**t I'd been through, having Dad back in my life was like a dream come true. He was my hero, and if I'd tried to emulate him before, I now ramped it up a thousand per cent. That meant copying not just his brilliance on the bike but his character and personality. After my victory in Cuba, followed up with a stack more wins at the British Championships in Manchester, *Cycling Weekly* did a big interview with me. I still have the magazine, and the way I speak is illuminating. 'When I'm at a race,' I say, 'I walk round like I'm the king. I tell myself I'm the best and no one is going to beat me.' Interestingly, I'm asked about my dad. 'We talk on the phone most weeks,' I tell the journalist, 'and before the Worlds he said to me, "You can win it. If you've only got one of my legs you'll win it." He motivates me a lot and told me there was nobody else in the race who was going to bother me. He drilled it into me that you've got to go out and think, "I'm going to kick your arse," because that's the only way you'll do it.' I'm asked to give four words to describe myself – 'Look after number one.' I've just turned 18 and I'm channelling my dad to such an extent that I might as well actually be him. There's something else. I'm talking like that because I know he'll read it. He'll see those words and glow with pride. 'That's my boy!'

I look at that article now and can't believe it's me. I literally don't recognise myself. It's Gary, *all Gary*. So everything I wasn't; everything I'm not. And yet that attitude, that desire to be just like my dad, definitely served me well as I sought to make my mark in the sport. I was also aware that it was success which had brought Dad to my door. Pretending to be him had actually made him real – another mess for the psychologists to untangle. If I hadn't been doing well, I really doubt he'd have been in touch. Had my path gone another way and I was in trouble with the police, in and out of juvenile detention centres, things like that, the sad reality is he probably wouldn't have wanted to know. After all, while we'd connected again, our relationship wasn't what you might call 'father–son'. It had no real emotional depth. For my part, all I was interested in was trying to show Dad my maturity and wisdom as an athlete. The last thing I wanted him to see was the traumatised individual hiding underneath. It never occurred to me, for instance, to tell him about Stan. By then I'd put him out of my mind. The last thing I was going to do when my dad rang up was go, 'Do you know what this guy's done to me?'

Reading that *Cycling Weekly* piece now, something else leaps out at me – a portent of what was to come in the aftermath of my success in 2012. I'm confident being myself with the cycling questions. I answer them all truthfully. Heroes – *Freddy Maertens and Danny Clark*. Favourite training ride – *Belgium, over the cobbled climbs*. But ask me about myself and I start reaching for things that deliver a cloak, an image. What's your most unpleasant characteristic? *I'm lazy, or so my mum tells me*. She never ever said I was lazy, but I thought it was a better look than saying I was 100 per cent focused and driven. Favourite film? *Beavis and Butt-Head Do America*. At the time it was cool to say you watched *Beavis and Butt-Head*, but in truth I hated it. The fact I felt a need to impress shows an underlying insecurity among the outbursts of OTT confidence.

Having won in Cuba and retained my national titles, my talent was clear and I was pushed into the Great Britain senior squad while still a junior. That meant me travelling to Kuala Lumpur to ride for England in the 1998 Commonwealth Games. I won silver in the team pursuit, but even more amazing was finding myself rooming with one of my great childhood heroes, Colin Sturgess, a former world champion in the individual pursuit who'd raced in the same team as Greg LeMond. Colin was almost 30 by the time he found himself in the same apartment as this skinny lad from London. There were six of us in all and as the youngster, nervous and totally lacking in social skills, I was the obvious butt of everyone's jokes. It was this tiptoeing around my elders that led to a rather unpleasant situation which to this day is referred to by all concerned as TowelGate.

One night, when everyone was asleep, I was desperate for the toilet. Problem was, I couldn't find any loo roll. It so happened that the organisers had issued each of us with a striped towel with 'Commonwealth Games' embroidered on it. In the absence of any toilet paper I used mine to wipe my arse. Of course, you can't flush a towel so I did what any other normal person would do in these circumstances. I chucked it behind the fridge. I then went back to bed, having not flushed the toilet – I didn't want my head ripped off for waking up the others. Of course, next morning there was an immediate inquest. 'Jesus, who's done that?' The lack of toilet roll also raised questions of personal hygiene. Initially, fingers were pointed at another rider and I wasn't about to inform his accusers of their error. Later, when, to much disgust, the towel was spotted behind the fridge, it was unceremoniously hurled off the apartment balcony, landing on a garage roof where it baked in the sun for the duration of our stay. I was very pleased with myself to have got away with something which had the potential to be a lifelong stain on my character – and then someone realised I was the only one without a towel. Straightaway, the smile was wiped from my face. From that point on all I heard for the rest of the Games was 'Wiggins, you dirty bastard!' Those who were there berate me to this day. TowelGate has followed me round for the best part of 30 years. I can be in the middle of nowhere doing a Q&A and someone will ask, 'Excuse me, Brad, what's this about TowelGate?' It wasn't until years later that I discovered how much esteem those riders held me in at that age. They certainly never let on at the time.

Scandal aside, I was blown away by the cycling royalty I found myself mingling with in Kuala Lumpur. In the next apartment was the road team, including Chris Lillywhite, who I'd watched win the Milk Race, essentially the Tour of Britain, when I was 13. Then there was Chris Newton, a genius on track or road who would go on to be a multiple world champion and triple Olympic medallist, and Chris Walker, an incredible competitor, always the man to beat in a sprint. I walked into the dining hall and there was another British rider, Shaun Wallace. 'Oh, you're Gary's son, aren't you?' he greeted me. 'I raced with your dad.' He'd ridden the Ghent Six Day in 1986. I've a picture of him and Dad at the track. That was just the British riders. Elsewhere, there were guys like the Australian Stuart O'Grady who'd worn the yellow jersey for three days in that year's Tour de France. I never really thought about it at the time, but to be holding my own with these much older and far more experienced riders was pretty much unheard of. They'd been round the block a hundred times and I'd not even had my first drink. Even when the Games were done and everyone went out, I was stood in a rooftop bar with a glass of water. All these big names, like the Welsh sprinter Iwan Thomas and Trinidadian counterpart Ato Boldon, were having a beer, and I'm there with a sparkling Perrier. As I surveyed this star-studded party, I felt pretty sure that no one else had gone to pick up their kit for the Games with their mum.

It felt like so much was changing in my life, and all of it momentous. One day Mum called me and Ryan into the kitchen. 'Your dad's moving out,' she said.

'What do you mean, moving out?' asked my brother.

'He doesn't want to live here anymore,' she told him. 'He's getting his own place. We're not together anymore.'

Ryan broke down in tears. I felt so sorry for him. My mum hugged him close. 'It's OK,' she reassured him, 'don't worry, you can still see him whenever you want.'

I knew why Brendan had gone. By now Mum was on the phone to my dad every night. I'm not going to criticise her for it – you can't change how someone makes you feel, if indeed that was the case – but it must have been a kick in the teeth for him. What was the point of him being there if Gary was going to be allowed back into the fold? Then again, one way or another, Gary had been lurking in the background the whole time they'd been together. Not only had Mum always kept Gary's wedding ring but she'd insisted in me and Ryan having the same surname. He was Brendan's son but was called Ryan Wiggins. I've no idea why my stepdad went along with that. I look at things like that and think, *No wonder he was overbearing towards me.*

Around the same time I was also identified as worthy of Lottery funding to help me make the leap to the next stage. I received £5,000, backed up by £3,000 sponsorship from a domestic cycling team. Where I grew up, £8,000 for a kid who'd just left school and was living with his mum wasn't bad. The idea was to help me prepare for a tilt at that medal at the Sydney Olympics. With huge talents such as Chris Hoy and Jason Queally coming through the ranks, British Cycling was on the up and it felt like we had a real chance of coming back with a decent haul.

As part of our preparation we headed to Melbourne for a six-week training camp. By now I'd been talking on the phone with my dad for more than a year and we both agreed that my trip Down Under offered the perfect opportunity to actually meet up. I mentioned the plan to Simon Jones, the national coach. 'You're 18,' he told me. 'Don't underestimate the impact that meeting your dad for the first time will have on you.' I never thought much about his words back then, but I see now how he recognised completely the psychological toll of meeting an absent parent after so long.

At that point, Dad actually appeared to have his life together. He was in a relationship, he'd just had a baby daughter, Madison (the only bike race that doubles as a kid's name), and was cycling again for the first time in years. He came to meet me at the apartment I was sharing with some teammates. I remember that moment vividly. When he walked up the stairs he couldn't look me in the eye. 'Hello, Bradley,' he said, averting his gaze. 'Hello, Gary,' I replied. Somehow, after he'd been absent for so long, it didn't feel right calling him Dad to his face.

I'm not sure what he was thinking, but Dad had come up with the bizarre idea of not just meeting me that day, but bringing all his children – so me, Madison and Shannon – together for the first time. His venue of choice for this jolly little get-together was a pizza restaurant in the faded seaside resort of St Kilda.

'I can't tell you how good this feels,' he said as I stared blankly at the menu. 'My three kids, right here. I've always dreamed of this.'

He was trying to generate an upbeat mood, but it was hard. Madison didn't understand what was happening and you could hardly expect me and Shannon, who didn't know each other from Adam, to be playing happy families. If anything, I felt a little resentment from her, as if I was in some way responsible for Gary leaving her as a little girl. I didn't blame her for that. Same as me, she'd been put in a very awkward situation. There we were, Dad's three kids, sat at this table. I was 18, Shannon 26 and Madison two. None of us had ever clapped eyes on one another. Dad had abandoned me and Shannon and now he had this baby he was doting on. At one point, he disappeared to the toilet. Shannon turned to me. 'Is this not a bit weird?' I had to agree. Gary and his trail of destruction. As so often, he just couldn't see it. Madison was lucky to be so young that the whole crazy situation washed over her. For me and Shannon it was just something else to deal with. There was definitely bruising, so much so that in interviews later in life I always used to say that the first time I met Dad was ten months later in Ghent. That day in St Kilda was so f**ked up I blocked it out. I wasn't consciously not telling the truth in interviews, I just couldn't face thinking about it. Although, as it turned out, the meeting in Belgium was hardly your classic heartwarming father and son reunion either.

It was November the same year when I went over to Ghent, fulfilling my ambition to actually take part in the Six Day that had so fascinated me since I'd watched from the stands as that little kid. I'd compete in the same races and on the same boards where my dad had made his name. To make the occasion even more special, I paid for him to fly over from Australia. What a proud moment, I thought, for him to see his own son travelling in his slipstream. And where better for us to properly bond and share some time together than this? Make no mistake, Ghent's Kuipke Velodrome is an incredible place. People have been racing bikes on this spot for the best part of a hundred years. You can touch and smell the history. Come those six days in November and the place is absolutely rocking. A crazily short track, just 166 metres compared with the standard 250, with really sharp slopes on the bends, means the riding is fast and furious. Add in a boozy crowd out to have the best possible time and it's basically like racing in a nightclub.

The day I met my dad, though, it was early and the velodrome was virtually empty. I heard him long before I saw him. I was waiting by the old soigneurs' cabins, where the riders receive treatment, when I heard a pair of shoes clicking along the concourse. I looked up and there he was in jeans and a Crombie overcoat. I was immediately reminded of when I saw him in Melbourne. Again, a complete inability to make eye contact. My guess is he felt nervous about coming back to the site of his biggest battles, his greatest nights. But even if you feel a bit uncomfortable, you generally say 'Hi!' the minute you clock the person you're meeting. Not Dad. He just kept walking, looking around, anything to take his eyeline away from his son. Finally, he reached me. 'How you going, mate?' But still he couldn't look me in the face. Barely had we said hello than he started showing me around. 'You used to be able to come in this way but they've blocked it off now.' I'd been there three days, I knew my way around! It was as if he was making a point, ensuring I understood this was his stamping ground. I found it bizarre. Why couldn't he just say hello and be normal? Why did he feel the need to be like that?

There was a shout. A soigneur had recognised him. 'Gary, f**cking hell! I haven't seen you for years!' That was it, his demeanour changed completely. Gary was back in town. Gary was the show. I watched as he hugged his old mate. All so relaxed, so jovial. Completely different to meeting me. I waited for an introduction. 'This is my boy, Bradley!' he said eventually. *My boy?* He said it like we'd been in each other's pockets for years.

The transformation from the bloke who'd walked meekly up the concourse to this big dominant character, laughing and joking, slapping old buddies on the back, was remarkable. In fact, if I'm honest, there was a part of seeing my dad slip so naturally into his old life, people recognising him, wanting to be around him, that made me proud. It was lovely to be able to share that moment with him. What was ugly was the message that came with it. *This is my domain! I'm in charge!* In a matter of minutes, I'd become subservient. His attitude was clear. Not so much 'I've come here to see you work' as 'I've come here to take you to work.'

From then on, he started telling me what to do. He wouldn't just let me be. At one point when the racing started he handed me a caffeine suppository – caffeine can stimulate an energy rush – something I'd never used before. I had no idea how to do what was needed. A quiet word from Dad would have sufficed. Instead he took the mick out of me in front of a load of strangers. 'Go on, push it right up! Push your finger right up!' He said something about 'probably not ever having had a cock up your arse', really demeaning stuff to a 19-year-old lad. He thought he was the king, but to me he was embarrassing. In the meantime, he was constantly asking me for money. 'I'm a bit skint. I'll sort you out. I'll pay you back.' I couldn't help thinking, *What does that say about him as a person? He hasn't seen me for years and now he wants to borrow a load of Belgian francs?* It summed him up in many ways.

You didn't need to be Hercule Poirot to work out I was basically paying for him to get drunk every night. By two in the morning, when the racing ended, he'd be completely gone. I was getting changed in a cabin one night and heard him arguing with a security guard. He must have barged his way through because next thing I knew both him and the guard were in the cabin with me. 'I'm Gary Wiggins! This is my boy!' The poor guy left us to it. 'Sorry, I didn't know. I just thought you were a drunk.' My dad looked at me. 'He doesn't f**king know how lucky he is I didn't hit him.' I got the impression he wasn't just saying that. I was taking part in the Six Day just 13 years after Dad's last outing – I actually competed against a few of the riders Dad raced against – and off the track people were queuing up to tell me stories about him. Time and again I heard the same thing. 'Your dad was crazy!' His reputation was as someone totally unpredictable. There was constant mention of punch-ups after he'd been drinking.

Such incidents went on all week, to the extent that by the fourth night I was thinking, *I wish you'd go home, I've had enough of you.* My dad was a liability, to himself and to me. Before one race he was going on about my saddle being too high. Behind my back he told my mechanic to lower it two inches. The first I knew of it was when I was out on the track. *What the f**k? My saddle's slipped down!* 'No, I told them to do it,' he revealed afterwards.

When he told me, 'You'll never be as good as your old man,' I felt sick. I held him in such high esteem that I was happy just to stand on his shoulders and emulate him. Being better than him hadn't even crossed my mind. My dad was my hero, and yet, when everyone else I'd met in cycling was happy to tell me I was going to be special, he, and he alone, had felt the need to tell me that I'd never be as good as him.

There's a photo of us at the end of the week shaking hands in the track centre. I'm trying to smile and he just looks pissed off. I'm glad he was there at Ghent. I'm glad he got to see me on that track. But me being glad he was there doesn't override the pain of what he said. Knowing how I feel about my own son, I find it impossible to comprehend that you'd never want to see your child do better than you. There was sadness when he said those words. There was sadness for a long, long time.

CHAPTER 5

DISTANCE

'Don't f**king embarrass me.'

There they are, all three of them in the same room – my mum and my two dads. Brendan, typically, is full of it. At one point he grabs me in front of my dad. 'I've looked after him, Gary, don't you worry. He's been like the son I never had.' The guy is moonwalking backwards about everything he's done for me. If it was just him maybe it wouldn't have been too bad, but they are all doing it. Mum, Dad and Brendan, all fighting to take the credit. 'He's got to where he is because of me.' Not one of them says, 'It's all his own hard work, you know.' It's all down to them. Brutal. I can't wait to get to Heathrow and get the hell out of here. I stick all my gear in the car, Brendan gets in the driver's seat and my dad gets in next to him. There's me in the back of this car looking at these two blokes, my real dad and my stepdad.

I've literally just remembered that now, as I'm writing. Literally just had that image in my head. Bearing in mind I've craved a dad for years, I've now got two in the front, both wanting to take me to the airport. I listen dumbstruck as they compete, flexing their muscles as to who's been the best dad, who is responsible for me being so talented; the truth being that at the point where I was being abused, where I really needed someone, neither of them has been there for me. They've both let me down in ways neither of them can ever imagine. Half an hour later they drop me at departures and drive back into London together. I mean, what the actual f**k? There are parts of my story that are so crazy that writing this now feels not so much like a book as a script for a black comedy. But of course it's not comedy, it's buried trauma.

By inviting dad to the Ghent Six Day, I'd seen full-frontal why those old cycling acquaintances of his I'd encountered when growing up had drawn breath when his name was mentioned. He was a loose cannon, a bully, and people were scared of him. The fact I was his son didn't seem to make any difference. There was nothing protective about his attitude to me. He could turn on me the same as anyone else. 'You have to be a hard bastard in cycling,' he'd say unapologetically, 'it's the only way to succeed.' But I met plenty of other great riders who rode with him and they were gentlemen. He might have seen his unremitting toughness as being a man, but actually it was toxic.

Something else happened that week in Belgium. I saw my mum and dad together for the first time. On the last couple of days, she came over to watch. I came off the track and there they were chatting together like nothing had happened.

If I thought that was bizarre, nothing could prepare me for what happened back in London. I walked into the flat one afternoon and there was Dad on the couch. It was a day I never thought I'd see. Here was this bloke who, until very recently, had been absent nearly all my life, sat there like nothing had happened. 'Hello, Bradley! How are you, mate?'

While Ghent had been something of a disaster, at least in the flat Dad was removed from the feverish atmosphere of the Kuipke Velodrome, a place which he clearly felt defined him. Without the distraction of the Six Day, we could actually spend some time together, although again it felt more like I was bringing him up to date on seven years of me being a cycling fanatic rather than the two of us catching up on nearly two decades of him not being there.

'Come and look at the posters on my wall!' I told him, something a kid much younger than myself might have said, but I wanted him to see just how massive cycling had been for me. I also fished out the photos I had of him – not the one where I'd written the letter on the back, that would have been embarrassing, but the others – and he explained exactly where each was taken and what was going on. Then there was my collection of old *Cycling Weekly* magazines from the 1970s featuring interviews with him. 'Look, I've always had these!' I pointed out where I'd highlighted his words with a pen. I wonder if he could see what I was telling him. *I never thought I'd see you again, but this is how much I think of you.*

Sitting with him, going through all those things, was the complete opposite of Ghent. It was the moment that finally I got to meet my hero. I know what they say, 'Never meet your heroes, because you'll only be let down,' but right there and then I couldn't be let down. I knew his flaws inside out. I'd always known he'd left us and I knew he could behave abominably. There was nowhere else to go. My only regret is that I've never known how those moments in the flat felt for him. Whether they meant as much; whether he felt the same closeness.

Not everyone was happy to have Gary back in London. One night, we went over to my grandparents' flat. They hadn't clapped eyes on their one-time son-in-law since 1981.

'Hello, George,' said my dad. 'How you going?'

Grandad looked at him on the doorstep. 'God, I never thought we'd see you again.' In all the time I'd known Grandad it was the only time I'd seen him unhappy about someone else's presence. He wasn't welcoming at all. Dad did manage to charm my nan, but Grandad? He was having none of it. His bearing that night never left me. I was reminded of it when I used to take Ben to see him as a baby. 'He's a lot better than his own father was,' Grandad would say. 'His own dad was useless.' Grandad always wanted me to be better than my dad. It made me wonder if there was more to Dad leaving than I'd ever been told.

Whatever the reception he was getting, Dad was clearly hanging around for a while. In that period I saw a reversal of the scenario I'd had with Brendan. Now my dad started being horrible to Ryan. I felt for him massively. His dad had moved out, my dad had moved back in, and it looked for all the world like he was going to get back together with his mum. I expect in that moment Ryan felt the exact same abandonment that had been mine for so many years.

A few days after Dad arrived, he and Brendan met one another for the first time. I was flying out to a race in Zurich, needed a lift to the airport, and Brendan, still in our lives because of Ryan, came to pick me up. Not long after I got back, Gary flew back to Australia. A few weeks later, Mum was on a plane heading after him. From what I could gather, she was doing so with a view to them possibly getting back together. I was baffled to say the least. *Hang on! What about all that stuff you told me about him before? You know, about how horrible he could be?* Later, my dad told me they had indeed discussed a reunion. I also heard on the grapevine that while he was staying at our flat and my mum was out at work all day he'd been sleeping with an old flame from 20 years ago behind her back.

When Mum returned from Australia, it was clear from her demeanour, if nothing else, that whatever small chance of a reconciliation had existed had wilted and died in the heat of the Victoria sun. As ever, I've no idea what really happened between them. None of it made sense then and it makes even less sense now. But I could sense that Mum felt rejected. She became very negative about Dad. Anytime I'd try to talk to her about him, she'd say, 'Be careful. I wouldn't want to speak to him if I were you.' She'd even take the phone out of the wall in the evenings. 'He's becoming a nuisance now.' She'd gone full circle from once doing everything she could to encourage me to talk to Dad to now getting totally pissed off about it.

Meanwhile, another chance had arisen for me to spend some time with Dad myself. In early 2000, a couple of weeks before meeting the Team GB cycling team for a training camp in Perth, I flew out to Australia and stayed with him at his unit, basically what the Aussies call a little flat, on a caravan park. In stark comparison to when we'd met in St Kilda, his life now seemed to be falling apart. Hair greying, weary and depressed, he seemed old beyond his years. He was 48 at that point, so only three years older than I am now, but physically he couldn't have looked more different. Working as a removals man, up and out the door every morning at 5.30 a.m., he was at least able to hold down a job, but it was obvious he was a mess, coming back at six every night with a slab of 24 Victoria Bitter cans and gradually working his way into oblivion. His own alcohol-drenched version of *Groundhog Day*. I wasn't drinking at that point. All I could do was watch him throw down can after can. The more he drank, the more I was on eggshells. It felt like whatever I said was wrong. He had some videos of himself when he was racing and one time I spotted the Australian Danny Clark, a fantastic rider, Olympic silver medallist and multiple World Champion, who I really admired.

'Wow! Danny Clark! What was he like? He's a real hero of mine.'

Dad looked at me angrily. 'Your dad was a pretty f**king good bike rider as well, you know.'

I quickly backtracked. 'No, no, you're more my hero than him.'

I'm 19, and there I am trying to navigate this tightrope. *Say the wrong thing and he'll turn on me.* His anger, his bitterness, frightened me. Genuinely frightened me.

By then the relationship with his third wife had crashed and burned. Who knows what was in the melting pot of that collapse but I wouldn't be surprised if somewhere in the mix had been Dad's increasing contact with Mum. Madison, however, was still allowed to come over on a Sunday. He'd dote on her, lots of love and cuddles. 'She's my world!' he'd say. Basically, everything I'd never had from him. Again, I was overwhelmed by a feeling of abandonment. *Well, if she's your world, what am I?* At the same time he'd be cooing at her. 'You call me Daddy, don't you? You call me Daddy! It's nice someone calls me Daddy!' It was all very pointed. *F**king hell*, I'd think, *someone get me out of here.*

This was our biggest chance to get to know each other, to add some cement to the relationship. But while there were brief occasions where it felt like we doing OK, sharing our love of boxing while watching old fight videos, for instance, more often than not his behaviour felt like a punch in the guts. One night we went to a cycling awards dinner. Of course, he got blind drunk. When we got back to his place he went out to a local bar to carry on his night and left me staring at my bedroom wall.

The final straw came when I competed at the Australian National Championships in Melbourne. The event was open to all nationalities and since I needed to maintain my fitness levels I decided to take part. Melbourne was Dad's local track and so he came down to watch. When word got round of the father–son cycling connection, we were brought together in the middle of the track and introduced on the mic. 'Junior World Champion and Commonwealth Games medallist Bradley Wiggins and his dad Gary!' Everyone gave a round of applause. Dad was revelling in it. As in Ghent, he hadn't been down to the track for years but was now suddenly getting attention again. I'd entered the madison and did a few warm-up races before the main event. At one point Dad came down to the centre of the track. I could tell immediately he was drunk. He grabbed me, squeezing my arm until it hurt, really forcefully imposing himself. 'Don't f**king embarrass me.' It was just awful and I hated him for it. I felt totally helpless. I had no backbone then. I couldn't say something, stand up to him. I felt that that had been eroded away by Brendan.

By the end of the fortnight, I couldn't wait to leave. I didn't feel sad, disappointed, anything. I just didn't care. I just wanted to go. Didn't want anything to do with him. Again, here was someone who was supposed to care for me and I'd ended up scared of them. No wonder I went through life seeking out a protection figure. But you don't expect to need someone to protect you from your own dad.

I'd hoped spending a decent amount of time with Dad would not only help us bond but fill the gaping information chasm about his absence left by mum. In the end, it did neither. Amid the passive–aggression and the maudlin regret, Dad did tell me things, but whether they were true or not is another matter entirely. So much of what he said seemed to clash directly with what I'd always seen as the accepted version of events.

'I bought you your first proper bike,' he claimed. *Did you?* I thought. I'd always been told my grandad had bought me that bike. 'It was for your sixth birthday,' he continued. 'I dropped it off at the bottom of your block because your mum didn't want me to see you.' When I got back, I asked Mum. 'Oh, he's lying.' But Dad was still racing in mainland · Europe, and occasionally even in England, at that time, so it seemed plausible that he might have dropped by the estate at some point. He also told me he'd sent Christmas cards every year to the flat. I'd never seen them and, from what I saw of his life, no way was he together enough to be sending festive greetings halfway across the world.

There were so many conflicting tales, so many things that didn't add up. Same with the story he told about how he'd got in touch with me when I was 17. According to him, he'd bumped into some old cycling friends at a funeral in Australia. They told him they'd seen my name in the results section of a cycling magazine and luckily he still had my nan's number in an old Filofax. But at that point he didn't have any of his old stuff. He barely had a pot to piss in. A Filofax? Really? Isn't it more likely that someone contacted him, rather than the other way round? This whole idea that someone saw my name in a cycling magazine and that was why he got in touch just seems a little too storybook perfect to be true. There must have been more to it. He must have known my whereabouts all along. My guess is he rang when I was 17 because at that age there was nothing to stop him. I was no longer a minor. Or maybe my mum let him get in touch because she considered me old enough to make up my own mind about whether I wanted him in my life. Either way, I'm pretty sure he didn't just get up one morning and go, 'I know, I'll ring Bradley!' Was there really never a point before that day when he thought, *I wonder what Brad's up to?* Did it really take a chance meeting at a funeral and someone to say, 'Heh, Gary, did you know your son's racing in the UK?' I'd been racing for four years at that point. And he didn't know?

The more I think about it, the more ludicrous it sounds. But talking to either Mum or Dad about my history or theirs was pointless. Whatever the subject, Mum would say one thing, Dad would say another. She'd say he was lying, he'd say it was true. 'It broke my heart not seeing you,' he told me once, 'but your mum said she didn't want me seeing you sporadically because it was no good for you.' I passed that on. 'No, he's lying,' was Mum's instant retort. 'He left and we never heard from him again.' At that age I didn't realise the effect this constant flip-flopping, this never knowing who or what was right, was having on me, and would do so for years to come. Jesus, could one of you not just tell me the truth?

Back in London, I tried to avoid speaking to Dad as much as I could. I also didn't see him when I went back to Australia for the Sydney Olympics. I was far too consumed with what we were trying to achieve on the track in the team pursuit. There was another overriding reason. After my nightmare stay at his unit, I really didn't want to. From then on I'd ring sporadically just to keep the peace, but that was it.

'Why are you only ringing me every three weeks now?' he'd ask.

'I'm busy, you know?'

'Too busy to speak to your old man?'

Where once it felt like he wanted to get to know me, he'd just go on and on about his own problems. By now his life had dropped off a cliff. He wasn't allowed to see his daughter, he was drinking to excess, everything had turned to s**t. The bloke who'd started out ringing up genuinely interested in how I was getting on now began ringing up drunk and rambling. 'I don't know why your mum doesn't want to talk to me.' I didn't know either, but the offshoot was I was lumbered with him on the phone. It had become burdensome, all about him, totally one-sided, and by the time I was 20 I'd reached the point of not wanting to talk to him anymore.

In the end I barely spoke to him for a year and a half. But then, towards the end of 2002, I took part in the Herald Sun Tour, a road race held in and around Melbourne. I was at the start when I spotted him. He was heading right for me. Straightaway he was really angry. Why hadn't I been in touch? All this kind of stuff. In an attempt to calm him down, I apologised and promised to phone him. I rang him once while I was still in Australia and then the minute I was out of the country didn't talk to him again. That period included me winning the Ghent Six Day in 2003. I can't help but wonder what he thought when he saw that I'd succeeded in that arena, on those boards that meant so much to him, but sadly I'll never know. The relationship, such as it was, had gone.

For the first 18 months, being in touch with my dad had been a great strength. My career was evolving at speed. I was breaking records and making a name for myself. I genuinely wouldn't have won the Junior Worlds without him on my side. My increased performance level and having Dad in my life were overlaid. I can't divorce the two. Not only that, but looking to the future I could actually talk to someone who'd done the races I wanted to do. Except when I actually started doing those races, and doing well, he turned on me. He was only happy when it was a subservient relationship, when I was on the end of the phone telling him he was my hero, asking him what it was like being in the big events, racing alongside the big names. He enjoyed that dynamic. But then suddenly I didn't need to ask those questions anymore. I'd become too successful too quickly for the relationship to work. His delight began to dissipate. Now he needed to put me back in my place. For every bit of pride he had in me for what I was achieving, I could feel his envy, his resentment, his jealousy. I'd tell him about the races I'd got coming up. 'I've got Gent–Wevelgem next week,' I'd say, excited to be part of a big one-day race in Belgium.

'I got third there one year,' he'd reply, 'behind Sean Kelly.'

'Wow!' I'd say. 'Did you?' And then after I'd put the phone down I'd look in the results and see that he hadn't even ridden that year. He did that a few times. Twice he told me he'd ridden the Giro d'Italia. But he hadn't. And it was so easy to find out that he hadn't. But I wouldn't pull him up on that stuff. I didn't dare. It wasn't worth the trouble.

More than anything, I just found it sad. Here was a man who I'm sure was only too well aware that his life had changed for the worse. He'd gone from being a very, very good bike rider, lauded, internationally renowned, to a man with three failed marriages living alone doing painting and decorating and removals jobs. At one point he was working at a supermarket collecting the shopping trolleys from the car park. I'm not demeaning that kind of work, I'm just saying that in his mind he must have felt he was worth more. But he didn't have to lie. I respected him as a rider and knew what he'd achieved. Dad said to me once, 'You're my son, there's a reason you're that good,' because he wanted to take some credit. Why mix my career with his? That side of him, that underlying element of competition, was ugly. If he'd thought for one second about how much I thought of him, and still do to this day, he'd have known he didn't have to do that. I have genuine love and affection for him. I put my whole career down to the person, and rider, he was.

I wasn't the first to see the more insecure and unattractive side of Gary Wiggins. Maurice Burton, a fantastic rider from south London who spent years on the Six Day circuit alongside him, told me something that's always stuck with me. 'Everyone's got a line, but Gary never did.' The evidence of the stories I've heard tells me Maurice is right. Dad could flip on people in a really violent way. After a perceived slight on a training ride, he chased one bloke, the New Zealander John Mullan, across a field and beat the s**t out of him. On another occasion, he battered the very well-respected Swiss rider Robert Dill-Bundi, gold medallist at the Moscow Olympics, and ended up on an assault charge. Former Team Sky head coach Shane Sutton, a fellow Aussie who knew Dad well from his own racing days, appears to have hit the nail on the head when he referred to Gary as a 'wild bastard'. A wild bastard with a malevolent side.

Others who knew him say he hated being alone. Maybe he was left on his own a lot as a kid, I don't know. But that need for company, combined with a narcissistic streak, meant, like a bully in the playground, he assembled people round him who he felt were inferior, who never challenged him and who inflated his own importance. He always had to be the one with the biggest balls, no doubt to hide his own self-worth issues. Add in his build, a tall, strong man, just a brute of a person, and he was able to dominate those around him.

It's not always easy persuading Dad's peers to talk. Often they're very coy about opening up, almost as if they don't want to break my heart with the truth. It's funny, my son Ben, himself a professional cyclist, is at the stage of his career where he's constantly meeting the people I worked with. He says how nice it is when they tell him affectionate little stories about me – the total opposite of my experience. Of course, no one ever actually says, 'Your dad was a horrible person.' They couch it in different language. 'Gary? Hmm. Let's put it this way, he was a character.' It's hard for people to tell me the truth. They think I've suffered enough. But the truth is exactly what I need.

Some riders do genuinely speak fondly of Dad. I've chatted with the Belgian Dirk Van Hove and he almost took offence at the suggestion Dad wasn't a great bloke. He was a big mate of his and had nothing but good things to say about him. Others say when the chips were down he was by their side. But I know Dad could use people. As I saw when he began to put me in my place, there was definitely an inflamed ego at work. I should have guessed that was there from the start. My full name is Bradley Marc Williams – BMW – a deliberate act on his part to reflect his love of flash cars. There's a photo of him having a massage which shows a big Rolex Daytona on his wrist, while his womanising ways fit the bill too. We all have ego. I showed mine in 2012, even if it was in a very insecure way. But Dad's ego got him into trouble time and time again, first during his career and then again when he retired. I'm sure a lot of his motivation was centred on a desire to show people he'd made something of himself. He did make something of himself, but by the time he retired and went home there was nothing to show for it. He was just this bloke constantly telling people how great he was, portraying himself as this big hotshot cyclist back in the 1980s, one of the best in the world. He lived in the past, totally unable to move forward. To do so he needed to accept his own part in the mess he'd created. But he didn't. He never took responsibility for it.

A psychologist might look at the evidence of my dad's life and say he was incredibly insecure. Maybe he was. I didn't spend enough time with him to discover the truth of the man underneath. Certainly, from the outside you'd say there was nothing insecure about him. He was just wired up wrong. I honestly don't know whether my dad thought of himself as a success or a failure. When I spent some time with him, I got the feeling he was aware of his failings in the family department. Maybe he also felt that about his time on the bike, hence him lying to me about his results. On his own, the only way he could deal with any of it was to drink to destruction.

In his defence, it's important to couch some of Dad's behaviour in the context of when it happened. Cycling was very different then. From a tough mining town in Victoria, Dad came over to London in 1974 with his cycling mate Dave Sanders, who himself would go on to a glittering coaching career working with, among others, Cadel Evans, the first Aussie to win the Tour de France and reigning champion when I won in 2012. Together they turned up at Heathrow with nothing but a backpack, a bike and a sense of adventure. The only lifeline they had was the phone number of Stuart Benstead at Archer Road Racing at Herne Hill and Paddington for bits of prize money that enabled them to scrape by. The scene was in no way glamorous. Maurice recalls him, Dad and Dave heading up to a meet in

Sheffield in a knackered old Transit van which the Aussie pair had bought for a tenner. So wrecked was this thing that the doors wouldn't shut. They had to cling on to the handles all the way there. Maurice remembers also how, because it was a nice day, both Dad and Dave didn't bother with shoes. Apparently, a bit of an Aussie tradition. Life on the track was equally unpredictable. Dad and Dave teamed up for the British National Tandem Sprint Championships at Paddington, making it to the final, only to be lifted up and over the fence when the opposition pairing crashed into them. Next thing either of them remembered was waking up in adjacent beds in hospital. Taking advantage of clean sheets and free meals, they made sure to stay just that little bit longer than was strictly necessary.

However tough it was to succeed in England, it was a thousand times more difficult on the continent. Over there, Dad was faced with hundreds of battle-hardened and wholly uncompromising riders who weren't going to be knocked off their perch by some brash young upstart from the other side of the planet. It wasn't to everyone's liking, but clearly he did what he thought was necessary to maintain his position. Unfortunately, it seems that on several occasions he completely overstepped the mark.

Like many others, Dad was also a victim of the drug-riddled period in which he rode. People often describe past cyclists as 'imperfect characters' but, for a long time, to succeed on the bike you didn't have much choice. The Six Day circuit was a constant slog round Europe. It wasn't uncommon for racers to finish one event at three in the morning and then drive eight hours to the next one the following night. Dad rode 73 Sixes in his career, indicative of the toll put on riders. He and his fellow pros had to work like dogs otherwise they'd slip down the rankings and would no longer be invited to the races where they earned their money. No wonder then that drugs were at the epicentre of that world. They'd take amphetamines to give them a boost on the track and then take more to keep them awake for the drive. To perform that night, they'd need sleep, and so they'd reach for another pill that knocked them out until race time. For a lot of riders, the Six Day scene was a constant round of uppers and downers.

According to some, my dad was actually known as 'the Doc' because he'd supply other riders with pills. Certainly, his own amphetamine use appears to have been prolific, to the extent that towards the end of his career he was actually barred from racing. Intensive amphetamine use over time is deeply damaging. I've looked it up and side effects include agitation, anxiety, paranoia, mood swings, depression and a propensity to overreact. That allows me to have some sympathy for Dad. When I stayed with him he would drink and get very depressed and angry, exacerbated no doubt by the long-term effects of the drugs he consumed when he was racing. I feel like he paid a heavy price for the success he had. Same as I would pay a heavy price myself.

Maybe if he'd been born into a different era Dad might have had a chance. As it was he grew up in 1960s and 70s

Australia, a time when blokes were blokes and life was tough. There was no one saying 'It's good to talk' back then. But that doesn't mean he was a bad person, same as there must have been a period with my mum when he was a normal bloke who wanted a wife and family. After all, she'd have never got together with him if he'd been an alcoholic amphetamine-user from the start. My guess is that when he started to find success he upped his drug intake to maintain and improve on that position. At that point, his behaviour became more extreme and their relationship fell apart. Again, I can empathise. I know from personal experience that drugs make you a very selfish person.

I've also heard it suggested that Dad only married Mum so he could get the relevant documentation to live and work in mainland Europe and the UK. Considering how self-centred he was, it wouldn't be the biggest surprise. But I don't believe he was that cold and mechanical. Look at it another way and maybe he wanted those work permits so he could be around for me. I don't agree that his relationship with Mum was solely transactional. My view is there was definitely an attraction between them. Sadly, that wasn't enough for my dad who, from what people say, was clearly a bit of a rogue with the ladies. Mum told me he left her to go off with the winner of Miss Dortmund. If that's true then I'm sure it must have been extremely painful and she had her own abandonment issues. It also illustrates his complete absence of accountability. Dad was aware that he'd caused damage to people around him, but he never expressed any responsibility or reason for it. Several times he told me, 'There's not a day goes by I don't regret leaving you and your mum.' At the time I thought, *That's a nice thing to say.* But 20 years later his words would be a torment. *OK, so why did you leave? What was so bad? Why did you have to do it? If there wasn't a day went past that you didn't regret it, what was the regret? And why so long before you got back in touch? Just let me know!* But he never did. Interesting to think about all this now. Very validating. Very cathartic. It means I can tell myself, *You've got every right to be f**ked up.*

I'd love to know why my dad was like he was, but at every turn I feel thwarted. We're all products of our parents, and there's no reason why he should be any different, but I met his mum and dad only once, very briefly, and other than him being a tearaway from a young age, and his mum ruling the roost, I know very little of his own childhood experiences, his history. What I have come to realise, though, is that whatever the reasons for his flawed character, it was part of what made him successful, and so, by extension, part of him being my hero. I've wondered also if that same flawed character lay dormant in me, only rising to the surface when I found extreme success in 2012. After trying to emulate him on the bike, perhaps now, subconsciously, I was trying to emulate him off it. There have definitely been times when I've been scared of turning into him. 'It's in your genes' – isn't that what everyone told me? Dad's DNA was to be treasured when it came to cycling, not so much when it came to the later years of facing up to the hurt and pain I was carrying.

Maurice and others who knew him say I'm nothing like Dad as a person, but I definitely inherited his constitution and talent so why not elements of his character and personality? Dad was an addict. He dealt with his emotional baggage with alcohol. Being around him when he was wallowing in that trough of anger and self-pity was horrible. But there was one saving grace. It showed me how far someone could fall; how easily treasured relationships could be ruined, never to be recovered. It showed me that addiction was destructive. I never realised it at the time, but maybe that was the biggest lesson Dad taught me.

As I've got older and had my own issues, I've definitely softened on Dad. I've looked in the mirror and seen his reflection staring back as I've come to realise what it must have been like for him when his life fell apart. That's not to deny his many bad points. There are days when I definitely don't want to be like him, same as there are days when I couldn't be more proud to be his son. It's a constant to-ing and fro-ing, with one undeniable truth. My dad is the most important influence on my life. How could a lad from Kilburn become the winner of the Tour de France? Because his dad was a professional cyclist. How could a lad from Kilburn be the one who changes the face of cycling in the UK, the catalyst for hundreds of thousands of people getting on a bike? Because his dad was a professional cyclist. It's all down to him. It has to be. Without him, I'd never have got into cycling. Whether I like it or not, I'm sat here today with a knighthood because of him, because he cycled, because he came to this country from Australia in the 1970s and met my mum, and because he was my hero. He remains my hero to this day. I get that it's strange. I know he let me down. I know he let a lot of people down. But my attachment to him is deep-rooted. I'm part of him and he's part of me.

And I'm glad of it.

CHAPTER 6

LIVING THE DREAM

'Oh, OK, what do I do now?'

Mum receives a letter from British Cycling. A complaint has been made about Stan by the parents of a 13-year-old boy. It's the moment I truly realise the scale of the seriousness of what has happened to me as a kid.

For a short while pre-Sydney, I'd lived with two other riders in Whaley Bridge in the Peak District. As its name suggests, the National Park offers suitably challenging training opportunities. It was also near British Cycling HQ at the Manchester Velodrome, somewhere I was spending more and more time. Ahead of the Games, however, I returned to my mum's. Going back to the scene of so much mental stress and physical pain might appear an act of self-harm, but actually I didn't mind. My stepdad was long gone, I was now the man of the house and my confidence was buoyed by my selection for the biggest sporting event on earth. Whereas not that long ago people had sneered at me for my love of cycling, now I was walking in and out of that flat in an

Olympic tracksuit. I'd be lying if I said there wasn't a little bit of *Look at me now!* In fact, looking back, I feel a little uncomfortable about it, as if I was too conscious of that element of *Well, I showed you, didn't I?* After all, it was totally false bravado. I was still the same non-confrontational person I'd ever been. But I can forgive myself a degree of satisfaction for feeling that I'd made it. I don't think there were too many others on that Olympic team who'd achieved the same from similar surroundings. After my success in 2012 I always used to say, 'Kids from council flats in Kilburn don't win the Tour.' But in 2000 I could just as well have said, 'Kids from council flats in Kilburn don't win Olympic medals.' Or go to Cuba, or South Africa or wherever for that matter. I was doing things that were completely alien to my surroundings. Pedalling a bike was taking me to different planets. That included Sports Personality of the Year, where I watched Steve Redgrave take the trophy after winning his fifth Olympic gold.

Only now when I look back do I see how meteoric my rise was. When I stood on the podium in Sydney it was just eight years since I'd rocked up as a complete novice at the Hayes bypass. In that time I'd won a world title, 15 British titles, been to the Commonwealth Games and competed across the world. It was, by anyone's measurement, an incredible ascent. And it wasn't going to stop at Sydney. I came back with my eyes fixed firmly on gold at Athens in four years' time. I'd seen Jason Queally win the top prize in Australia and I knew I wanted the same. My entire life was focused on cycling, aiming for the next goal, and the next, and the next. That's why going back to Kilburn laid a few demons to rest, I wasn't going to be hanging around. I'd shown my potential on the track and was equally keen to do the same on the road.

At the end of 2000 I signed up with the Linda McCartney Racing Team, formed two years earlier to promote her vegetarian food range. I headed off to the team HQ in Toulouse in my old Ford Fiesta, recently acquired thanks to a gift of a thousand pounds from Grandad. It says a lot for how proud he was of me that he wanted to do that. I really was the apple of his eye. Before the Fiesta, I'd been getting around in my stepdad's Volvo that my mum now owned. When I got invited up to the Sydney Olympics training sessions in Manchester I'd just messed my driving test up by going too slow on a 40-mph bypass. I didn't see the sign, crawled along at 30, and the examiner failed me. I didn't let that little detail get in my way. I packed all my cycling gear in the back of the Volvo and drove up the M1 with no insurance or driver's licence. *F**k it!* I thought. *If I get caught, I'll just tell the police I'm going to the Olympics and they'll let me off.* That was my attitude to most things at that point. *Don't worry about it! No one's going to find out.* I'd watched far too much *Only Fools and Horses*.

By the time I drove to Toulouse I had actually passed my test. Trouble was, no sooner had I arrived than I was doing a U-turn. The team's funding collapsed and I was back at Mum's. I finally said goodbye to Kilburn a few months later when I signed for the better-established Française des Jeux team and moved to Nantes for a year. Better established Française des Jeux might have been but I personally felt totally invisible. Most of the time I was left to my own devices, seeing my teammates only sporadically at races where I'd struggle to make an impression. Turning professional so young, I also found myself racing alongside the faces from the posters on my bedroom wall. Coming face to face with endless legends of the sport was a confidence killer. *I'm not good enough for this.* On the track I could hold my own, I felt I belonged, but thrust into the road scene I couldn't help thinking, *Oh God! What am I doing here?* At the same time, I felt very alone. After training or a race I'd head back to an empty flat. I had no one to pick me up, to cheerlead me. I wasn't living as a professional road cyclist should, and the result was unhappiness and insecurity.

As was the case throughout my career, the track came to the rescue. The 2002 Commonwealth Games were on home territory in Manchester and I won two silvers, in the individual and team pursuit. More significantly, it was where I finally got a girlfriend. I'd had two fears as a kid. The first was drinking the water abroad and getting the s**ts. The second, because of how it might affect my cycling, was getting a girlfriend. Now I'd done both without any hint of disaster. Cath would go on to be my wife. Some people find it odd that someone should marry the first person they got together with, but for me it was perfect. I never wanted to be one of those people who 'play the field'. I just wanted to meet someone, settle down and be happy. Being with someone close was a comfort to me. That was what I wanted, not all that blokey stuff.

Meeting Cath was another huge step towards taking charge of my future, creating something of my own, totally removed from my past. But barely had we got engaged when Mum received the letter from British Cycling. If British Cycling had launched an investigation into Stan then something was very, very wrong. I never saw the contents of the letter, but Mum said they wanted to talk to me. 'He never did anything like that to you, did he?' she asked. Caught off guard, and not knowing how to react to such a huge question with such major personal ramifications, I found myself blurting, 'No, no, he didn't.' All sorts of things were going through my head in that moment. High among them was the fact I was now with Cath. After years of not being able to express my masculinity, finally I was getting on to a confident level. Now, out of nowhere, I was supposed to admit to having been sexually abused? My mind was set. *I'm not going to say anything about this, she might leave me.*

Equally, my career was taking off. I became individual pursuit world champion in 2003. Right now, great things were happening to and for me. The abuse in my past was the last thing I was ever going to mention. Until Mum received that letter I never expected it to crop up again. My attitude had always been straightforward. *Just forget about it. Pretend it never happened. Take it to the grave.* I didn't need what Stan did to me to be front and centre in my life. I didn't need everyone knowing about it, any more than I needed a headful of it myself. I was going to stay quiet. Lock it away in the darkest, dingiest corner of my mind. With any luck I'd never have to think about it ever again.

I busied myself setting up home with Cath. I'd had enough of being marooned in France and so we bought a house in Chapel-en-le-Frith, again within easy reach of the Manchester Velodrome, where I'd prepare for Athens. The move worked for my road career too. While it still lacked the kind of structure and planning on which I thrived, I was happier because I was now operating from my own home rather than an empty flat. I'd arrive at races feeling more excited than overwhelmed, which reminded me of why I so wanted to ride on the road in the first place. Finally, I could appreciate that I was actually living the moments I'd dreamed of as a kid. I remember once hearing the footballer Ian Wright talking about his first FA Cup final, playing for Crystal Palace against Manchester United at Wembley, and how massive it felt to be involved in this thing that he'd watched for years on TV; how desperate he was to get off the substitutes' bench and actually be part of it. I understood so well what he meant. Every time I did a big race for the first time I was exactly the same. *I'm doing the Giro d'Italia! I'm doing Paris–Roubaix! I'm doing the Tour of Flanders!* It felt like every week I was part of cycling folklore. Everything that had started out as a distant dream was coming true. There was an element of getting all that wide-eyed wonder out of my system for a couple of years, but at the same time I wasn't just pootling round with my jaw hanging open. I was ambitious, desperate to perform, get results and be noticed by the big teams. Like every professional out there I was desperate to ride one race in particular – the Tour de France.

On and off the bike, everything seemed to be happening at hyperspeed. The night before the Olympic individual pursuit final in Athens, Cath told me she was pregnant. She thought I was going to be angry. She couldn't have been more wrong. I was over the moon. I had no reason not to be, I loved the idea of being a dad. Next day I powered to victory against the Australian Bradley McGee. At the side of the track was the person who'd first sparked my fascination with the Olympics. Twelve years on from his own success in Barcelona, Chris Boardman had masterminded my own charge to gold in Athens. With silver in the team pursuit and bronze in the madison, I returned home with three medals.

I wasn't conscious of it at the time but those months after my first Olympic gold were another portent of what was to happen, on a much vaster scale, after the Games in London. With gold medal in hand, I'd often be the special guest at cycling club events, asked to pull the lottery tickets out of the hat. There were times I'd get so pissed I was barely able even to do that. I see now that a big part of hiding behind pint after pint was the fear of being seen as myself. I used alcohol as a crutch. Ironic, really, since I could hardly stand up half the time. I reached for it because, in moments when the spotlight was on me, it delivered, or I thought it delivered, a perceived edge of self-assurance off the bike. That need for a confidence booster, something to shut out the low self-worth, was the first sign that I hadn't been given the tools in childhood and adolescence to grow into a strong, secure adult. The contradiction is that had I been given those tools I probably wouldn't have achieved anything on the bike. As it was, cycling was life and death for me. It was all I had. Not winning at Athens wasn't an option. I couldn't imagine what kind of life I'd have if that didn't happen and my cycling career faltered. Some people have a safety net. If cycling fails, they've got other skills to fall back on. I had no skills, academic, practical, interpersonal or otherwise. I had cycling or I had nothing, and that stayed with me throughout my life.

There was something else about that period. It was the first time I'd really stopped since I raced that first time on the Hayes bypass. While there was an element of freedom in getting off the bike, and in my surroundings, far from the stifling atmosphere of the flat, there was also an abundance of aimlessness. I'd spent four years striving for something, aiming towards one single moment, and then in four minutes 16.304 seconds it was done. I was overcome with a sense of anticlimax, something I'd experience a few times more with the Olympics. I had a two-week downer after Beijing, for example. But it's only natural for there to be a certain element of emptiness. The World Championships are big but the Olympics is the really big one. And then you do it, and win, and it's like, *Oh, OK, what do I do now?* Everything seems so trivial in comparison. It's like suddenly part of you has been removed. Even just getting back on your bike feels slightly pointless. *Well, it's four years to the next one. I don't need to.* That might have been OK had I not become totally institutionalised to cycling, another result of my psychological as well as physical relationship with the sport. I was unusual among athletes in that I loved the process and application of reaching a goal, rather than the goal itself. I thrived on focus and routine. When it was gone I felt like I was floating in a void. Post-Athens, that was definitely the case. I'd imagined winning a gold medal would bring radical change to my life, financially if nothing else, my days filled with invitations to meet sponsors and the like. But actually it altered nothing. Offers to make a few quid were far from forthcoming. Don't get me wrong, doing *A Question of Sport*, on the same team as Shane Warne no less, was great, but you don't spend four years training to identify the mystery guest.

Ultimately, with time on my hands, and Cath out at work all day, I spent a lot of time in the pub.

I have occasionally pondered if, subconsciously, I was testing the waters of what it was like to be my dad at that point, but I don't honestly think that's the case. The questions swimming around my head were more connected to the fact I was about to become a father myself. The main question being *How the f**k do I do that?* After all, I'd never had anyone in my life who could justifiably say they'd adequately filled the role. Combine that with the fact I'd just achieved my lifetime's ambition, only to find it felt totally different to how I expected it to, and no wonder I was attracted to something which, on the face of it, helped me feel a bit better about myself. I realise that sitting at the bar of their local all day isn't quite the image most people have of Olympic champions, but for me alcohol, per se, wasn't a massive problem. Only when I retired did it take on a different, darker role.

I do wonder, though, if part of that post-Athens drinking was related to the first rumblings of childhood trauma coming through. Cycling was the wall behind which all the bad stuff lay. Whenever it was absent, as it was now, the wall would crumble a little and I'd become vulnerable. Bear in mind my success in 2004 came just a year after my mum received the letter about Stan, and maybe what happened to me as a child was starting to manifest itself. My mental process had always been to tell myself that the abuse by Stan hadn't really bothered me. But of course it had. When echoes of that time were allowed to get through, all too often self-destruction was my answer. Spending days in the pub wasn't exactly personal ruination, but it could be seen as the foothills of what was to come.

The last few weeks of Cath's pregnancy didn't go well. She was in and out of hospital suffering from pre-eclampsia and then the delivery itself was complicated by Ben having a knot in his umbilical cord. Sadly, I missed the birth. I kept flying back from races thinking it was going to happen and then inevitably it wouldn't. In the end I was away for the weekend and couldn't get a flight back in time. Finally, I made it to the maternity unit and held my son in my arms. I have the photo. I look so young. I've no idea what it is to be a father. So much had happened so quickly. At 22 I'd got a girlfriend for the first time; at 23 I'd become a world champion; at 24 I'd won three Olympic medals at the same Games, got married and become a dad. I even had my own house, for Christ's sake. *Jesus, Brad, you're actually an adult!* As if all that wasn't enough, a year later my daughter Bella came along. That's a lot of very big life events in a very short space of time – life events with a very large potential to rub up against my past. Looking back now, I was taking things in my stride that really should have been moments for deeper reflection. But because I was so used to dealing with everything on my own, my attitude was simple. *It'll be all right, I'll just get on with it.* I thought that was what you did when something big happened – you just got on with it. And that, outwardly at least, was what happened. Inwardly, however, fatherhood proved a definite trigger for thinking about my own childhood. As weird as it sounds, I didn't realise I was abandoned until I saw my own children not being abandoned. I felt loved by a parent only for a short period when I was very young. I looked at Ben and Bella and wondered how my own mum and dad could have allowed that to happen.

That feeling was exacerbated by another crushing thought. For most new dads, the idea of introducing their children to their own father would be accompanied by a sense of excitement and anticipation. In my case, the prospect of Dad wanting to see Ben and Bella hung over me like a dark cloud.

I didn't want his chaos around them, but the prospect of telling him he couldn't see them made me feel sick. The inferiority I felt in our relationship meant I knew I didn't have it in me to assert myself and say, 'Leave my kids alone!' Whether he'd ever ask, I didn't know. The last time we'd spoken was very briefly after Athens. One part of me didn't want to know what his reaction was to my gold medal, another wanted him to say, 'I'm so proud of you, Brad!' I can't remember exactly how the conversation went, but him saying he was proud of me definitely wasn't part of it.

The result of me re-adjusting to my post-Athens reality was 18 months where I lost focus on the bike. I'd become a professional cyclist, won an Olympic gold medal, become a world champion and won the Ghent Six Day. I'd also surpassed my dad. While it was never my goal, there could be no argument that I was better. At that point, when winning the Tour de France was way beyond anyone's imagination, mine included, what I'd achieved was enough for me. In many ways, it was only natural there was a slump. By the end of 2005, however, I finally got my act together. I could always rely on Team GB and they put together a good support structure which allowed me to concentrate on the Road World Championships in Madrid, where I finished seventh in the time trial. On a level playing field, I might actually have finished in the medals. Kazakhstan pair Alexander Vinokourov and Andrey Kashechkin were both banned for doping two years later, while a couple of other riders in the places above me were implicated in Operación

Puerto, the high-profile Spanish police investigation into a large doping network.

It was disheartening to know that one of the reasons why my results on the road weren't matching my potential was that so many others were operating on another level. I look back now to my first Giro d'Italia in 2003 and I was riding against the likes of Marco Pantani and Mario Cipollini, whose careers were beset by doping allegations. They're just the most high-profile examples. Dopers were everywhere. That period in the early to mid-2000s saw the sport rocket to entirely new levels of performance enhancement. How was I, riding on bread and water, ever supposed to compete? In all honesty, there were times when I felt like packing up.

In 2006, having moved to another French team, Cofidis, I was selected for my first Tour de France. Again, there was an element of pinching myself. I'd be riding against huge names like Jan Ullrich, who won the Tour in 1997, and one of my heroes, the two-times Giro winner Ivan Basso. At least I thought I would. Before the Tour even started both were kicked off the race after being linked to Operación Puerto. I was just a spectator in that Tour. While I managed to get in the break one day, overall it was a case of just getting round. When finally I crossed the finishing line in Paris, my overriding feeling was, *Whatever else happens, I can always say I've finished a Tour.* I had no inkling whatsoever that one day I might win the thing.

By the time the Tour came round again in 2007 I was flying. I felt in a good place. I was happy at home, loving being a dad, and had rediscovered my confidence and identity by going back to the track and winning two world titles. On the road that self-belief showed with a win in the time trial at the Four Days of Dunkirk and the prologue at traditional Tour warm-up, the Critérium du Dauphiné. That child, so excited at actually being part of these legendary races I'd always dreamed about, hadn't left me. What had changed was me becoming capable of succeeding in those races. I wasn't taking part anymore, I was actually achieving.

I'd had my eye on the 2007 Tour ever since it was revealed that the race was to start in London. The announcement had come just a year after the capital won the bid to stage the Olympics in 2012. It was barely believable, two massive events, happening not just in Britain but a few miles from where I grew up. Not only that, both would be happening in my peak years as an athlete. If that didn't get me out of bed in the morning, nothing would. My objective was clear – win the 2007 Tour prologue and 2012 Olympic time trial in my home city. *Whatever happens after that, I'll retire happy. That'll do for me.*

The London départ was huge. It was embraced by the city, even more so since the day itself, 7 July, marked the second anniversary of the 7/7 bombings which killed 52 people and injured almost 800. The prologue, a five-mile individual time trial, started in Whitehall, went through Westminster, past Buckingham Palace, took in Hyde Park and finished on The Mall. The crowds were huge, like riding through a party in my backyard. Five years later I'd have the same experience on a far more epic scale. In the end I didn't win that prologue, but finishing fourth, a single second behind George Hincapie in third, was no disgrace and was a marker for the good form which continued throughout the race. On stage 6, a flat 199.5 km run from Semur-en-Auxois to Bourg-en-Bresse, I won the combativity award for the most aggressive rider, having made one of the longest solo breaks in Tour de France history. Shocked to find myself alone off the front after just 2 km, I was away for the next 190.5, at one point 18 minutes clear of the chasing pack. Again, it was one of those *Is this really happening?* moments. Well, not so much a moment as five exhausting, but hugely exhilarating, hours. That's how long I was away, beamed into homes and cafés across Europe at the head of this incredible race in which I'd always dreamed of leaving my mark. Eventually, as tends to be the case with big solo efforts, I was reeled in by the chasers with a few kilometres left. Given that 13 July was the anniversary of the death of Tom Simpson, the legendary British cyclist who died toiling up Mont Ventoux in the 1967 Tour, and someone whose life resonates with me deeply, my achievement that day felt extra special.

A week later I finished fifth in the time trial on stage 13. And then 72 hours later my race imploded. Barely had I crawled over the line at the Col d'Aubisque after a torturous 218.5 km through the high passes of the Pyrenees than one of the Cofidis soigneurs was trying to usher me into a team car. As he did so, he explained breathlessly that my

Italian teammate Cristian Moreni had tested positive for elevated levels of testosterone. This a day after Alexander Vinokourov's Astana team had been thrown off the race because the Kazakhstani had tested positive for blood doping after winning the time trial. I'd seen enough doping scandals play out in front of the cameras, which, as I took in what the soigneur was telling me, were now very much pointing in my direction, to know that being hurried away in a team car was not a good look. Instead, I freewheeled down to the team bus at the bottom of the mountain, where, immediately, the police arrested me and the rest of the Cofidis riders while they carried out an investigation.

We were taken first to a police station so the bus could be searched for drugs, and then by car to our hotel while a similar examination was made of our rooms. The media followed us everywhere, which was exactly what the police wanted, illustrating that they were actually doing something about the ingrained and widespread doping which had beset the sport. The cameras clicked and next day a picture of me being led into the hotel by a uniformed gendarme was all over the front page of French daily sports paper *L'Équipe*. Look at that photo and you'll see a bit of a smirk on my face, not because I thought what was happening was funny but because, as scary as it was being arrested, the whole thing just seemed so utterly surreal. I mean, how many other sports are there where one minute you're crossing the finishing line after the best part of seven hours killing yourself, and the next you're in a cop car on a potential drugs charge?

The upshot of this insane saga was that, while none of the rest of us were found to have doped, the team withdrew from the race. Enraged at the decision, and feeling sick to have been dragged into a doping scandal, next day I threw my Cofidis kit in a bin as I waited at Pau Airport for a flight back to the UK. I took what happened very, very personally and immediately on my return gave a press conference in Manchester. Everyone in that room could see how angry and pissed off I was. I spoke that day not because I wanted to be some sort of martyr for clean sport, but because I knew that if I didn't take a stance I'd soon get tarred with the same brush. Cristian was a lone ranger in what he did at Cofidis but it still meant drugs were in our team. I took great offence to that and I wanted to do all I could to avoid being tainted by association. What I really did, however, was create a rod for my own back, becoming the media's go-to person for comment whenever there was a high-profile doping case. Later, when I started winning races, I preferred not to keep talking about doping because I didn't need the distraction. Of course, then came the backlash. 'Oh, he used to be such a staunch advocate for clean riding. Now he doesn't want to talk about it. That must mean he's cheating.' As I would find out in retirement, there are always those who actively want to believe you've done something wrong. Given the opportunity, they'll bang that drum so loudly that eventually you start falling apart.

With distance, memories of the ugliness of the way it ended at Cofidis have faded. I was good mates with Cristian

Moreni before the incident and I'm still good mates with him now. Just because someone has cheated as a sportsperson in the past doesn't mean I feel the need to condemn them as a human being forever. I've softened on all the drugs cheats, not because I agree with what they did, but because their actions are indicative of the time in which they rode. Now cycling has cleaned itself up, one person cheating everyone else is difficult to forgive. When it comes to someone doping 20 years ago, when virtually everyone was doing it, it's more difficult to judge. Look at the British rider David Millar. He tried to ride clean in that era and in the end was so crushed that he started doing what everyone else did. There's never any guarantees, but it's an undeniable fact that the playing field is a lot more level than it used to be. Worth pointing out as well that, whatever the industry, there will always be people seeking to gain an unfair advantage. I go back to what was said about my dad – 'most people have a line they won't cross, others don't have a line'. All you can do in any situation is control your own actions. Worry about other people's and the result is you talk yourself out of a perform-ance.

While my 2007 Tour had ended shambolically, there had been several moments where I'd shown my potential to leave a real mark on the road. But I still never imagined that that would equate into a pitch at the podium one day. In fact, with 2008 being an Olympic year, my aim was to miss the Tour and try to add to my medal haul on the track. I felt happy with that aspiration, same as I felt content and settled with my life off the bike. Being a dad, immersing myself in a family so different from the one in which I'd grown up, suited me in a way I could never have imagined.

For once, the course of my life was running smoothly. But then, at 6 a.m. one winter morning, the phone rang.

CHAPTER 7

MURDER

*'Idolising him meant I achieved my dreams,
but it also left deep emotional scars.'*

The mental image of Dad lying in a ditch cut me to ribbons then and does so still to this day. I think about the moment his attackers dumped him in the dirt to die, the thud as he hit the ground.

Whoever was on the other end of that phone wasn't giving up. It rang and rang. It was Cath who eventually stumbled her way down the stairs. 'Hello?' She heard a familiar Aussie voice – Shane Sutton. She put him on to me. 'Listen, Brad, I've got some bad news.' He paused. 'Gary's died.' A bloke in Australia who knew Dad had got a message to Shane. The details were sketchy but it seemed Dad had been beaten up in the street and left for dead.

The first thing I did when I hung up was go into Bella's room. I lifted her out of her cot and held her. In her tiny form I satisfied my own need for comfort. I expect in my mind she also perfectly embodied the vulnerability of human life. I clung on to her all morning and then in the afternoon I went out and bought a guitar, a Rickenbacker 360. Comfort again. I've always loved the way guitars can transport you to a completely different mental space.

Sounds ridiculous, but I think part of my inwardly quite calm and collected response was that Dad's death came as no great surprise. While it had been a few years since I'd seen him, I never for one minute imagined he'd have turned himself around. My expectation was that his everyday life would only have got more messy. Rather than being overwhelmed by grief, I found myself constantly questioning my emotions. *How am I supposed to be feeling? How am I supposed to be behaving? Am I sad or am I pretending to be sad? If you really are sad, Brad, you've got no right to be. It's not like you watched him walk out the door this morning and never saw him again. You hadn't spoken to him for the last four years. You didn't actually know if he was still alive.*

Meanwhile, the phone rang non-stop. 'You're going to have the press on you all day,' Shane had warned, and he wasn't wrong. An Olympic champion's father found dying in the street is just the kind of story the newspapers like. Nowadays maybe it would be different, but back then I had no one from British Cycling, a press officer or whatever, to help fend people off. I answered a few calls but spending the day dealing with the same questions over and over again isn't what anyone needs in these circumstances. Anyway, at that point I had no more information than anyone else. It was only over the next few days that the detail began to emerge. Dad had been to a party at a house in the small

Hunter Valley town of Aberdeen, New South Wales. He was badly beaten, 'bashed' as the Aussies say, at the property before being dumped in the street, one suggestion being that his assailants hoped he'd be run over, or even ran him over themselves, so the subsequent injuries would disguise the assault. A passing motorist saw Dad stagger to his feet but he either collapsed or was attacked for a second time further down the road. He might even have been chucked in the back of a car and dumped in the dust and dirt. Whatever happened, Dad was found unconscious in a ditch early the next morning. He was flown to the nearest city hospital, in Newcastle, but nothing could be done to save him. An inquest determined the cause of Dad's death to be a heavy blow to the back of the head. With a lack of reliable eye-witness evidence about what had happened at the party and, therefore, the cause of Dad's injury, the coroner was forced to record an open verdict.

But there's no doubt in my mind he was murdered.

Once the police released Dad's body, the funeral could take place. I didn't go, something people expect me to regret, but actually I still feel comfortable with the decision. My relationship with Dad was complex and the funeral would only have added another layer to the confusion in my head. It would also have literally been a case of turning up at the service and flying straight home.

Dad's murder came just weeks before the Track World Championships in Manchester. As ever, cycling provided the ideal distraction from trauma. Elite sport is an environment where pause for reflection, grief or sentimentality gets you nowhere. In the individual pursuit, any chink in my armour and I was beaten. In the team pursuit, if I messed up, my three teammates also suffered. In the madison, if I wasn't on it, then my partner's chance of gold was gone. As it turned out, I won the individual pursuit, helped to set a world record in the team pursuit, and, with perfect symmetry, won the madison, Dad's speciality, with Cav. I was world madison champion and Dad would never know it, a bittersweet sensation I couldn't help mentioning in my post-race interview. 'It was his event,' I reflected, 'but he never managed to win the world title, so that one's for him.'

Around the same time, I flew to California for a training camp with my new team, HTC-Highroad. My fellow riders were so nice, offering constant consolation, and me being me, I didn't know how to react, putting on a brave front and making out things were OK. Yet again I was kicking a huge ball of stifled emotion down the road. Death isn't the end of anything. It just means you've got a whole different set of thoughts, questions and memories to deal with. Therapy would have been the track to go down, but it wasn't on my radar. As far as I was concerned I'd got this far working things out for myself. Meanwhile, an Olympic year meant more opportunity to bury myself in competition. I'd set my sights on winning three gold medals at Beijing, and then, shortly before the team left for China, I got really ill, so ill in fact that there was a fear I had meningitis. Whether my sickness was a reaction to my dad's death, I don't know, but for someone who rarely got ill, its severity was unusual. I recovered enough to haul myself onto the plane, defending my individual pursuit title, and just about holding my own in the team pursuit, before finally capitulating in the madison.

That last race at Beijing aside, 2008 was an incredibly successful year, heralding the start of the most glorious period of my career. As hard as it is to admit, once my dad died I flourished. Maybe that's just coincidence. Or had his presence, somewhere out there, been holding me back? I'd be lying if, among the mixed bag of feelings I felt when Dad died, there weren't occasional waves of relief. Dad was gone and I didn't have to worry about him anymore. I get that people who've never had someone deeply dysfunctional and disruptive in their lives will find it hard to understand, but there can be an element of liberation when they're gone and you don't have to deal with their chaos, or the spectre of their chaos, anymore. That's not easy to say, but it's true. Part of me thinks I'd never have had the success of 2012 if Dad had still been alive. You need everything in your favour to win the Tour de France. Absolute focus from the minute you set out to achieve the goal is the most important element of all. My relationship with Dad would doubtless have been gnawing somewhere at the back of my mind. I say that as an observation, not as something that's in any way important. What I mean is that, just as his existence somewhere out there had been an inspiration in my childhood, by 2008 it had become a black cloud.

Even when Dad wasn't in my life I was on tenterhooks, waiting for the day that everything blew up again in some way, be it him making an unexpected and potentially disruptive appearance at a race, or the thing I really feared, asking to see my kids. Other possibilities felt similarly difficult to contemplate. While our relationship seemed beyond repair, maybe at some point he'd have given an interview in which he talked fondly about me, said he was proud of me or something, and I'd have felt obliged to put my hurt to one side and make amends, the complexity of emotion lost in a shallow reunion played out for the benefit of a TV show or a newspaper. A reconciliation that was honest and heartfelt would have been different, but such an occasion seemed unlikely when so much of what I'd felt from him was jealousy and resentment. He hadn't told me he was proud of me. He'd told me, 'You'll never be as good as your old man.' And so, in 2008, Dad's death felt like the closing of a chapter. I didn't have to worry about him anymore. As hard as it is to admit, there was an element of freedom. Without him in the picture I could focus on painting a happy future for my family and career. My life is full of ugly contradictions, and prominent among them is that, in death, Dad contributed to so much I achieved.

As time has passed, the relief I felt in 2008 has faded, replaced by the massive part of me that wishes Dad was still here. Had he lived, we would, inevitably, have met again at some point. No way would I have gone on and on not speaking to him. Who knows? Maybe a miracle would have happened and he'd have turned his life around. I know from personal experience that rock bottom is a place that brings out the worst in us. I know also that we're all capable of change. But it did seem like Dad had run out of road. He'd had multiple opportunities to get his life back together and never taken them. Today he'd be in his seventies, but the way he lived his life he was never going to make it that far. I hate to say it, and I'm making assumptions based on the little amount I saw of him at his lowest, but I think in so many ways he was a lost cause. In all honesty, I think he'd have been a nightmare had he been around the last 20 years. I say that from an entirely personal point of view. Clearly there's more than just me in Gary's story. Two other children, one just a little girl, lost their father that night, same as a sister lost her brother. Gary's family will always carry an immense burden of hurt. The circumstances around his death will forever be a torture to us all. There had always been a chance his life would end in a violent manner, but that doesn't negate the shock when that actually turns out to be the case. No one ever expects to be told their dad's been murdered.

Dad's case has never been solved. His sister Glenda has campaigned for years for the killer or killers to be brought to justice, but as of now they remain free men. For whatever reason, the police have failed to gather the evidence. What is clear is that by the time Dad died his life had careered out of control. Sadly, it appears that fights were a common feature. There are stories of Dad hitting a man who was harassing a woman in a pub and the bloke ending up in a coma. Another time a guy threatened him with a baseball bat only for Dad to wrestle the weapon from him and dish out a beating. For that little misdemeanour he ended up in jail for a while. It seems certain that he made enemies and there were people who wanted rid of him. Violence is a common thread through Dad's story. Ultimately it was what ended his life.

The tragedy of Dad's final moments on this Earth really breaks my heart. Whoever he was in those last few months and years, he was still the man who held me in his arms as a baby, still the man who made me a cyclist, still the man in those photos who saved me as a child. The fact I hadn't seen him for so long would spark flashes of regret, sadness, self-hatred and guilt. I couldn't help feeling I'd cut him out of my life at the exact moment he needed me most. Then I'd swing completely in the opposite direction and reassure myself that staying away was absolutely the right thing, both for me and my family. I can see now that what I should have done in 2008 is taken time out to reflect properly on his death; to come to terms with the different relationships I'd had with him over the years and how they'd impacted me. I needed help and support. By throwing myself back into racing I never allowed myself to process the effect his loss had on me. If anything, I felt not grief, but fear. Sounds odd now, but I was scared for a while. The headlines were all about how Gary was my dad. Every time I won anything his murder was brought up. The killers weren't going to be allowed to slink easily back into the shadows and there were times when a little bit of paranoia would slip in. *Are they going to try to shut this down? Are they going to come and kill me as well?* I know, crazy! But until you find yourself in alien territory you can never predict what games your mind will play.

I do know, however, that the success I had that year felt somehow different. There was a definite undercurrent of not quite being able to appreciate or celebrate those World and Olympic titles. I think now, without ever understanding it, I was numbed by shock. In the shadow of Dad's murder I'd convinced myself I was fine, but inwardly I was suffering. Cycling was the pillow I used to suffocate those feelings. The non-stop surge towards the ultimate success of 2012 steam-rollered any chance of reflection. Only as my career ebbed after 2012 was there room for Dad to re-enter my conscious-ness. I'd wonder if I was better off for meeting him or if it had been a connection better left unexplored. I'd ponder the non-relationship we had at the time of his death and then think back to a decade earlier when I was showing him the posters on my bedroom wall. In the end, I've concluded that, as painful as much of it was, I'm happy I had the chance to spend time with a man who for so long existed only in my imagination. I got to see him not as a photo, in sepia, but in full-colour flesh and blood. Experiencing the difficult side of him was part of making him real. I had to go through all those episodes – his absence, his presence, his encourage-ment, his envy – to be the person I am now. I wouldn't change that. It's not for me to change anything about my life in those early years.

I've inherited Dad's genes in a lot of ways but the cyclical nature of actually being like him, something which for a long time I feared, never happened. There was a certain malevolence to him which I don't have. He'd flick someone, reject them very quickly, and violence appeared central to his character. It's undeniable that, for one person, he left an awful lot of wreckage. When I talk about that side of him, it baffles me why I'm still so fond of him; why I have pictures of him up in my home. Undeniably there are versions of Gary which are impossible to respect, and maybe I've struggled to accept that down the years, clinging instead to the incarnation of him that suits me better, the cyclist who provided me with an escape route from my childhood despair. After all, most of those photos in my house are of him racing.

In many ways Dad was a role model for how not to live my life. So, in a weird sense, still a role model. Either become like him or learn from him. I did both. Growing up, every time I got on a bike I thought about being him. I wanted to ride like him, win like him, think like him. In adulthood, I'm realising the impact he's had on me, good and bad. I'm understanding that idolising him meant I achieved my dreams, but it also left deep emotional scars.

I realise also how hard it must have been for him to re-enter my life at a point where I was really beginning to shine as a cyclist, having never been part of that journey, and knowing my mum had overseen my progress to that point. The complexity of that dynamic from his perspective isn't lost on me. The ball was very much in his court. Sadly for him, as time went on he became less and less likely to pick the right option. Imagine if he'd left me with the memory of him saying, 'I wasn't there at the start, but you make me so proud, you'll be a far better bike rider than I ever was' rather than 'You'll never be as good as your old man.' But that was Dad – never quite able to see a situation through other people's eyes. When that's someone you drink with or race against, it's not so bad. When it's your own son, it's different.

While winning the Tour and four more Olympic gold medals may never have happened if Dad had lived, part of me can't help but ask what he'd have thought of the success I went on to have after he died. In the end, I've concluded that he'd have been proud of me winning the Tour. The envy I'd seen in the past had come when I'd surpassed his ability in races in which he himself was competitive. Surely even Gary Wiggins would have had to admit the Tour was beyond him. I expect the problem would have come in a need for reflective glory to paper over his own inadequacies. If Ben wins the Tour, I'll be the first to say he did it all off his own bat; that it was nothing to do with me. Dad, I'm sure, would have revelled in the genetics – 'I was a pretty good rider myself, you know!' But perhaps he'd have proved me wrong.

I see some of his competitive attitude with me as being a side-effect of his more reflective and sorrowful nature, the part of his personality that felt free to tell me, 'There's not a day goes past I don't feel guilty about having left you.' His only way to keep that more meaningful and very non-Gary emotion in check was to go in entirely the opposite direction.

Had he just allowed that tenderness to be, he'd have seen what I really thought of him. But then again this is my dad so I don't know whether he was truly eaten up with guilt or if he just thought it sounded like the right thing to say. *Because Dad, why did you leave me? If you were deported and you couldn't come back, I'd understand. But I don't know why you left. No one's ever told me.*

It feels sometimes like me and Dad were shouting at each other silently, never quite able to let the other one know what we were feeling. When Dad died, Madison told me, 'He was so proud of you. He had all these clippings of you on a shelf.' I appreciated her telling me, but at the same time how am I supposed to feel about that? Good? Bad? I'm not sure, because I can't ever really know how he felt about me. Same as I've got mementos of his career, and he doesn't know how I feel about him – that he's my hero and I love him. It's why the Kuipke Velodrome will always be somewhere incredibly special to me; the place where I feel myself and Dad most closely intertwined. There's a big picture of every winner of the Six Day up on the wall. That includes me, who won it twice, once with Cav, the first British pairing ever to do so, and once with the Australian Matthew Gilmore, who, in another barely believable twist, was the son of Graeme Gilmore who raced the Six Day with Dad. I'm honoured to have my picture up in that epic arena, but at the same time I know it wouldn't be there without Dad. In 1984, he won the European Madison Championship, which at the time was effectively the world title. He knew the madison inside out and that meant so did I. I'd studied it from as far back as I can remember. I might not have gone to university, but I've got a degree, with honours, in the madison! I had a sixth sense for it, never crashed, despite it being a physical race with lots of thrills and spills, and knew exactly where to position me and my partner. My relationship with the madison is in my veins. It looks like the DNA has been passed on a further generation, for Ben became Junior World Champion in the madison in 2023.

When Dad and I tentatively started rebuilding our relationship in my teens, a big brick in that wall was that very European Madison Champion's jersey he won in 1984. He gave it to me and I hung it in my bedroom, my most prized possession. Fast forward to 20 November 2016, and I'm making my very last professional appearance, in the madison at the Ghent Six Day, on what would have been Dad's 64th birthday. All day, people have been telling me that victory is written in the stars, but, while I do win, what actually happens is so much more than some kind of weird celestial alignment. I'm riding round the track when I have a full-on out of body experience. Dad is actually with me on the bike. I know that sounds mad, but it's true. He is there, pushing the pedals round with me. I'm not emulating him. I *am* him. We are each other. All our history has become one. There's a photo of me as a baby with Dad at the Kuipke Velodrome. Now, after all that's happened in the years in between, here we are, finally, racing together in this place that's a church to both of us. It was here, right here, he told me, 'You'll never be as good as your old man.' But nothing I've ever done on a bike has been about me telling him, 'I'll show you!' It's all been about gratitude and love, and in that moment those feelings are made real. There I am, madison World Champion, winner of the Tour de France, five Olympic golds, riding with Dad on my shoulder, the end product of all I've achieved, all that he's made me.

The laps unwind and gently Dad fades into the ether. But the memory never disappears. Me and my dad riding those boards. As one at last.

CHAPTER 8

LE TOUR

*'My mindset that whole Tour was simple
– I was indestructible.'*

I've been asked many times what's it's like winning the Tour de France and I've given many different replies down the years. Now, however, I have the definitive answer. It's like doing drugs. It gives you everything you've ever asked for in that moment, but it takes so much more from you in return.

When I left for the Tour in 2012, I never for one moment realised just how famous I was going to become. I was known in cycling circles but otherwise not too many people had heard of me. Three weeks later I returned to find myself just about the most famous man in the country.

My elevation to superstar status was in itself the culmination of one of the most remarkable sporting transformations Britain has ever known. For decades cycling was very much a minority sport but then, due largely to the mantra coming from British Cycling performance director Dave Brailsford, the track squad earned a reputation as a medal factory, following up mine and Chris Hoy's gold medals in Athens with a further eight in Beijing. Emboldened by that success, then came the audacious statement – or at least it seemed that way at the time – of trying to win the Tour de France with a British rider, at the heart of a British team.

In 2009, when the first whispers of this ambition emerged, I was enjoying what I still consider to be the most enjoyable year of my career. Having joined US team Garmin, I'd moved the family out to live with me in Girona, Spain. The weather was beautiful, the lifestyle was relaxed and the kids were happy. After Dad's death the previous year, and all that had come before it, finally I felt like I'd found a steady level. I was at peace with myself, and that translated to my performance on the bike. Both the team and myself had started to identify that I could really achieve on the road as well as the track. At the Giro, there were several days where I found myself climbing and finishing with the front group, and by the time I got to the Tour the insecurity that had accompanied me at times on the road had gone. More than that, I found myself riding in pockets of supreme confidence. My mindset that whole Tour was simple – I was indestructible. I knew I could finish in the top ten, and nothing that happened during those three weeks dented my belief. Team leader Christian Vande Velde clearly saw my potential to finish high in the general classification (GC). He'd big me up daily – 'If I get dropped, Brad, you don't come back for me, you stay up front.'

I just went from strength to strength, reminded constantly in my own head of those times when I'd sit on the turbo trainer in the flat in Kilburn watching videos of the Tour, pretending I was climbing the high mountains as I turned the pedals. Now, not only was I doing it in real life, but I was up there with the best, alongside eventual winner Alberto Contador and the Schleck brothers, Andy and Fränk. Ridiculously, I actually found myself battling for a podium position with my childhood hero Lance Armstrong, such a big figure, not just in cycling but in the entire world of sport and beyond. This was Lance's comeback Tour after winning the race seven times in a row between 1999 and 2005. The aura he had was the equivalent of sporting legends such as Maradona and Michael Schumacher, not that everybody was impressed. It was incredible to see up close the abuse he was getting on the climbs. On the hellish ascent of Mont Ventoux, the 'Giant of Provence', the Spanish fans were actually throwing urine on him. Riding on his wheel, what missed him went on me. In that position all you can do is keep your mouth closed – not easy when you're toiling up one of the hardest climbs on the Tour.

Urine splatters aside, I loved racing with Lance. There were times when he'd come up alongside me in the peloton and start chatting to me, asking how I was doing, offering me support, just being a friendly face. The cycling journalist Paul Kimmage wrote a story during that 2009 Tour suggesting my performances were abnormal, questioning how I'd made the leap from hanging around at the back with the grupetto, the cyclists who can't keep pace with the climbers on the mountain stages, to being at the front of the race. The insinuation was clear – I was doping. I kicked off about it in a newspaper article. Afterwards, Lance came up to me in the peloton. 'I read that interview you did. Good on you! You can see the s**t I've had to put up with the last few years!' He was trying to draw a comparison. Our stories weren't exactly the same – Lance, infamously, would go on to admit widescale doping during his career – but I appreciated where he was coming from at the time.

While Kimmage preferred to take the cynical view, one of the actual reasons I did so well in 2009 was the complete lack of pressure. Not considered a threat, I could ride totally under the radar. Every time I moved up at the top end of the GC it was a bonus. In essence, I couldn't fail. The only way that could happen is if I blew up one day and lost 40 places. In the end I finished fourth in Paris. It was a great, great feeling. Better than winning the entire race in many ways. That might sound mad, but I go back to Ian Wright and the FA Cup – it's not always winning that provides the greatest sporting memories. I couldn't have been happier with my achievement. As a Briton riding the Tour I'd equalled the position of Philippa York in 1984 and surpassed the legendary Tom Simpson's sixth in 1962. *This is it now*, I thought, *I'm in the history books forever! If I never do anything again, I finished fourth in the Tour de France.* Look in the record books now and you'll see I finished third. Following his admission, Lance's own third position was declared void.

While Dave Brailsford's attempt to win the Tour with a British rider was already in the pipeline in 2009, he couldn't talk to me as I was under contract with Garmin. Well, officially. Two weeks into the race, me and Dave met clandestinely in a supermarket café. As a British rider at the top end of the GC, getting me on board to spearhead the assault on the Tour was a no-brainer. I had not only the pedigree but the profile to head up a UK professional team, backed by Sky, the media and telecoms conglomerate, seeking to break the stranglehold of the big continental and American outfits that dominated the sport. There were other big-name British riders around at that time, and I'm not denigrating their achievements in any way, but because I was at the centre of so much on both track and road, chances are if you'd asked anyone in the street to name a cyclist the first one they'd have said would have been me.

Naturally, having suddenly found themselves with what appeared to be a genuine Tour GC contender, Garmin weren't keen to let me go, and, if I'm honest, I wasn't particularly keen to go either. I loved being at Garmin. On the bike I'd thrived in the relaxed environment the team engendered, and off it, with our family life in Girona, I'd found a degree of contentment that had for so long been lacking. It was a big ask to tear all that up and return to the UK. In the end, however, Team Sky made the deal so lucrative, so attractive, that it became irresistible. I saw their offer of a four-year contract worth almost £5 million as not just as a wage but a pension, something that would last me the rest of my life. It was way, way beyond the £350,000 a year I was on at Garmin.

I went to see Garmin team director Jonathan Vaughters. 'Sky have offered me this much – can you keep me?' Jonathan was a straight-up guy. 'I can maybe pay double what you're on now, but I can't afford that.'

I also knew that if Team Sky were hellbent on taking what British Cycling had done on the track and transferring it to the road, then everything performance-related, equipment, training, staff, development, was going to be the best. If I held genuine ambitions to win the Tour de France then it was the place to be. What I didn't know was just how big a sacrifice I'd have to make along the way.

Of course, just because I'd agreed to go to Team Sky didn't necessarily mean it was going to happen. Garmin weren't going to let an asset walk out the door just like that. Eventually, Team Sky had to pay £3.5 million to buy me out of my contract. The football-like sums they were throwing around were unheard of in cycling, an indicator of just how far they were willing to go to achieve their goal. Dave Brailsford could have bought Steven Gerrard for that price, and might very well have wished he had done the way the 2010 season panned out.

If 2009 was the happiest time of my career then the following year would definitely be in the running for the most miserable. After all the hype, all the big talk of a British team winning the Tour with a British rider, I crawled into Paris in 23rd place. The form of the previous year was entirely absent. At the end of stage 14, the first of a trio of difficult stages in the Pyrenees, having lost more time on the leaders, I was approached by the Australian journalist John Trevorrow, funnily enough an old cycling mate of my dad's, which maybe, subliminally, was why I threw the bullshit handbook to one side and told him just exactly how f**ked I was feeling. Generally, this is the sort of thing you don't broadcast during a race; instead you toe the party line about 'anyone can have a bad day' and 'there's plenty of time to turn it round'. But I've never really done PR. 'I just feel consistently mediocre,' I told John. 'Not brilliant, not s**t, just mediocre.' As I say, not quite what the Team Sky bosses were hoping for, but then again I'd just ridden five hours over several high mountains to a ski station while they were sat at the bottom of the road in a top-of-the-range team bus. After chatting to John, I freewheeled down to them. I was sneezing all the way, struggling to get my breath, a sign of the allergies that would later place me at the centre of a violent and relentless storm that I never for one minute saw brewing.

The 2010 Tour was a massive ego-dent for Sky. They'd invested a lot in me and expected an immediate return. But back in the UK I had bigger things to think about. Two weeks after the race, Grandad died. He was only in his late sixties but had a heart attack. It was devastating. Growing up, Grandad was the single solid male role model in my life. He'd treated and loved me like his own. My happiest childhood memories all surrounded him. It was unthinkable that he'd gone, and so I did what I always did – turned my internal computer off and failed to process it. I wasn't conscious

I was pushing my emotions to one side. I was just a natural avoidant. Instinctively, I'd swerve anything that might be painful in any way I could.

At the funeral, Mum suggested I go and look at Grandad. I wasn't keen but I went across to the coffin in a side room. Immediately I regretted it. Nan was in there crying her eyes out, totally lost in grief. Eventually, she left Grandad's side. I walked over and looked at George, this dear old man who'd always been there for me; my grandad who, from as young as I could remember, I'd shared so much with. To this day I wish I hadn't. I should always have remembered Grandad in life, how he truly was.

Immediately after the funeral I had to fly out to a race. It was a disaster. I should never have been there. I should have been encouraged to grieve, but that was how it was at Team Sky. Sympathy and success were rarely seen as compatible. Over the next few weeks, Grandad's death began to hit me hard. Team Sky wanted to stage a post-mortem on a disappointing season but my head was in an entirely different place. Cycling seemed secondary – because it was secondary. Grandad's heart attack was difficult enough to deal with, but it also reawakened thoughts of the loss of my dad just two years earlier. I went off-grid for a while, Sky trying to get in touch, me not responding, and by the time we reconvened at a meeting in Manchester they were doubly pissed off. The season hadn't gone well and then, in their eyes, I'd disappeared. Their attitude was simple. If I didn't start performing they'd cut my salary in half and find a new team leader. Bear in mind this was before we really understood what 'performing' was. Neither they nor I knew what my limits were at that point. I still hadn't fulfilled my true potential. One of the ways they pushed those limits was by instilling fear. Firstly, by telling me that if I didn't pull my weight someone else would take my job, and secondly by telling me they'd slash my wages.

Occasionally at Team Sky I'd think back to Garmin and that Tour of 2009. I knew, had I stayed, the pressure wouldn't have been the same. I knew I'd be enjoying it. But I knew also I'd never have a chance of success at the Tour, whereas at Team Sky, same as British Cycling, winning was the standard. Team Sky made me a different animal. It made a lot of us different animals. It was a factory, a production line. You went in one end as one thing and, if everything went to plan, came out the other a winner. That was the entire reason for your existence. That might sound obvious, but other workplaces aren't like that. You can exist elsewhere without having to be the best in the world. It damaged me in a way I never quite appreciated.

By the time the Tour came round in 2011, Sky had moulded me into the rider they wanted. In March my good form showed with a third-place finish in the weeklong Paris–Nice stage race, and then in June I won the Critérium du Dauphiné, traditionally a marker for who's going to be competing for the podium in Paris. I went into the Tour right up there with the race favourites – and then 40 km from the end of stage 7 I was in a heap on the floor. I knew straightaway I'd broken my collarbone. All that work, all that effort to reach peak competitiveness, gone in a nanosecond. I did, however, salvage a lot, and again indicate my progress as a climber, by finishing second in the third Grand Tour of the season, the Vuelta a España, a race which gave me more belief than ever that I could take the ultimate prize in 2012.

If I'd shown good form in the run-up to the 2011 Tour, then a year later I was absolutely flying. By the time the race rolled out of Liège, I'd already won Paris–Nice, the Tour de Romandie and the Dauphiné. Everything I did went to plan, and that soon extended to the Tour itself. After months of the most intense preparation, I understood in minute detail precisely how to ride that race. What I never understood was the effect my pursuit of glory was having at home. In a three-week Grand Tour you live in a bubble. You get up, eat, race, go to the hotel, eat, have a massage, sleep, and that's it. On repeat. I got that I was doing something extraordinary – these days it's totally normal to have a British rider in yellow, but when I took the jersey in 2012 I was only the fifth, after Tom Simpson, Chris Boardman, Sean Yates and David Millar, in the history of the race – and I completely understood the magnitude of what that meant for me and British cycling, but I never for one minute thought I'd ignite the interest of the public as a whole. After all, Mark Cavendish had been winning stages of the Tour for years, and had even been voted Sports Personality of the Year, but he could walk down the street without getting mobbed.

The man who made me: Vague memories of early days with Dad are all I have – he'd soon disappear from my life. I was delighted when my absent hero re-entered my world as I started to make a mark in cycling, but the relationship would prove difficult.

Butter wouldn't melt: Actually, it would! 'I don't want them bloody things on it!' I declared when my first bike arrived complete with stabilisers. Encouraged by Mum, the older I grew, the more obsessed I became. I was determined to make it and was soon noticed by British Cycling.

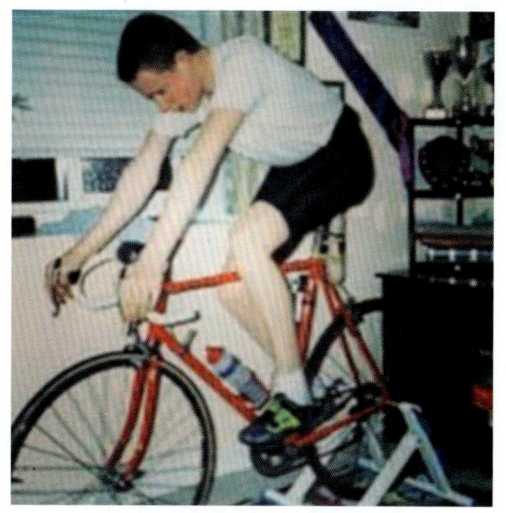

'Kids from Kilburn don't win the Tour': I'd train in our living room, while my bedroom became a shrine to my cycling heroes. All the time in the background was Stan, the coach whose years of abuse I'd try to push to the back of my mind.

Yellow jersey: If winning the 2012 Tour de France was a dream come true, then leading my 'brother' Mark Cavendish to victory on the final stage was the icing on the cake. Sir Dave Brailsford masterminded Team Sky and British Cycling's dominance, but our relationship was about to hit a downhill slope.

Precious: Having grown up with an absentee dad, I always wanted to be front and centre in Ben and Bella's childhood. They loved nothing more than lying in the middle of the 13 cuddly lions I brought home from France – one for each day I was in yellow.

Will the real Bradley Wiggins please stand up?: Nothing could prepare me for the attention that came my way in 2012. My answer was to hide behind a completely differently personality. But, whether it was the 'Victory V' sign after the time trial at the London 2012 Olympics, the infamous 'Susan' incident at BBC Sports Personality of the Year, or an increasingly outlandish wardrobe, being 'Wiggo' came at a huge personal cost. Being knighted by the Queen was a rare moment when I could reflect proudly on my achievement.

Lowest ebb: With my life collapsing around me, and echoes of childhood abuse reverberating around my mind, drugs felt like an escape. Instead, they dragged me into a bleak world where hotel room drug binges and being high in public were my daily norm. There were times when I'd wonder if I'd be found dead.

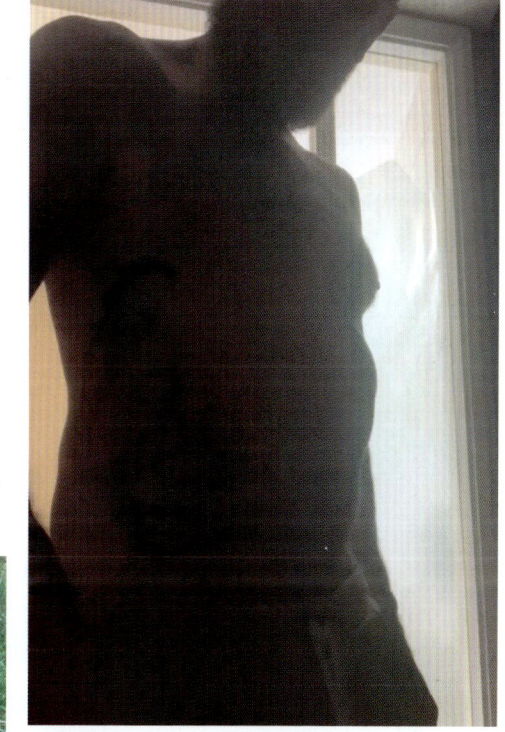

So much to live for: My children, Ben, Bella and Ava are my saviours. They pulled me from the wreckage and showed me the way to a better future. Cav too has been right at my side. I am now with Courtney, someone who has helped me re-find my love of being back on a bike. I'm so lucky to have such remarkable people in my life.

Even as the race got closer and closer to Paris, I had no sense of the growing excitement across the Channel. I knew that TV and radio would be giving updates on my progress, but I wasn't reading the papers or looking at social media. Absolute unbending focus on the goal had to be the way. There might be more room for error on the road than the track but the margins remain minimal. For two weeks and 13 stages I led the Tour de France by around two minutes. Puncture at a bad time, or find myself under a heap of bodies in a pile-up, and the advantage was gone. I was living in a pressure cooker with a very real chance that the lid could blow off at any moment. In that situation, every waking second is possessed with extreme nervous energy, a burden of anxiety you carry not just for yourself but for your team-mates, backroom staff, mechanics, everybody.

Most people, me included, think of the moment I crossed the line when winning the penultimate stage, the time trial from Bonneval to Chartres, as the point I won the 2012 Tour de France. But even on the final stage, considered a 'parade' due to the longstanding convention that the leader shouldn't be challenged, there's nothing to stop you crashing and not being able to finish. Clearly, leading Cav out to victory in Paris was a dream but there was also a practical element – ride at the front and I had a better chance of staying out of trouble. All in all, for those three weeks I could be forgiven for not being overly bothered whether I was the first item on *News at Ten* or slotting in somewhere behind a skateboarding duck.

The propensity for things to go wrong in a Grand Tour meant that when finally I did cross the finishing line, the feeling I got was relief rather than euphoria. I'd carried off our plan 100 per cent and made it to Paris. It's why, while winning the Tour was incredible, the absolute pinnacle of my cycling career, I'd be lying if I said it was hugely enjoyable. 'Businesslike' is how I'd describe it. I'd won so much already that year and was so well equipped to add the Tour to the list, that coming first basically boiled down to staying upright. The only time a deeper realisation of the magnitude of what I'd achieved hit me was as I slumped into a seat on the Sky team bus, Ben and Bella climbing on board to see me. The moment was caught on camera. Ben on one side, Bella on the other, and me in the middle. The look on my face says it all. *What the f**k's just happened?* Beforehand, I stood on the roof of a Sky team car, channelling my inner Liam Gallagher, grinning and celebrating. In other words, there was a public me and there was a real me.

Those few short minutes were, in hindsight, a huge signal of an almighty crash ahead.

CHAPTER 9

LONDON 2012

*'When you've got helicopters landing in the back
garden, you know the world's gone mad.'*

With 'Wiggomania' building and building, there are thousands of people milling around, not great when the last thing you want is your focus to be diverted by being recognised. I stick on my shades and pull my cap down but there are still some people who can spot me a mile off. 'Daddy! Daddy!' I hear as I walk past a little café, from where Ben and Bella come running out. I stare straight ahead. I can't look at them. I know if I do, I'll start crying. An outpouring of emotion is the last thing I need. To win that time trial I can't in any way be dislodged from a state of absolute single-mindedness. It is plain cruel to ignore my children, but I do it, and it upsets me to this day. In my head, I can still see them standing there, watching me walk past, thinking, *Why's Dad done that? Why couldn't he just say hello?* In high-level sport, so often you end up exchanging success for happiness.

The anti-climactic feel to the Tour de France was exacerbated by the fact I didn't have time, as is traditional, to celebrate in Paris. I was out of the French capital that night and heading to England to prepare for the Olympic road race six days later. The upside of that quick turnaround was there was no opportunity for a slump in performance. But it also meant I never had the chance to digest such a huge event in my life. There was simply no time for any of it to sink in. Shane Sutton, who'd remained back in Britain preparing the Olympic track squad, said at the time, 'He might realise what he's achieved when he gets back and he can't open his front door.' He was right about the door if not the realisation. There'd be times in the coming weeks I could barely reach it, let alone open it.

My house was always a very important space to me. Returning from Girona, we'd bought a property in Eccleston, near Chorley, in Lancashire. Situated at the end of a track, it had a measure of isolation I always appreciated. It felt very much like our own little world that we'd created. The Sunday night we came back from Paris, there was actually no one there waiting. It was like nothing had happened. By the next morning, however, word must have got round. Half the world's media appeared to have assembled in the lane. We were besieged. We also needed a pint of milk, and so, like I would any other time, I set off for a stroll down to the village shop. Immediately, I was followed by a phalanx of press and photographers. Never has the purchase of a pint of semi-skimmed caused such a stir. Back at the house I needed to go for a ride as part of my Olympic preparation. As I tried to get out the lane there were cars all around me – journalists, film crews, anybody and everybody. It was complete bedlam, like riding through an obstacle course, so much so that the police ended up coming down to try to sort it out. By the afternoon, I'd formulated a plan. Cath and I needed to go out to a nearby pub for a little bit of filming for the *A Year in Yellow* documentary, picking up the kids from school on the way. At that point I had a Mercedes Vito van. I crouched in the back while Cath drove out the gate. It didn't work. The newspaper snappers were wise to the trick, pushing forward, shoving their cameras against the windows, like when you see a prison van emerge from the gates at court.

Despite the madness outside, going home for those two days was heaven. Being able to relax with my family, even wipe my son's arse (which to this day he denies actually happened), delivered a restorative dose of normality, just the best feeling ever. I'd look out the window and there'd be Ben, riding around the garden, lap after lap. It reminded me of when I was his age, looping round the courtyard at the flats, the only difference being Ben was proudly clad in his own miniature yellow jersey. After all the time and effort that had gone into winning the Tour, there I was, a family man back in his safe haven. Forty-eight hours later, to avoid more craziness outside the house, the decision was made to send a helicopter rather than me drive down to London. When you've got helicopters landing in the back garden, you know the world's gone mad.

Maybe had it been just the Tour, the attention, the excitement around me, would have died down. The fact that straightaway we had the Olympic Games, *in London*, only threw a whole load of petrol on the fire. The media were actually referring to the sudden fascination in all things Bradley Wiggins as 'Wiggomania'. The only other mania I could remember was Beatlemania. I was never quite in that bracket but for a while my sideburns were definitely as famous as Ringo Starr's were in the Sixties. Both the *Sun* and *Daily Mirror* printed mock-ups of my trademark facial hair. 'Every *Sun* reader can back the 32-year-old's time trial bid by cutting out and taping on his lucky sideburns,' declared the tabloid. I'm not sure winning an Olympic time trial does actually hinge on how many people have paper sideburns Sellotaped to their face, but I'm sure it helped to sell newspapers and build up the hype.

There was the road race to deal with first. Coming on the first day of action, myself and the rest of the team would be resting up rather than attending the Opening Ceremony the night before. But then at the last minute, on the day of the ceremony itself, Dave Brailsford pulled me to one side and told me that Sebastian Coe, who'd headed the successful London 2012 Olympic bid and was now chairman of the Games' Organising Committee, had contacted him and asked if I could ring a bell to set the event in motion. I had no real idea what this meant but it sounded a nice-enough idea, and so that afternoon I was driven down to the Olympic Park, stopping off at the canteen in the Athletes' Village on the way for a bite to eat with Chris Hoy. Me and Chris had moved up through the cycling ranks together, racing at the Games in Sydney, Athens and Beijing, and now here we were not just competing in, but at the forefront of a home Olympics, him as the flagbearer for Team GB at the Opening Ceremony and me ringing the bell.

If that wasn't surreal enough, no sooner had we sat down than we were surrounded by sportspeople from across the globe. 'It's Bradley Wiggins! And look who he's with – Chris Hoy!' Everyone was trying to speak to us, asking us for photos. I suppose I can just about understand it. After all, Chris was one of the most decorated Olympians of all time while I'd just won the Tour. I'd also witnessed a similar outbreak of veneration at the Olympic Village in Beijing. US basketball star Kobe Bryant walked into the food hall and was immediately surrounded by 200 people. In our case it was just 20 or 30, but even so, to be pounced upon by other athletes really is quite something. Mine and Chris's conversation wasn't quite so exciting. 'You haven't got a razor on you by any chance?' Chris asked. I was a little bemused. 'No. Why?' Chris, it transpired, was an ambassador for Gillette. As part of the deal he had to be clean shaven, but because of the security in the Village he was having trouble getting his hands on a blade. His sponsor was unlikely to be impressed if he marched out at the Opening Ceremony of the biggest sporting show on Earth with a five o'clock shadow.

Sounds ridiculous, but at no point until I got to the actual stadium did I fully understand the magnitude of what the organisers were asking me to do. And then it struck me. *F**k! I'm actually opening the Olympic ceremony!* Myself and Dave Brailsford were shown into a backstage area. Straightaway, the band McFly, one of the many acts playing free concerts during the two weeks of the Games, came over to say hello, another reminder of how my winning the Tour had transcended sport. Meanwhile, I was given a pair of dark trousers, a yellow T-shirt, and fitted with a pair of earpieces. 'The doors in front of you will open,' I was told, 'at which point you'll walk forward, wave to the crowd, turn around, wait until we tell you, pull the rope on the bell and walk back.' Sounded simple enough. Except, offputtingly, when the doors did open, so blinding were the flashes of several thousand phone cameras I couldn't see a thing. Nor could I hear the crowd – the earpieces blocked any kind of reaction. I could only hope they were cheering. I followed the instructions in my ear, rang the bell – at least that's what it looked like, it was actually all done mechanically – and that was that. 'Superb,' Dave told me as I changed straight back into my tracksuit, before the both of us were ushered into a black Mercedes with police cars front and rear. With blue lights flashing and police motorcycle outriders stopping the traffic it was a real 'pinch yourself' moment. I was a kid from a council flat being treated like the president of the USA. Whizzed straight back to our hotel at Hyde Park Corner, I literally stepped straight out of that car and into the tactics meeting for the road race. There was Cav, putting his cleats on his shoes. 'How was that?' he asked, like I'd nipped out for an ice-cream.

I rang the bell at the Olympics Opening Ceremony in front of an estimated global television audience of one billion people. I was on a bill including David Beckham, James Bond and the Queen. It's the kind of experience you could be forgiven for still unpicking two weeks later. And in 30 seconds it was like it never happened. Crazy as it was, that had to be the way because of the athletic performance that was needed the next day.

Opening the Olympics and then just a few hours later being out racing says a lot about my ability to compartmentalise my life. It's either my greatest skill, or my most damaging, depending on how you want to look at it. But for years I actually forgot about ringing the bell, and that's more difficult to explain. Only a decade later, when I was watching a programme about another Olympic athlete, and it happened to show my part in the ceremony, did that huge occasion in my life come rushing back. It prompted me actually to go back to the Olympic Park and see the bell for myself. Now situated away from the stadium, it seemed a little sad and forlorn, a mere lump of metal, its moment of glory long forgotten. Carrying on to the arena, now better known as the home of West Ham United, I looked up at where I'd walked out in front of the world. As I did so I realised for the first time just how big a part those few seconds in 2012 played in the twisting and mangling of who I was in my mind. Perhaps that explains why I locked the memory away for so long. I know who I am now, but in 2012 I had no idea.

Sadly for Cav, the road race turned out to be a damp squib. Other teams seemed more concerned with snuffing out his chances than winning the race themselves and when a strong group of riders broke free it was too big an ask to chase them down ourselves. Outside of the velodrome, all hopes of cycling gold lay with me in the time trial in three days' time. Half the problem with the Olympics is what can often feel like an endless wait for your event. For those three days I was doing my best not to see any of the TV coverage of the Games, instead focusing on my own little world. I wanted to go out and deliver that time trial in exactly the same way I'd done so many times before. *It's just another race*, I'd tell myself, a mindset easily sent askew if you spend your time watching other people trying to achieve goals that will define the rest of their lives.

Of course, it was impossible to escape the Olympics completely. This was, after all, the biggest sporting event the country had hosted since the 1966 World Cup. It felt like a massive moment because it *was* a massive moment, something in which everyone in the country had emotionally invested. Every now and again I'd catch little bits of conversation around the hotel. 'We've not won a gold yet!' someone would say, or I'd pass an open door and hear the telly – 'The pressure's mounting for Britain's first gold' – reflecting Team GB's slow start on the medal front. It was like that episode of *Whatever Happened to the Likely Lads?* when Bob and Terry are trying desperately not to hear the result of an England football match before they watch the highlights on the telly. It was all but impossible to tune out. 'Bradley Wiggins is going tomorrow,' I'd hear on a distant radio. 'The nation's counting on him to bring home the gold.'

On the morning of the actual race I went against every instinct in my body and did actually flick on the telly in my room. Michael Hutchinson, the former British time trial champion, was on *BBC Breakfast*. 'What's Bradley's chances?' he was asked. 'Well, he's been unbeaten in time trials for a year and a half,' noted Michael, 'but who knows? We don't know what effect the fatigue of the Tour de France and the road race might have had.' *F**k this*, I thought, *I'm not watching that*, and turned it off. It's a very odd, and in all probability unhelpful, thing to see punditry about yourself in the build-up to a race.

Eventually, the time came and I left the hotel to walk the short distance to the warm-up zone at Hampton Court. That should have been the most inconsequential part of the day. Instead, with my feeling the necessity to ignore my own children, I've come to see it as the perfect example of how top-class sport damages people, requiring them to behave in ways that would otherwise be unimaginable. Despite, or because of that incident, in front of a TV audience of millions and hundreds of thousands more at the side of the road, I executed that time trial perfectly. And then, this being Hampton Court, seat of Henry VIII, himself no stranger to executions, they asked me to sit on a throne. The whole idea totally threw me. Sat there on this vast ornate golden seat in front of a bank of media and photographers, I just felt so silly. And that's when, without even thinking, I did the Winston Churchill victory 'V' sign. I could ride 44 km, with an estimated quarter of a billion people worldwide watching me, and not be bothered by that attention one bit. But the second I got off the bike I was that proverbial rabbit in the headlights. That character, that laid-back bloke, legs crossed, skinsuit unzipped, chest exposed, sat languidly in that chair was complete deflection; someone who could ride to the rescue and take the glare off me.

Half an hour later and he was still there in the press conference. 'I can't believe I won a fourth Olympic gold medal,' I tell the assembled media. I reach for a glass. 'A vodka tonic helps!' I hold my drink up for everyone to see. Except it isn't a vodka tonic, it's a glass of iced water. I'm sat there drivelling on about how I never believed I'd do this, never believed I'd do that, and in my head I'm thinking, *What are you talking about? From the very first time you got on a bike as a kid, you never for one minute believed you wouldn't succeed. Right from the start you identified success on a bike as your escape route.* But now, when I'd actually done it, my default position was, *What, little old me? I've done all that? I'm going to need a few drinks to let that sink in.* Why? Why do I need to clutch at a prop to accept what I've done? It's bizarre, like suddenly I've detached myself from the athlete. For 50 minutes and 39 seconds I've held precisely the power output, the watts, I need to win the gold medal, but then I unclip my feet from the pedals and I'm thrust back to being me. It's as if I can't handle the enormity of what my physical self has done.

The gap between what I knew I'd achieved and how I then portrayed it was crazy. *I* was crazy. Asked about winning first the Tour and now Olympic gold, my reply should have been all about the months of training, the mindset, the diet, the sacrifice, that made those achievements possible; in other words exactly how I'd answer that question now. These days I'm more than capable of standing up in front of an audience and talking in depth about performance and achievement. I can analyse how I won the Tour de France or anything else from my career. But the person I displayed in 2012 was the complete opposite. I couldn't talk like that. I didn't have anything like the confidence to look someone squarely in the eye and talk seriously about what it took to win on such an epic scale. All I could do was laugh and go, 'Vodka tonic!' I've just won the time trial in my home Olympics, hundreds of thousands of people screaming my name along every inch of the course. I should feel 50 feet tall. Instead, I'm sitting there, unable to look anyone in the eye, a bundle of absolute and utter insecurity. I'd started cycling as a child with a clear vision of where I wanted to get to and then, 20 years later, when I got there, I was transported straight back to being that child again.

I recognised my performance in the Olympic press conference all too well. After winning the Tour time trial in Chartres ten days earlier, I'd shown exactly the same insecurity. No sooner had I punched the air in triumph as I crossed the line, a real show of just how much that moment meant to me, just how much I knew I could deliver that effort, than I found myself walking into the media hall and apologising, all meek and submissive, to the assembled journalists. 'I know I can be a pain,' I say in a little boy's voice, 'so thanks to everyone for the last couple of weeks for putting up with me.' I've just won the Tour de France at that point, not that you'd ever know it as I stand there, shoulders hunched, speaking to the floor. I'm like a dog, with its tail between its legs, skulking back to its owner, knowing it's done wrong. I'm that 13-year-old kid bowing down to my stepdad. I'm that 19-year-old treading on eggshells around my real dad, nodding my head when he tells me he was third in Kuurne–Brussels–Kuurne even though I know full well he wasn't. I look at that footage of myself in that press hall now and think, *Stand up straight!* But I know as well that back then I couldn't. It wasn't who I was. I wasn't self-assured enough to handle the success as me. I always found it so hard to be that person who's articulate and gracious. It was as if I was looking at myself from the outside, seeing my own discomfort and awkwardness. It's sad to see those images of the aftermath of the Tour and time trial now. I can barely look at them, they're so painful, especially with the knowledge that they were mere forerunners of several more equally excruciating episodes of self-flagellation, all played out in the glare of intense and unremitting fame.

With the time trial done, myself and the family stayed in London, near St Paul's Cathedral. The plan was to hang around for a week and catch some of the other Olympic events. But the realisation soon dawned on us that wandering around enjoying this great summer of sport like any other family was going to be impossible. The day after the gold medal I took Bella to the Apple store on Oxford Street. I'd promised to buy her an iPod as a way of making up for the time I'd spent away. The minute I appeared it was absolute bedlam, like being in the middle of a rugby scrum. People were pushing and shoving – 'Wiggo! Wiggo!' – desperate to get my attention. Such was the mayhem the police turned up. 'You can't walk around like this now,' they told me. 'Sorry, but we're going to have to be there if you want to go out.' And that's exactly what happened. Wherever we went, whatever we did, two undercover CID officers accompanied us. As mad as that might sound for a bloke who rides a bike, I was told it was vital because there'd been a threat to my life. I never knew the details, who was after my blood, but clearly the police took it seriously because I'd look up from our table in Pizza Express and there they'd be by the door, ready to pounce. My management even assigned me a bodyguard. His CV was impressive. His previous post had been with Roman Abramovich.

I'm not totally naïve. I get why people latched on to me, saw me as a hero. I was this kid from Kilburn, sat on a throne doing the 'V' sign, not taking myself too seriously, being a little bit sweary in interviews. In many ways it defied belief that someone like me, with the outlandish sideburns, the cheeky attitude, the underlying unpredictability, could win the Tour de France and Olympic gold. And it was precisely that which made me relatable, a classic case of, 'Bloody hell, if he can do it, anybody can!'

In Britain, we like sports stars who remind us of ourselves. Roger Federer is a sporting great, but in no way is he relatable. It's imperfection and vulnerability that make someone relatable. Paul Gascoigne, Maradona, Eric Cantona, they're the ones we warm to. We see the holes in their armour, the pure emotional reaction to events both good and bad. When Freddie Flintoff stumbled into the street from the England team hotel the day after winning the Ashes in 2005, most of us smiled and thought, *I'd probably be like that!* No disrespect to an excellent footballer, but growing up not many of us want to be the next James Milner, same as in music no one wants to be the next Cliff Richard. Not when there's Liam Gallagher out there.

Untouchable heroes, those who go about their business calmly and predictably, are respected. Anti-heroes, those who turn the blueprint for success on its head, are idolised. More often than not they also come from working-class roots. While now it's decidedly middle-class, attracting those with a bit of disposable income, historically cycling was always a sport of the people. Back in the day, factory workers and miners formed clubs, heading out cycling on a Sunday, no doubt enjoying the open air after six long days of dust and dark. I might not have been working down the pit, but my background was definitely no frills. We love it when someone breaks free of those shackles and causes a bit of a stir, especially since they're generally the ones who wear their heart on their sleeve as well. Take the answer I gave after stage 8 of the 2012 Tour when a journalist asked what I thought of the cynics who say that to win the race you have to be on drugs.

'I say they're just f**king w**kers,' I replied. 'I cannot be doing with people like that. It justifies their own bone-idleness because they can't ever imagine applying themselves to do anything in their lives. It's easy for them to sit under a pseudonym on Twitter and write that sort of s**t rather than get off their arses in their own lives and apply them-selves and work hard at something and achieve something. And that's ultimately it. C**ts.' I'm sure somewhere there was a Team Sky press officer with their head in their hands, but I just can't do the whole robot thing. If I've got some-thing to say I'll say it and that's that.

No matter what happened in my career, there was a big part of me that remained resolutely untouched; a definite element of 'you can take the kid out of the council estate, but you can't take the council estate out of the kid'. I never cleared off and lived in a tax haven. I wasn't blasting around in a Ferrari. I did the school run in a van. I was like the guy next door, and again that appeals to people in this country. I'm still like that now. I walk round, jump on and off the Tube, like everyone else. Why wouldn't I? If I didn't I'd be the first person to ask myself, *Who the f**k do you think you are?*

But even bearing in mind all the above, I never for one minute thought a cyclist could capture the nation's imagination in the way I did. In a matter of days I went from a relative unknown to being one of the most instantly recognisable figures in the country. I also never understood the price I'd have to pay.

As a deeply insular person, I relied on privacy. By winning the Tour de France and London 2012, I lost every bit of it. Most distressingly, that included our home, somewhere I not only loved, but considered a sanctuary. After every day in yellow on the Tour you're presented with a cuddly lion. I had 13 of them on my sofa. Ben and Bella liked nothing more than lying in the middle of them. They took up a lot of space. And that's exactly what we, physically and mentally, as a family gave up. That space just to exist as us.

To begin with, there was a novelty to the attention. There was actually an element of comfort that a British person winning the Tour de France had been recognised as something incredible. It was validation that something extraordinary had happened. I mean, what if I'd come back from Paris and no one was bothered, there'd been no press interest, no cameras? How would I have felt about that? So the interest was actually nice. The problem was it never seemed to stop. After three or four weeks, when all we wanted was a bit of normality, to be able to take the kids to school like everyone else, or go to the shops, and the cameras were still following us everywhere, it began to wear a little thin. The press were outside our house constantly. For a while I'd go out and have a chat, try to give them something, a few words, or pose for a photo, in the hope they'd be satisfied and go away. But they were never satisfied. I could have stood there all day and they wouldn't have been satisfied. There were still journalists out there three months later. The situation veered from an initial burst of understandable and good-natured media interest to something better resembling harassment. Team Sky would send a press manager down, and on occasion the police were even called, but there was nothing they could do. While we lived on a private lane, the press and photographers were stood on a public footpath so they weren't breaking any laws.

No one could anticipate what was going to happen when I came back from the Tour, what I was going to have to deal with from a fame point of view. Other riders live out of reach in the south of France and places like that. I was up north on my own, taking the kids to school and trying to go out training through a pack of reporters and paparazzi. Concentrating on the road at this point in my career meant I couldn't just drive to the velodrome, shut the doors and crack on. One time we tried to escape by flying out for a holiday in Majorca where I'd done so much of my pre-Tour training. Ideally, we'd have stayed in the apartment I'd used at the time, but the complex was packed and so it was out of the question. Instead, a friend kindly lent us a villa in a gated compound, but even then there were paparazzi trying to take pictures from outside. Leaving a restaurant on the island late one night, I leant against a wall with a cigarette and a gin and tonic. Somewhere there must have been a photographer hiding because a couple of days later, there I was on the front page of one of the papers. The headline wrote itself. 'Ciggo!' Again, it differentiated me from other sports stars, not least my London 2012 peers. You weren't going to see Katherine Grainger stood by a wall with a fag on, and that's what appealed to people, that's what amplified the fame. Like Shane Warne dancing on the balcony at Trent Bridge after winning the Ashes, or Gazza with a pair of plastic tits on the open-topped bus after Italia 90, these things come to define you. Except they're not you. They're just a version of you, captured in a moment. You couldn't ever be like that all the time. It's totally unsustainable. But no one wants to publish a picture of you sat picking your nose in front of the telly.

The never-ending fascination in anything and everything Bradley Wiggins meant that, back in Eccleston, all sorts of people would walk up to the house or drive down the lane to get a peek. Some would literally knock on the door asking for signed photographs. It felt like people would stop at nothing to get what they wanted, and we were particularly worried about the kids. Bella's bedroom was on the roadside of the house. By necessity, her curtains were always shut. Eventually we had a privacy film put on her window so people couldn't see through. She was five years old. At that age, you're in no way equipped to understand the madness that's happening around your family. Only a year earlier she couldn't properly comprehend that the Bradley Wiggins she'd see on the telly was actually the same person as her dad. When I rang home after breaking my collarbone in the 2011 Tour, she couldn't wait to get on the phone. 'Daddy!

Daddy!' she told me, 'Bradley Wiggins has crashed!' I wished I could have heard her so excited after I won in 2012. She didn't really say much for two years after that.

You're almost not allowed to complain in these circumstances, because seemingly you've got everything anyone could ever want – success and the reward that comes with it. But, as I say, it wasn't that I wanted to hide away – I understood the interest in me – it was just that every semblance of normality had been stripped from our lives. How can you, or your family, feel settled and secure when there's strangers stood by your gate for months on end?

One 'stranger' was particularly dangerous. He should never have been allowed to take a hold on me, but he did – because I deliberately left the door open and invited him in. Faced with an avalanche of pressure from all sides, external, internal, everywhere, I saw him as the one able to stand in the way and absorb the deluge. I was wrong. It was me, not him, who was so very nearly swept away, buried, gone. Forget the Tour de France and London Olympics, the fact I'm still here to tell the tale is my greatest victory of all.

CHAPTER 10

WIGGO

'How could being Bradley ever be enough?'

I'm with the family in Morzine in the French Alps. It's New Year's Eve, 2012. One last chance to celebrate a remarkable year.

I reach for my phone. 'I'm really struggling,' I write. 'I'm scaring myself with some of the thoughts I'm having.' I send the email.

My phone pings. I look at the reply. I can't quite believe what I'm seeing. The gist of it is simple – 'Pull yourself together.'

I'm telling someone at Team Sky I'm falling apart and this is what I get?

I was drinking all day before Sports Personality of the Year. I was so scared at the thought of being myself on such a big stage, with thousands packed into the Excel Arena and millions more watching at home. I'd tried my hardest to pull out of the show in the days before. 'I really can't do it,' I told Dave Brailsford. He looked me in the eye. 'It'll look terrible for you if you don't.'

If I thought the booze was going to deliver a confident, self-assured me to this landmark event in the British sporting calendar then I was very sadly mistaken. The minute I stepped from the car, my insecurity took over. As a nominee, the idea is you do a couple of interviews on the way into the venue, pose for a few photos and look a bit humble. No way could I do that. I hovered back and waited for someone else to set off down the red carpet before running behind them waving my hands and messing around. I watch those few seconds now and it's embarrassing. It's really adolescent behaviour, like a kid refusing to have their picture taken. 'Come on, Bradley, be serious for the photo!' 'No, no, I can't!' Somewhere underneath that ridiculous display is a need for control. I didn't want to be seen through somebody else's lens. What I saw through my own lens was bad enough.

It says everything that, rather than a celebration of my cycling achievements, the 2012 edition of Sports Personality of the Year is best remembered for me calling the host Sue Barker 'Susan'. It says even more that I was totally happy with that. Like so much of what I did at that time, the 'Susan' thing was a way of detracting from the praise. It wasn't planned, but it didn't need to be. I was always going to find something to divert attention away from the real me. I knew from long experience that making people laugh offers deflection. It means you don't have to talk seriously about yourself. It's non-acceptance of who you are. You're reaching for humour, but what you're actually reaching for is a barrier.

My acceptance speech was exactly the same, dotted with self-deprecating 'humour'. 'Nan, the cheque's in the post,' I say at one point, 'because you pushed redial God knows how many times.' It's a joke, but it's one that's sending a message. *I'm just little old Bradley Wiggins, I don't think I deserve this.* I hear it in the way I speak. Like the press hall in Chartres, my voice sounds childish. 'Fanks very much.' My demeanour is similarly submissive, as if I'm unworthy of the amazing accolade I'm receiving. Why? Why did I have to be like that? I knew I was liked and respected for what I did on the bike, and I was proud of myself for what I'd done. So why in moments like this did I always need to throw in a load of self-deprecating nonsense? Recently I saw a video of myself at school. I'm about 12. I've made a drum in art and now I'm having to talk about it. And there I am again, this shrinking, hesitant character. 'This is a drum, and you hit it, and it's makes this noise.' Like I'm about five. Twenty years later and I was still receding into that personality when all eyes were on me. That's despite 492,000 people, 30.25 per cent of everyone who rang in, voting for me in possibly the best year for British sport ever. Second-placed Jessica Ennis-Hill had won gold in the Olympic heptathlon under the most intense pressure as the poster girl of the Games, while Andy Murray, in third, had won the Olympics and become the first British man to win a tennis major for 76 years. Mo Farah, Ellie Simmonds, David Weir, Chris Hoy, Ben Ainslie, Sarah Storey, Rory McIlroy, Katherine Grainger, Nicola Adams   any one of my fellow nominees would have walked away with the title in a different year. But I won it.

I got the most votes ever recorded for a winner. The people who'd watched all that sport said they wanted me. And yet as I accepted the trophy from the Princess of Wales all I felt was an impostor. I just could not be me in the present and accept the adulation. I absolutely couldn't face it. Even when I'd won the ultimate prize in cycling, I couldn't accept praise for what I'd achieved. Again, there's a contradiction. The only thing that ever gave me confidence was cycling; the belief that I could succeed. Then, when that success came, I didn't think I was worthy of it. The insecurities I had as a person overrode any feelings of self-value from winning the biggest bike race in the world. I didn't even consider the athlete side of me as worthy. And so there I was, a 32-year-old man unable to say thank you properly. A 32-year-old man doing anything to avoid the praise that felt like sandpaper against my skin. And of course it was complete self-sabotage. Playing the joker that night backfired horribly. The more I acted the fool, the more the media was interested in me.

When I won the Tour de France and Olympic gold in 2012 my pathway appeared to be one of lifelong happiness. Satisfaction born of ultimate personal achievement. What I actually discovered was that sporting glory can never magic away scar tissue. In my case, it just tore open wounds that I'd tried so long to pretend weren't there. The deep insecurity that came rushing out was matched only by a crushing lack of self-respect. I'd reached the peak of my sport without ever knowing or valuing who I was. Cycling was the only thing that gave me a semblance of identity. Without it, I'd have been nothing. But then cycling got conflated with fame. With the attention trained on Bradley the person, rather than Bradley the cyclist, I felt totally exposed, and so reached for a persona to hide behind. The man who called Sue Barker 'Susan' at *Sports Personality of the Year* was just that – a disguise. The latest of many. A lifelong lack of self-worth meant I'd been wearing disguises for years. It was the most natural thing in the world to me. They shielded me from the spotlight I feared – the one that would illuminate my truth – that as a person I had nothing to offer. Self-belief was never given to me as a child. I was always told I was destined to be great on the bike – 'Your dad was brilliant, it's in your genes' – but off that bike I didn't have a clue who I was. The only difference was, where once I'd been hiding the real me from a few people at school, now I was hiding it from millions.

After the Olympics, that was my season done. Normally that would mean a quiet few weeks with the family. When, virtually overnight, you've become the most famous bloke in the country that's impossible. Suddenly you're thrust into an endless round of award shows and media engagements. The only way I could deal with that was the total avoidance of being me. The camouflage I chose was about as far away from the real Bradley Wiggins as humanly possible. I looked around the fancy dress shop of my mind and found some-thing that would allow me to appear confident, irreverent and unorthodox. I chose rock star. The most lurid incarnation of this look came at October's Pride of Britain Awards, the annual event run in association with the Prince's Trust – well, if you're really going to go for it, you might as well do so in the presence of the future King. Team GB and Paralympics GB were being honoured with a Special Recognition Award for their achievements at London 2012. All the well-known names from the Games would be there, with me accepting the accolade for Team GB. While everyone else dressed smart but sensible, I arrived at Grosvenor House in a three-piece silver suit that wouldn't have looked out of place on the set of *Goodfellas*, rounded off with a pair of two-tone brown and white brogues. This might not have been too bad had it not been for the £10,000 Rickenbacker guitar, in its case, I was carrying, having stopped on the way at a music store on the King's Road. As the paps snapped away, I couldn't help feeling I looked more like some kind of mobster, complete with St Valentine's Day Massacre machine-gun case, than a bloke who'd just won the Tour de France. I look at that image now and think, *Who the f**k are you? What on Earth did you think were you turning up for?* Not just that, but I see the guitar for exactly what it is – another prop. That Rickenbacker is a thing of great beauty, and it sounds as good as it looks, but in that moment, like the 'vodka tonic' at the time trial press conference, it was nothing more than a diversion tactic. I'm a cyclist, not a guitar player, but carrying a Rickenbacker, same as the 1920s hoodlum get-up, took the attention away from my true identity.

At least when the time came to receive the award I didn't take the guitar up on stage with me. But I was still desperate to be different, to escape being 'Bradley the Olympian'. Mo Farah was present and so all the Team GB members, and Prince Charles himself, came together to do the double gold medal winner's famous hands-on-the-head 'Mobot' victory dance. All the Team GB members, that is, except me. My thought process was clear. *I'm not doing the Mobot, don't include me in this lot.* And so next day a picture appeared in the papers of everyone laughing doing the dance while I'm stood there, arms glued resolutely to my side, with a fixed smile on my face. I find it difficult to look at that picture now. Thankfully, I can offset it a bit with a lovely image of me shaking hands with Prince Charles at the start of the evening. I liked Charles, and had already met him a few times during and since the Olympics. He never wanted any formality, none of this 'Your Royal Highness' business. 'All right, Charlie,' I'd say. 'All right, Bradley,' he'd reply. He was really enamoured with the cycling at the Olympics. 'Camilla and I watched all the events, you know,' he told me. I liked the thought of them feet up at the Palace watching what was going on just the other side of the railings.

While the three-piece silver suit and two-tone brown brogues definitely weren't me, the Rickenbacker actually was. I was about 15 when I started tinkering on a guitar, another little mental escape amid the claustrophobic atmosphere of the flat. No coincidence that my interest was piqued just at the moment Oasis went massive. I'd sit on my bunk listening to *Definitely Maybe* and trying to mimic the chord patterns. 'Rock 'n' Roll Star' had been a particular inspiration. Its lyrics about pursuing your dreams, escaping and finding a better life were always going to resonate with me. Imagine how totally bizarre it was then, 17 years later, to find myself at the GQ Men of the Year Awards, on the same table as Liam Gallagher. Right there, alongside Texas lead singer Sharleen Spiteri, and opposite style icons Domenico Dolce and Stefano Gabbana (you don't get these sorts of tables at cycling dinners), was one of my all-time musical idols. Liam wasn't there just to make up the numbers. Liam could never be anywhere just to make up the numbers. My hero was there to give me – me! – a Lifetime Achievement Award. Up on stage, Liam handed me the trophy. 'Not since Phil Daniels,' he told the audience, 'has someone looked that cool on two wheels.' Brilliant! I'd always loved *Quadrophenia*, in which Daniels plays Jimmy, the disillusioned office boy who finds escape from his humdrum life on the back of a Lambretta. When asked later by ITN what makes a great man, Liam responded, 'Obviously someone who gives his missus a foot massage every minute of the day and takes the dogs for walks and puts the dishwasher on and wins gold medals at riding a bike really fast.' Hard to disagree.

Afterwards I went for a drink with Liam, particularly pleased he'd mentioned *Quadrophenia*, because the whole mod ethic was one I'd always favoured. That meant when searching for a role to hide behind it was a scene natural for me to amplify. I already had that look about me. My grandad always wore a suit and I loved that 'always look your best' element of working-class culture. Similarly, I liked those quintessentially British, yet slightly alternative, films of the 1970s and 80s, like *Babylon*, about racial tension in Brixton, and the borstal drama *Scum*, again starring Phil Daniels. Meanwhile, the music of Paul Weller, who exemplified the mod look, had been the soundtrack of my life. I also loved mod royalty The Who, the late John Entwistle especially. The way he used to stand there playing those great basslines in his skeleton suit was just phenomenal. When, after 2012, I started collecting guitars, one of Entwistle's basses was my pride possession. I hung it with the others on my stairwell, something I knew Entwistle himself had done after seeing pictures of his country estate. There's something else Entwistle inspired. Everyone thinks I copied the sideburns from Paul Weller. No, it was John Entwistle. Add in the trademark long-at-the-sides, slightly feathered haircut and the streamlined, narrow lapel, sharp-cut suits, and I was soon able to cultivate a man-about-town persona of old-school English eccentricity which seemed to fit in with a personality already seen as flippant and funny. My dad's anti-authority side, which appealed to me, was 100 per cent in the mix too. I'd be shocking and contentious. I'd go to awards ceremonies and get drunk, be a bit of a geezer, and say things I shouldn't in interviews.

In so many ways, mod culture felt easy to reach for, the perfect way to distract people from the real me I was desperate to keep hidden. And so it was that pretty much overnight I became the new 'Modfather', something which made me feel like a massive fraud, but was much better than the other option – being Bradley Wiggins. It was the oddest thing. Whereas once I'd been mocked and abused, sneaking out of the flat in my cycling gear, now I was inspiring a trend in fashion. Sales of classic mod labels like Ben Sherman shot up. I actually signed a five-year agreement with Fred Perry. That was great, but in my head it meant I felt the need to play my new character even more. *Channel 4 News* even did a piece about me being a 'style icon'. 'The mod look is everywhere on the high street,' their report stated, 'perhaps it never went away. But the high-end pinnacle is Bradley Wiggins, all cool, quirky and well-tailored. So has Wiggo put the mod into modern Britain?' I didn't know whether I had or not. I was too busy engaging in my own retail therapy, which I found provided a temporary fix for the underlying unhappiness I was feeling. I'd obsess over certain things. I had five scooters at one point, SX200 Lambrettas and the like. I never had a licence to ride them, but that wasn't the point. I just wanted to buy the best scooters around. I even appeared on the front cover of *Scootering* magazine.

The whole mod/music crossover climaxed two nights after *Sports Personality* when I was stood in the wings at the Hammersmith Apollo watching Paul Weller play a show for homeless charity Crisis. I'd met Paul through the renowned Soho tailor Mark Powell, who came up with so many of the suits I wore at that time, cementing our friendship by co-hosting a BBC Radio 6 Music show where we played our favourite tracks. Watching Paul from the side of the Hammersmith Apollo stage was mesmerising, but then, before the last number of the night, 'That's Entertainment', there was a pause. Another guitar was being plugged in. I never twigged what was happening until Paul and the other band members looked across at me. It was a proper *What? Hang on a minute!* moment. I was totally unprepared for performing in front of a huge live audience and it took a fair bit of coaxing to drag me out. In the end, chants of 'Wiggo! Wiggo!' from the audience meant I didn't have much choice. And so there I was, on stage with one of my absolute all-time heroes, Paul Weller, playing one of the greatest songs ever written, 'That's Entertainment', with a crowd chanting my name. I looked around. On one side of me was Paul, on the other was another rock god, longtime Weller collaborator Steve Craddock from Ocean Colour Scene. And in the middle was me, a Tour de France winner. In that moment I was as glad to have Wiggo there as they were. I needed to be him. How could being Bradley ever be enough?

So perfect a fit was my alter ego, the stranger that I had invited into my life, that I was even singing at one point. That's what you really do call impostor syndrome. Those few minutes were like a whirling, swirling dream. I looked out at the crowd, thousands of bobbing heads illuminated as spotlights flashed across the auditorium. *How the f**k have I ended up here?* I've been back to the Apollo a few times since to watch Jack White, Fontaines DC and Sleaford Mods, and it's surreal to think of myself up there where they are. I never took him up on it, but Paul did actually invite me to play at a couple of other gigs. My whole life, I'd been a bedroom guitar player, three chords, Oasis, The Jam, etc, and now it was like I was a part-time member of the band. Post-Hammersmith, we all went drinking together. Jake Bugg was there, Miles Kane. As ever, the pictures appeared in the next day's papers. Their readers, I expect, either loved me or hated me at that point. They either saw me as someone doing exactly what they'd have done in my position, milking newfound fame for all it's worth, or they saw me as someone who'd got a bit too big for his boots, out boozing all the time, hanging around with rockstars, pissing my talent down the drain. In fact I was neither of those things. I was just an actor, self-cast as Wiggo. I was hiding in plain sight, as they say. Going unnoticed despite being in full view.

For a while, this strange brew of sporting achievement and appropriated personality traits, with a little bit of me sprinkled on top, brought a level of fame that allowed me to walk through practically any door I wanted. But it wasn't just me who was attracted to the country's great cultural figures, they were attracted to me. Roger Daltrey declared it was an 'honour' when he heard I listened to The Who while training. 'He's got a backstage pass for life,' he stated. I never took him up on it, but I did go backstage at a Stone Roses gig in London, actually meeting their genius guitarist John Squire, himself a big cycling fan, so much so that he was asking me the best kit to ride in. 'Tell me, Bradley, do you like Assos?' He appreciated the cultural aesthetic of cycling, same as I appreciated the cultural aesthetic of guitars. Later I sent him a signed yellow jersey from the Tour. Two months down the line I received a 'Beano' Les Paul in the post. Engraved on the back was 'John Squire, Warrington Parr Hall'. It was the guitar he'd played at the Roses' legendary comeback gig in 2012. Phenomenal. As if meeting one globally revered guitarist that night wasn't enough, I also found myself chatting to Jimmy Page from Led Zeppelin. I could be more myself when I was one on one with people, but I still felt self-conscious, especially when they were my heroes.

Mad encounters just kept on coming. One night I found myself in Soho drinking at the Groucho, the private members' club and renowned cultural hangout. I was talking to the artist Tracey Emin at the bar when someone tapped me on the shoulder. 'Excuse me, are you Bradley Wiggins? Peter Blake's round the corner. He'd like to meet you.' I couldn't believe what I was hearing. Sir Peter Blake, a design icon, who'd co-created one of the most instantly recognisable album sleeves in history for The Beatles' *Sgt. Pepper's Lonely Hearts Club Band*, wanted to meet me? But it was true, and I sat with him as he told me how much he'd been into cycling during his younger days in the 1950s and 60s. If I wasn't actually meeting these revered individuals, I was receiving letters and emails. Elton John, who I'm still in touch with to this day, sent me a message congratulating me on my achievements. Three-time Oscar-winner Daniel Day-Lewis, star of *Gangs of New York* and *Last of the Mohicans*, invited me for lunch in New York. He'd watched the Tour and been massively inspired by my performance. At one point it looked like our worlds might collide. There was talk of a film being made about me, with *Notting Hill* actor Rhys Ifans in the starring role. I'm not sure what Rhys is like on a bike but he did look a bit like me.

Then there were the politicians. I met then Prime Minister David Cameron and Chancellor George Osborne at an awards do. Grandad would I'm sure have disowned me had he seen me talking to such Tory grandees, but the thing is you meet these people and in the moment they're actually all right. When Cameron turned to me and said, 'I just want to say, Bradley, what you've done for this country is amazing,' I was hardly going to say, 'F**k you, Dave!' was I? For the record I have met Labour politicians too. Gordon Brown visited Manchester Velodrome, I sat next to Ed Balls at a dinner, and a few years later, as guest editor of Radio 4's *Today* programme I interviewed Jeremy Corbyn. Royalty had their eyes on me too. Prince Harry wanted me to launch the Invictus Games with him. I was unable to do so because of my cycling commitments but I felt hugely honoured to be asked.

There's a dichotomy at play here. While so much of what happened in the wake of the Tour and Olympics came from playing a highly exaggerated variant of myself, I'd be lying if I said there weren't elements of it that were hugely enjoyable. It wasn't like I was living in a world of total bleakness. I still had my family around me and I met some true heroes, people who'd genuinely affected me and lifted me throughout my life. Despite my trepidation, playing on stage with Paul Weller was amazing. Same as meeting so many other people from the cultural world who I loved and admired, who really meant something to me, was amazing. Amid all the madness, the endless swirl of attention, the lack of privacy, the press encamped outside the house, there came a barely believable stream of once-in-a-lifetime occasions, moments that I could soak up, look at myself and just think, *F**k!* To be invited into the midst of a scene I so admired was beyond my imagination. But I know also that transcending sport is something that cost me a lot. Take the glitter away from that night at the Hammersmith Apollo and what was actually happening? I was a cyclist playing with Paul Weller in front of several thousand people. I was in no way equipped to do that. The only way I could do so was to reach for my veil. Doing things like that was damaging for me. Like so many other moments in that period – ringing the bell at the Opening Ceremony, chewing the fat with John Squire from The Stone Roses, receiving an award from Liam Gallagher – I barely even had time to think *What the f**k just happened there?* before the next bit of insanity was upon me, splashed, inevitably, all over the newspapers the following day. It suited the tabloids for me to be this other character as it filled their pages. It also suited them to build me up, because they knew at some point I'd be equally easy to knock down. They were right to think that. Wiggo was a character crafted in sand. Every time I wore his face there was an underlying unhappiness from knowing that what I was doing wasn't really me. I'd hate the person I saw in the mirror but I still thought it was more likeable than Bradley.

More recently I've come to see a greater truth about the me I portrayed after my success in 2012. I'd always thought I was bothered about what other people thought of me. Actually, I was bothered about what I thought of myself. Which was nothing. That's the real reason why I invited this stranger into my life, dressed him up and pretended he was me. The fact that other people, in my head at least, seemed to prefer this strain of me only served to emphasise just how right I was to dislike myself on such a grand scale. As ever, somewhere at the heart of that wreck of a personality is a traumatised child. As an adult, I was holding shame and embarrassment from those years of abandonment and abuse. The bike was my safe place. On it, I had extreme confidence and believed 100 per cent in my ability. Off it, I was lost and empty. Ask me to do an interview or accept an award and I was constantly reaching for Wiggo to hide the insecure mess I was underneath.

By the end of that tumultuous year, I'd had enough of being famous. I was beginning to feel swamped by the falsehood I'd created. If Mum had unwittingly fashioned a monster, unable to deal with daily life, then I'd taken that monster and bastardised it by adding several more layers of insecurity and self-hatred. The result was this mongrel, this thing, Wiggo. From the moment he first appeared on the throne at Hampton Court, that creation became more and more outlandish, as embodied in an ever-increasing eccentricity of appearance, by the end not so much mod as nineteenth-century English dandy. I did that deliberately. The more extreme the look, the bigger the screen to hide behind. But in so doing I sparked so much confusion in myself. Who I was had become inescapably tied up in Wiggo and the public's perception of that character. It felt like I'd been poured through a sieve and the real me had been lost in the dregs. Wiggo offered a shield but he also slowly suffocated the real me, snuffing out my last few remnants of self-esteem. I did the Tour of Britain that year, basically a lap of honour, with crowds of people coming out to cheer. But which one of me were they cheering? Me? Or Wiggo? Even Ben didn't seem to know the real me. When asked at school to draw a picture of his family, he showed his mum and sister in normal clothes and his dad in a yellow jersey with a medal round his neck.

There was only person who knew full well who I really was – Cath. She'd look at the photos of me in the tabloids and despair. 'This isn't you!' For the same reason she'd get embarrassed watching me playing the fool at Sports Personality and other functions. She'd have her head in her hands. *Oh, God, what's he doing now?* The way I acted wasn't me and the way I looked wasn't me. She had a right go at me one day. 'Look at you! Look at your stupid sideburns! What do you think you're doing?' That was the day I shaved them off. I knew she had a point. Who was this person getting photographed coming out of the Groucho with Miles Kane? Since when had hanging around with rock stars at Soho gentlemen's clubs been me? The bollocking off Cath was the line in the sand. The end of that rock star version of me. Interviewed round about that time she gives a great description of me as 'a bit of a twat'. And she was right. The whole 'Wiggo' thing had become a burden on me and those around me. As a family, everywhere we went people would constantly ask for photos. It was difficult and tiresome. My own kids would have to stand and watch while I posed for pictures with other people's. Even in team hotels, there'd be people scouring the corridors looking for me. Just as I'd finally sit down with my family there'd be somebody tapping me on my shoulder asking for an autograph. I understand that it means something to meet your sporting heroes, but it can be hard, especially if there's a problem going on in the background they don't know about.

At the same time, Team Sky were getting pissed off. I was going AWOL when it came to fulfilling my duties. They wanted me to make a video message in acceptance of an award for Most Inspirational Sportsman of the Year at the Jaguar Academy of Sport Awards. I hadn't done it, same as I hadn't been on the bike as much as I should have. Amid a welter of other commitments, cycling had stopped being a priority. I was stealing time on the bike as and when I could, desperate to escape the chaos and get back to something resembling normality, but because I was so often tied up during the day that could mean scraping a couple of hours in the dark. The situation wasn't helped when, one evening, I went out for a ride only to be knocked off when a car pulled out of a petrol station near the house. I hit the deck hard and it took me a couple of minutes to get myself together, by which time people had started to twig who this bloke clutching his side and groaning on the tarmac was. The media was alerted and that was that. All I'd wanted was to get out on my bike and once again I was headline news. The only person who didn't seem to have heard was Chris Evans. Next morning I was supposed to be on his Radio 2 breakfast show, impossible since I'd spent the night in hospital with a broken rib. Thinking I'd just not turned up, he proceeded to give me an on-air roasting. As a big music fan, I was more bothered about missing out on another engagement later that same day when I was due to guest present *Never Mind the Buzzcocks*. But again, the fact I was expected to combine cycling with so many high-profile bookings shows just how impossible a juggling act I was trying to pull off. While I wanted the whole Wiggo thing to end, and had started pushing back on these big commitments, trying to take back a bit of control, there was still part of me relying on him to hide behind. The whole charade was unsustainable. Everything was falling apart. Including me.

Being Wiggo had allowed me to externalise the extreme focus that came my way after the success of 2012. Now, as I tried to rediscover the real me, I began to feel crushed and overwhelmed. The only thing I could see clearly was that life would never be the same again, and not in a good way. Wearing a disguise had offered short-term freedom in exchange for a long-term trap. Wiggo wasn't really me and I didn't want to live his life anymore, but in the eyes of the vast majority of people he was Bradley Wiggins. You can say that was a self-inflicted wound, but Wiggo was born of an absence of self-belief. He existed so people didn't see me. I'd been thrust into the limelight and dealt with it in the best way I could – with a character I could adopt at the click of a finger. Now I was left drowning in the aftermath.

It had been just five months since I'd won the Olympic time trial, and in that time I'd skipped from one sparkling experience to the next without ever realising the final destination was going to be somewhere very dark indeed. And so there I was in Morzine on New Year's Eve contemplating whether it had all been worth it. Questioning the role of cycling in my life was dangerous for me. It was then and it would be again in retirement. It allowed cracks to appear in my psyche in which negative feelings, rooted deep in my past, could germinate and grow. When I describe myself as 'suicidal' at that point, I wasn't literally on the verge of killing myself, but I was definitely having thoughts of not wanting to be here anymore. There's a distinction between the two, but either way it's a terrible and all-consuming place to be.

Had they ever enquired about my psychological state in the wake of becoming the most famous person in Britain while wearing their logo, Team Sky might have seen that I was struggling. Sadly, I didn't consider that sufficient after-care was forthcoming. During that time I don't recall them proposing any professional help for me to deal mentally with the madness that was happening around me. Never did I feel they were interested in my welfare and health. My words that New Year's Eve in France – 'I'm really struggling. I'm scaring myself with some of the thoughts I'm having' – were a very obvious cry for help. The 'pull yourself together' reply wasn't really in the ballpark of what was needed. It was followed up with talk of getting back into a routine on the bike and booking in with Steve Peters. An eminent psychiatrist, Peters was revered for his mind-management model that hinged on understanding your 'inner chimp', essentially that unseen entity that sits on your shoulder dripping negative thoughts into your brain. He was seen as integral to Team Sky's success, on hand if riders needed psychological help. But his position as consultant to the senior management team as well as the riders meant that, in my opinion, his role was compromised. Sky was an elite sports team run by hard-nosed ultra-competitive people. They brought in a psychologist because, ultimately, they thought it would help them win races. As far as I was concerned, Steve Peters was there to help get a performance out of me, not tell Dave Brailsford and Shane Sutton I needed six months off, although I accept that I never properly assessed my situation with Steve. To me, his presence felt like a tactic. Sitting down with him wasn't an option. It was therapy with a twist.

To make matters worse, barely had we touched back down in England than Lance Armstrong gave his landmark interview to Oprah Winfrey, admitting to winning his seven Tours on performance-enhancing drugs. As the reigning Tour de France champion, guess who came under scrutiny? Guess who everyone wanted to question about doping? At a time when I just wanted to hide away it was the last thing I needed. At least, though, I was an adult, able to defend the sport and myself. What I couldn't handle was my kids getting it in the neck at school. Ben especially found himself on the end of jibes. 'If Lance Armstrong was doing it, your dad must be doing it as well.' It was only a handful of kids saying stuff but it was bad enough for us to move him to a different school. Bella was too young to understand but she still had kids saying, 'Your dad takes pills to get up hills.' With kids that little, such nasty comments could only have been passed on from their parents.

It's not uncommon for people on the outside to sling arrows. In the age of the keyboard warrior we see it more and more. When it happens, your natural instinct is to find comfort and solace in those you trust. In my case I felt that should have been Team Sky. But just at the point I needed some security, some hope, all I felt was ignored. Slowly, but surely, I came to feel that they were pushing me over the edge.

CHAPTER 11

SKYFALL

*'I felt I was disposable to him. I felt I could
be rinsed of all use and chucked in the bin
with the rest of the rubbish.'*

There were times when I thought of Team Sky as family. What tripped me up was the belief that they thought of me as family too.

After my success of 2012, everyone thought I was living the dream. What I was actually feeling was the world closing in on me from all sides. I expect some people would have had a breakdown, flushed it out of their system that way, but cycling had always been my escape in times of crisis and as far as I was concerned that's precisely what was going to happen again. Except post-2012 even cycling felt different. As the reigning Tour de France champion you'd think I'd have felt secure at Team Sky. I had, after all, given them exactly what they wanted. Not only had they achieved their goal of winning the Tour de France with a British rider two years early, but they'd also become the dominant force in professional cycling. So how come I found myself operating in a world of distrust and anxiety? A world where I never quite knew what was paranoia and what was reality?

Punching the air at the end of the time trial in Chartres wasn't only a celebration of winning the Tour de France, it was a release of anger. The only threat to my victory had come from within my own team. On stage 11, with 4 km to go to the finish at the Alpine ski resort of La Toussuire, Chris Froome, in third place overall at that time, and whose job it was to support my push for victory in Paris, attacked. Eventually, after about 500 m, he relented and dropped back. From where I was sitting, I was in prime position to win the Tour, leading the race by more than two minutes, only for an attempt to topple me to have come from someone in my own team. It was the last thing I ever expected to happen and it unsettled me massively, to the extent that later, at the team hotel, I threatened to walk. My mind was clear. *F**k it! I don't need this!* That might sound mad, but to win the Tour you need to be in control of as much as humanly possible. On the road, your team is there to deliver that control. So for a threat to come from your own flank is hugely disconcerting. If you can't trust the guys in the same kit, who can you trust? In the end, Dave Brailsford and Sky sporting director Sean Yates managed to talk me down. But from that point on, I never felt able to trust Chris. Like I say, riding on the front during those last few kilometres around Paris was partly to lessen my likelihood of crashing. But I was also determined that Chris shouldn't benefit from any last-gasp hiccup and end up on top of the podium. I didn't get the feeling that if I hit the tarmac he was going to hang around at the side of the Champs-Élysées for two minutes, that's for sure.

From the second Chris attacked me at La Toussuire, relations between Team Sky's two top riders were in tatters. At the start of 2013, they put us both in the team for the Tour of Oman to see if we could race together. It didn't work. Neither of us trusted the other an inch, and in a team sport that's a problem. There were a couple of showdowns with Dave. Once he put me and Chris in a room together. 'You need to apologise to each other,' he told us, 'because I'm going to lose my job if you don't. The board are asking questions.' We did as he asked, trying to reassure the other Team Sky riders that we'd buried the hatchet by actually shaking hands in front of them. But it was totally meaningless. We couldn't stand a second in each other's company and that was that.

It's both uncomfortable and unnerving to find yourself on the inside of a split like this. For me, it was something else to contend with, something that felt wholly unmanageable, on top of all the other turmoil I was experiencing. It was just horrible, reaching a point where I couldn't even go on training camps where Chris was. I started to feel like I'd become something of a pariah at Sky and couldn't help but compare my situation to other riders who'd won the Tour, seeing how much better they were treated by their teams, and wondering why none of that seemed to apply to me. It was a really disturbing period, and one which the bike couldn't ever quite drown out.

In May, I set out for a tilt at the Giro d'Italia. Initially all was well. On day two, the team time trial, I stayed on the front for so long that at the end of the 17.4 km, one of my teammates told me, 'You could have gone faster on your own instead of hanging around waiting for us!' Sky won and I was in second position on the road. But then the Italian heavens opened. It rained constantly, stage 7 being particularly treacherous as my wheels went from under me a few kilometres from the finish and I negotiated the rest of the descent into the coastal city of Pescara at a snail's pace. My mood was going downhill much faster than I was. I was obstinate in interviews and refusing autographs. Basically, I was being an arsehole and didn't like myself any more than anyone else did. In the end I left the race halfway through with a chest infection but felt I was crumbling mentally more than anything. After the New Year's Eve email I'd given up asking for help and papered over the cracks as best I could myself. But the Giro was a clear sign that something wasn't right. Back in the UK, meanwhile, I spent the next six weeks suffering from vertigo, a condition often triggered by stress, that made me feel like I was going to fall over every time I stood up. I was struggling, and, with the Tour approaching, was unable to reassure Team Sky that I was going to be OK for the race. Not that it mattered. From a performance point of view, they'd long since identified Chris as a better prospect. That meant he was able to impact who should be riding alongside him. Unsurprisingly, after our set-to in 2012, and all that followed, I certainly wasn't top of his list. And justifiably so. If I was him, I wouldn't have wanted me there either. There was no guarantee I wasn't going to climb off after a week and go home. You can't blame Chris for wanting a team that he knew was 100 per cent behind him, and in the end he was right. He won that Tour without me.

A year later, the Tour, to great national excitement, would start with three stages in Britain. You could argue that having become the first British winner two years earlier, which in itself had led to a UK cycling boom termed, imaginatively, the 'Wiggo effect', it would have been appropriate for me to have been on the starting line in Leeds. But the situation with Chris still hadn't been resolved. The bonus of him winning in 2013 was that he'd taken some of the focus off me, which suited me fine. I didn't like being the face of the team and had always felt much more comfortable as an underdog. Left to climb the ladder again, by the time the 2014 Tour came round I'd won the Tour of California, shown strongly in Paris–Roubaix, and then, with just a week until the Grand Départ in Yorkshire, won the British Time Trial Championship. My success put Team Sky in an awkward position. Chris still didn't want me in the team, his power over selection further bolstered by his win in 2013, and by that point it was almost 18 months since we'd raced together. We'd spoken at least, but fair to say our relationship remained fractious. He'd lost a lot of faith in me and was unable to allay his concerns about whether I really would put his interests first and ride in his service. If, say, he fell on stage 5, which included tricky sections of Paris–Roubaix cobbles, could he know for sure I'd wait for him? In the end, Dave decided he didn't want to take me. I was told I couldn't be trusted and that was that. I could hardly argue. While I would happily have ridden in the service of Chris – to have taken part without the pressure of going for the win myself would actually have been nice – I wasn't doing much to show that was the case. Weirdly, had I started, I'd have definitely been a very valuable Plan B. In fact, I think I'd have won. Chris did fall on stage 5, before the race had even reached the cobbled sections, and was forced to pull out. With the form I was in, there's every chance I'd have run eventual winner Vincenzo Nibali pretty close.

More importantly, not riding in 2014 was a missed opportunity to reseal that partnership with Chris. To have gone back as a support rider would have been the perfect way to make amends for the collapse of trust. I know people will think that after the La Toussuire incident it should have been Chris making amends, but I have to take some responsibility for how I treated him. I had my faults. I wasn't the easiest to get along with. I wasn't very communicative. There was a lot more I could have done to iron out our differences rather than sulking and making them worse. In October 2012, I staged a star-studded fundraiser, the Yellow Ball, at the Roundhouse in Camden. I invited the whole Sky team, everyone who had helped me win the Tour, except Chris. I look back now and think how pathetic that was. How must that have made him feel? It was only ever going to make our relationship more difficult, and I take full accountability for that.

In the end, I reached out to Chris. I spotted him at a function at the end of the 2021 Tour and told him straight, 'Chris, I'm sorry.' I wanted to settle it. The awkwardness had been going on for so long and it was paining me. I'd really liked Chris before we fell out. He'd overcome his own difficult upbringing in Kenya, an incredible story in itself, and far surpassed me as a cyclist, a phenomenal athlete and the best Tour rider of our generation. It was stupid blaming him for one moment on the bike. As racers we all do what we feel is right. More than anything, though, Chris was a genuinely lovely guy, and I hurt him, and I shouldn't have. To be able to speak to him again, to say sorry, was so liberating. It was unhealthy for me to carry that bitterness around. Being Chris's friend again means an incredible amount.

I don't blame either myself or Chris for those horrible years of non-communication. I understand Dave Brailsford's goal was likely to get as many Tour de France wins as possible, and that he had his own pressures from the higher-ups to deal with, but it felt like Dave got between Chris and me at times. If we couldn't ride together, I guess it made leaving me out of the team easy. But there were times when I wouldn't like Dave, wouldn't trust him, and others when he'd be the likeable and charming guy everyone would see on the telly. Often when I was with him, I'd be thinking, *Dave's all right, he's OK.* And then a few days later something would piss me off and I'd be standing there open-mouthed thinking, *How's this happened again?* All too often it felt like he was telling me one thing and doing entirely another. Over time I found Dave's approach to winning to be ruthless. So when it came to my relationship with him, winning the Tour was the beginning of the end.

Ultimately, the damage between me and Chris was camouflage for the deeper damage between me and Team Sky. Most people probably still think, 'Bradley Wiggins and Team Sky – a partnership made in heaven'. But the truth is the relationship was complex, layered. Writing this book, coming to understand the effect my childhood had on me, has made me realise that throughout my life I looked for people who could act as family. As a kid I never felt anyone had my back. I don't need that reassurance now, but for many years that basic desire for someone to protect me was certainly there. I failed to form a close relationship with either parent, and the result was I sought security from other people – maybe the wrong people. Thinking of your team as family is natural in any sport, and the closeness remains with the riders who went through those years with me. When that sense of kinship is shattered it hits very hard.

Dave had always been like a big brother to me. We'd been through a lot together, his repositioning of British Cycling as a global force coinciding with my own rise to glory. I saw him as a defender, someone I could be open with, who'd look out for me and always have my best interests at heart. I didn't consider, however, that our relationship had been more client based. I thought we had that kind of friendship where we could have a bit of a laugh with each other. He seemed to take himself a lot more seriously.

When it came to Dave, the mistake I made was thinking the ties we had were unconditional. They didn't seem to be. I felt I was disposable to him. I felt I could be rinsed of all use and chucked in the bin with the rest of the rubbish. Maybe I was naïve to think I was different to anyone else. After the success of 2012, Dave hosted Manchester United manager Alex Ferguson. The velodrome was only down the road and Fergie was interested to see if there was anything he could take away and incorporate at Old Trafford. Dave told me later he'd asked Fergie the secret of his success. Fergie, he said, leant over. 'The biggest thing in any organisation, any big sports team, is get rid of the c**ts.' Fergie was brutal when it came to people who challenged him. Dave seemed to be in awe of that bit of advice. I distinctly remember him repeating it to me: 'Get rid of the c**ts!' I couldn't help but wonder whether there was an element of him doing that with me. Maybe he thought of me in the same way Fergie thought David Beckham had become bigger than Manchester United and Roy Keane had become too dominant as the captain. Like them, I felt I was basically driven out.

My other key relationship at Sky was with Shane Sutton, a definite father figure in my life. In fact, he'd say it himself – 'You're the son I never had.' I felt safe around Shane. A father figure offers unconditional love. They'll do anything for you. And with Shane, while he could be tough and uncompromising, there were times it definitely felt like that.

Everything fitted the father–son dynamic. He was old enough to be my dad, and, like my real dad, was an Aussie and a cyclist. They actually knew each other, for Christ's sake. But as my relationship with Dave disintegrated, that closeness with Shane disappeared too. I've never really understood what happened with Shane, and for many years I had no communication with him. Amid so much emotional invest-ment, for those relationships with both Dave and Shane to crumble was difficult in the extreme. The result was a recur-rence of those feelings of abandonment I'd experienced as a child. Life was repeating itself. Rejection as a regular pattern.

There'll be some who'll say the environment at Team Sky and British Cycling was to be expected. This is sport at the very top level after all. In some ways, I agree. Make no mistake, elite competition is tough. You have to be resilient and able to take criticism because that's part of pushing an athlete to the next level. But in elite cycling, the line between critical and derogatory was so blurred as to be meaningless. Put it this way, would I have wanted my daughter in that system? Absolutely not. The way women were spoken about was especially awful. Before a World Cup meet in Manchester, the team pursuit squad gathered in the middle of the velo-drome. Around us, on the track, Victoria Pendleton was putting in a training effort. 'How's Vicky going?' I asked one of the staff.

'She's good,' came the reply, 'but she's going to get better because the painters are in this week.' Essentially, they were telling us that her performance peaked when she was on her period. The silence was deafening. We were four lads, definitely not choirboys, but we all understood that what was being said was totally out of order. This was a senior person at British Cycling talking about an Olympic champion athlete, not a football changing room in the 1970s. I looked at Vicky tearing round the track, doing everything to deliver success for British Cycling and her country, a woman who'd given cycling such a boost, and thought, *Is that what she's up against? As a woman is that the kind of bullshit she has to deal with?*

Sadly, it wasn't a one-off. When the BMX rider Shanaze Reade came on to the track programme, I heard similarly offensive language. At the time, the World Sprint Champion was a big guy from France called Grégory Baugé. Both Shanaze and Grégory are people of colour. 'God,' said the same person, 'imagine if we could get Shanaze to mate with Baugé. Can you imagine the athlete they'd produce?' Again, a jaw on the floor moment for anyone within earshot.

It didn't end with the athletes. I heard the word 'faggot' to describe a gay member of British Cycling's senior management team. In the end, the guy quit his role, stating that he couldn't work with someone whose homophobia was on another scale. Clearly, if anyone had to quit, it should have been the person who made the comment. But then again double standards were all over the place. Victoria Pendleton fell in love with her coach and he lost his job, while another person in the organisation was having an affair and a blind eye was turned. I mean, for crying out loud, you can't pick and choose who you fall in love with. It's not a crime last time I looked.

I learned a lesson at Team Sky. The people who are there for you when you're at your lowest are the most amazing you'll ever have in your life; the polar opposite of those who only want a part of you when you're at your best. Whichever way I looked at it, the divide between me and them had become unbridgeable. The trust had gone. A complete break-down. Paris–Roubaix in April 2015 proved the end of the road. I didn't want to have regrets, to walk off into the distance like Eric Cantona, and so an exit strategy was drawn up. I wanted to develop my own team, one that brought through upcoming riders on track and road and would facilitate my own return to the velodrome with a mind to one last crack at the Olympics at Rio in 2016. Team Sky backed the idea financially. From their point of view it allowed young talent to be nurtured. It also meant I remained tied to them – it was a way for them to keep me saying the right things, keep me on board. The result was Team Wiggins. Under that banner I looked for challenges that I could concentrate on as an individual, like the Hour record which I broke at Lee Valley VeloPark in London in June 2015, completing a distance of 54.526 km in the allotted time. The Hour was important on many levels. It gave me a goal, was an iconic marker in the sport, first set on a penny farthing in 1876, and was another occasion which, screened live on TV, gave cycling fans a moment to remember. Solo targets worked in other ways. In particular, they kept me away from the constant turmoil of the day-to-day at Team Sky. They also meant I could fit training around the family rather than living on top of a mountain at altitude.

Some might say I should have stood up for myself more at Team Sky, and occasionally I did wish I could be more like my dad, drawing on his character like I had when winning the Junior Worlds. But the hard edge I took from him dwindled away over the years. The last time I remember displaying his steel was the Olympic individual pursuit final in Athens when I needed everything in my armoury to see off Brad McGee, an opponent who'd got in my head as being virtually unbeatable. After Athens, I was left solely with extreme ability, which proved enough for me to excel, but a tougher mentality would have come in useful in certain situations, not least when the relationship with Team Sky was in freefall. Instead I was resolutely anti-confrontation for a long time. More than that, I had a proclivity to blame myself for most things, and still do.

I might have internalised the pain of the collapse of those supposedly trusted relationships at Team Sky but the visible signs of my distress were there. Facially, there's a notable decline in the years after 2012. By the end of 2014, I think I look like a hostage – drawn, tired, broken. It's there in the photos for all to see. At the time I thought I was normal but with distance I can see how the unrest took its mental and physical toll, leaving me looking lost, haunted and sad. It's actually frightening to look at – a portrait of a man losing his mind, becoming very unstable. It's also totally understandable. Slowly and steadily I'd been declining in happiness for the best part of three years. Such was my stress that grey hairs began appearing, my insecurity revealing itself in the dye I was using on my beard. I only wished I could find a magic potion that would hide my entire self. Once again I had no idea who I was. With my mod cut now replaced by a slickback, I was ping-ponging versions of myself to and fro, only to find none of them could rid me of my underlying self-hatred.

The mod look might have gone, but trying to shake off Wiggo had proven nigh-on impossible. Just because I'd seen that he was incompatible with life as a professional athlete, far removed from the thorough, utterly meticulous person who'd prepared for the 2012 Tour de France, didn't mean other people were going to let me revert to my previous self. While cycling had always been my escape, I wouldn't be able to use it to escape fame.

I met Noel Gallagher once. I was with Bella, loitering round reception at Soho Farmhouse, when his daughter came over. 'Excuse me, are you Bradley Wiggins? My dad's a big fan of yours. He'd love to come and say hello but he's a bit scared.' *Noel Gallagher scared of meeting me?* I thought. *Surely that's the wrong way round!* Noel was watching Manchester City on TV at the bar. We chatted for a while about Paul Weller, a mutual friend of course, and the new Oasis documentary, *Supersonic*, which had just come out, charting the band's rise to fame. 'The mad thing is, it's all true,' Noel explained. 'It was such a great time.' His fondness for those early days reminded me of something I'd heard him say once before, that the day you find yourself on the front page of the tabloids, everything changes. It's not fun anymore. He was talking from a musician's perspective but as a sportsperson it's exactly the same. Once you're on the front of those newspapers you're doomed to remain there for a very long time. The tabloids hound you. Wherever you go, they're on you. Everything you do is captured through their lens. And then, when you get back to the sport, and the results don't go quite as well, they turn. 'You know why he's gone s**t? Because he's living the good life.' When you're winning you can get away with being pictured with a beer in your hand. You're 'good old Wiggo', always up for a laugh. Snapped when you're no longer being picked for the big races and it's a completely different story. All of a sudden, the rhetoric changes. Those same publications which were lauding me in 2012 now had an entirely different narrative. 'Look at the state of him! No wonder he can't get in the Tour team!' Obviously, back in 2012 I didn't realise this was the U-bend they flushed you down. It was all new to me then.

I hoped retirement would bring me, and the family, some relief from the relentless attention, and so in many ways the Rio Olympics couldn't come quickly enough. But even then I couldn't resist a bit of self-sabotage. Having won the team pursuit, me and my fellow riders, Ed Clancy, Steven Burke and Owain Doull, were stood on the podium, national anthem playing, flag going up the pole, when the camera closed in on my face. I spotted myself on the big screen in the velodrome and, in that second, opened my eyes as wide as I could and stuck my tongue out. I was mocking the moment. Just the same as at London 2012, I was showing a complete inability to take seriously what I'd done. It had been four years since the Hampton Court throne and nothing had changed. I still hadn't processed that gap between the person I was and the person I felt I had to be. Yet again I'd achieved, was being offered appreciation, and my reaction was to act the clown. Classic impostor syndrome – unable to accept the spotlight being on me in the moment of glory.

What I craved in retirement was not being that person anymore – this alternate me that I didn't seem to have any control over. Of course, the reality was that my psyche existed for deep-seated reasons. Bringing calm to me and my life was never going to be as simple as ending my cycling career. You can throw your cycling shoes in the back of a cupboard but you can't throw who you are with them. Especially when you don't really know who you are. Truth was, aside from my family, the bike was the only thing keeping me sane; a sanctuary from the real world I found so hard to deal with. It was the lifeline that stopped me drowning. Which leads to an obvious question. What happens when the bike is no longer there?

The answer is total and absolute collapse. The catalyst was something I could never imagine.

CHAPTER 12

CHEAT

'Bradley Wiggins Faces Drugs Quiz'

I am at home when I hear the news. My medical records have been released by the Russian hackers' group Fancy Bears. It is four days after the 2016 Tour of Britain. My last ever race. Four days of retirement. Four days of peace and quiet. Four days of not being someone else. And then that was it. Gone. My life will never be the same again.

I left Team Sky, but Team Sky wouldn't leave me. It was like being in a mafia movie or *The Sopranos*. You know how a character will say they've had enough, they're quitting the game to lead a calmer, more peaceful life? Only whatever they do, they can't escape their past? That's what happened to me. No matter how I tried, I could never get away. It was as if the minute I retired, someone pushed the button on the next phase of the relationship, one which I would have absolutely no control over.

Believed to be revenge on the World Anti-Doping Agency (WADA) for highlighting state-sponsored doping across numerous sports in Russia, Fancy Bears published the stolen medical records of some of the world's biggest sportspeople, showing when they'd been given permission to take banned substances to treat medical conditions, therapeutic use exemptions, or TUEs, as they're known. In my case that meant injections of the anti-inflammatory triamcinolone before the Tour de France in 2011 and 2012, and the Giro in 2013, to treat a pollen allergy which had long bothered me as a road cyclist. At times it would feel like I was breathing through a straw. I'd be sneezing, eyes watering, snot pouring from my nose. It was deeply uncomfortable and had the propensity to massively affect my ability to compete. While elements of the media jumped on the leak as if I'd been hiding something, the latest to enter cycling's hall of shame, it was hardly breaking news that I was asthmatic. Puffing, wheezing and coughing up phlegm tends to be a giveaway. I'd had exercise-induced asthma from childhood, for crying out loud. Mild panic attacks had also affected my ability to breathe normally. If I was in a potentially confrontational situation I'd hyperventilate and feel like my breathing was out of my control; a reaction, as ever, more than likely linked to childhood trauma.

Initially, then, I wasn't bothered by the Fancy Bears leak. *Well, this should get cleared up pretty quickly.* After all, the reason my medical records were there to be hacked in the first place was because I did everything above board. I'd be more worried about those who didn't have properly maintained medical records. But in no time at all there were people – journalists, ex-riders, doctors – lining up to say what I'd done was questionable, that I'd in some way been seeking an unfair advantage, that the drug I'd taken was a performance enhancer. The innuendo was clear – I'd cheated my way to victory in the Tour de France.

Faced with a barrage of insinuations and accusations, none of what I'd ever said or done in terms of calling out doping seemed to stand for anything. It became very clear very quickly that any chance of heading off into the sunset for a bit of well-deserved rest and relaxation was well and truly gone. A runaway train had been set in motion and the only way I'd ever get any peace was if I tied myself to the tracks.

I've got no issue with journalists. I understand they have a job to do. But the opprobrium heaped on me by some sections of the media was as nasty as it was unjust. It felt like certain journalists totally lost any ability to take a balanced view in what they were writing. For them it had become personal, as if they took delight in my achievements being brought into question.

To rebuff the speculation, I was advised by my then-management to go on *The Andrew Marr Show*. I should have refused. People were used to switching on BBC1 on a Sunday morning and watching Marr, a seasoned political journalist, eking uncomfortable truths out of evasive ministers. I went through what had happened, explained that I'd been struggling with asthma before the 2012 Tour de France and had been advised to take triamcinolone, but by appearing on his programme I just looked like the latest in a long line of public figures with something to hide. It was a terrible platform to argue my case and the interrogation just added to the feeling of being under attack.

A better approach was sitting down with the *Guardian* cycling correspondent William Fotheringham. Doing so allowed me to give chapter and verse on my relationship with asthma and how it had been treated down the years. I explained how my pollen allergy had first shown at the Giro in 2003, affecting me so badly on one stage that the next day, exhausted, I was eliminated for being outside the time limit. From then on I'd used inhalers, antihistamines, nasal sprays and eye drops to keep the condition under control, varying in quantity according to both time of year and environment. Let's face it, when it comes to a pollen allergy, riding Paris–Nice in March or training on a volcanic island like Tenerife is never going to be the same as racing through the lush countryside of France in mid-July. During periods where I was indoors concentrating on the track, of course, I wasn't bothered by allergies at all. It was ahead of the 2011 Tour that one of the Sky doctors, Richard Freeman, suggested I see an independent specialist with regard to my medication. I'd struggled with my allergies during that June's Dauphiné and he thought seeking advice would be a positive move. The specialist did three hours of tests and recommended triamcinolone. His finding was then put to a committee of at least three sports doctors at the sport's governing body, the Union Cycliste Internationale (UCI), who would decide whether to authorise a TUE certificate. Journalists tend to either ignore or conveniently forget the fact that the committee could have turned that request down. But they didn't. They said it was OK. Not that it made any difference because that was the Tour when I ended up on the floor with a broken collarbone.

The following year was pretty much a carbon copy. Again I won the Dauphiné, and again I was granted a TUE for triamcinolone before the Tour. People say, 'How come, if you could win the Dauphiné twice without the drug, you needed it for the Tour?' But I'd been managing the condition for years. I could still race, still train. I just did so while carrying symptoms like runny eyes and a blocked nose. The Dauphiné is a one-week race and so the effect isn't as pronounced. Carrying those symptoms for a three-week struggle like the Tour is much more debilitating. Dr Freeman felt if there was a way of helping me deal with that then it was worth exploring. I was a cyclist, not a doctor. I was going on medical advice. It wasn't like I was sat round a table at Team Sky with everyone talking about triamcinolone and how it might help. I listened to the doctor, saw the specialist, and that was that. Come the Giro in 2013 and it was exactly the same set of circumstances. But again, for me it was never about obtaining a TUE. It was more a case of being checked out by a specialist, an annual MOT like any professional sportsperson would have, and a TUE being advised.

Funny how the language changes when you're on the end of a kicking. Triamcinolone is an anti-inflammatory, but every time my name was mentioned it was being referred to as a 'powerful steroid'. Even if we go with that description, the amount I was taking wasn't enough to have any effect. But I was still lumped in with those who'd taken it to cheat. After the Fancy Bears leak, David Millar, who was banned for two years for doping in 2004, spoke about how he'd had an injection of the drug because it had the potential to cause weight loss while not compromising power. David had lied about a tendon injury to get his TUE. I have no doubt that triamcinolone has been misused by cyclists, but it's way too simplistic to say that's why every cyclist has ever taken it. The drug's effect must, I'm sure, depend on the quantity taken and the physicality of the person involved. Also, I expect many riders who've abused triamcinolone will have done so while taking other banned substances, such as EPO, the hormone associated with increased red blood cell production, and testosterone, which allows cyclists to ride harder with less need for recovery. Also, losing weight during a race is far from ideal. It can leave you feeling drained and weak, which is exactly how I was starting to feel in the 2011 Tour before my fate was decided by a crash. Then there's that other undeniable truth, one which was so speedily forgotten in my case – triamcinolone is prescribed for allergies. Which is exactly why several totally independent doctors thought it was right that I should take it.

Ironic, isn't it? Had I actually acted irresponsibly and taken that same drug off my own back two days before the Tour, it wouldn't have been detected and none of the subsequent furore would have happened. You work within the rules, do everything right, have the correct paperwork, record it all digitally, and you're the one who's the target. Meanwhile, the ones who bypassed the proper procedures, the ones who were doing something wrong, slip under the radar. But those who had the knives out for me didn't want to hear that, same as the fact I'd already won Paris–Nice, the Tour de Romandie and the Dauphiné in 2012 without a TUE seemed to pass them by. It wasn't like I was having a terrible year and then turned up at the Tour with rocket boosters. I'd been performing exceptionally for the previous 18 months. But reporting the nuance doesn't sell you newspapers, doesn't get you followers on X. No one, it seemed, wanted to listen to the truth; that the rules are there, the sport's medical experts decided those rules, and they're black and white. You can either do something or you can't. Suddenly everything was about 'grey areas', 'twisting the regulations', 'pushing against the line'. It was like around every corner an angry mob was waiting, pitchforks in hand. But that was nothing compared with the nightmare ahead.

A few days later, the *Daily Mail* published an article stating that UK Anti-Doping (UKAD) were investigating myself and Team Sky about a Jiffy bag delivered to the team bus at the end of the Dauphiné in 2011. The allegation was that the package, which the media speculated may have contained triamcinolone, was meant for me. Some reports suggested its contents had actually been injected into me at the back of the bus. Had that been true, because I had no

TUE at that point, it would have been a clear doping violation and potentially I'd have been stripped of my 2012 Tour title. But it wasn't true. The first I heard of any package was the same as anybody else – when the story appeared in the *Daily Mail*.

The journalist responsible for the Jiffy bag 'exclusive', Matt Lawton, seemed to enjoy being on my case. Barely had he written that article than he was back at it again. 'Sir Bradley Wiggins in new drugs storm after British cycling star's test blunder just three months before the Rio Olympics is revealed' screamed the headline. This time he'd dug up a non-story about a mix-up with WADA, which requires athletes to provide a one-hour window each day during which they can be tested. I'd given them a time but then subsequently booked a long-haul flight from California. In the meantime, they'd turned up to do a test and I wasn't there. That's automatically deemed a missed test. Three of those and you're facing a ban. I appealed, my explanation was accepted, and it was recorded as a filing failure rather than a missed test. End of. But in Matt Lawton's world that counted as a 'drugs storm'. It's a great example of how not very much can so easily be twisted into something sensational. And that's exactly what was happening with the package. The only known fact about that Jiffy bag is it was delivered by Sky coach Simon Cope to Sky doctor Richard Freeman. And yet to this day the impression is given that it was delivered to me. Like I signed for it! God knows how many times I've answered the question, 'What was in the package?' I never even knew there was a package! Why would I? It wasn't for me. It was for a doctor. But no matter how many times I've pointed that out, I still get asked the same question again and again.

Of course, as time went on and UKAD's investigation continued, it became clear that nobody, be it British Cycling physiotherapist Phil Burt, who had originally assembled the package in Manchester, Shane Sutton who asked for it to be delivered, Simon Cope who travelled out with it, Richard Freeman who received it, or anyone else at Team Sky or British Cycling, could confirm what was in the Jiffy bag. You might reasonably expect with medical supplies, especially those being dispatched by a public body, that there'd be a carefully kept record of what, who, where and when. But the paper trail in this case was in complete disarray. Every time a potential source of a definitive answer was identified, the door was slammed shut. Richard Freeman's laptop containing medical records, for example, was, he explained to UKAD, stolen while he was on holiday in Greece. Every last trace of proof of the contents of that Jiffy bag had been erased from either memory or planet. Which was handy for Team Sky and British Cycling, these two organisations, one commercial, one publicly funded, which overlapped untidily and, some might say, unhealthily, but not so great for me, who was left with a whole load of insinuation hanging over my head. I'd listen to whatever the latest 'story' was and invariably think, *How can they say that? That's so unfair. That's not how it happened.* But once that narrative is out

there, people believe it. I'd been looking forward to retirement, desperate to reclaim my own space, my identity, only
to be grabbed by the throat and chucked headlong into a
doping scandal. The severity of it, the sinisterness of it, the
inescapability of it, was overwhelming. I'm not sure what
that package weighed, but to me it felt like I was carrying an
anvil on my back. Short of saying again and again that I
hadn't anything to hide, there was nothing I could do.
Someone had decided I was to be fed to the wolves and that
was the end of it.

Except it wasn't just me they fed to the wolves, it was my
family. The furore over the package brought the press to our
doorstep once again. In 2012, they'd revelled in building up
a new British sporting hero. Four years on, and some of them
couldn't wait to tear him down again. The harassment was
disgusting. I'd wake up in the morning and there'd be a TV
crew on the doorstep. I'd be out there remonstrating with
them in my pyjamas.

When the attention takes on a bleaker and more accusa-
tory tone, it's not just you it affects, it's the people you hold
close. My kids were in the house. What was it like for them
seeing their family under siege? What was it like for them to
have lies all over the TV and newspapers about their dad?

So bad did the situation get that eventually we were driven
from our home. For our own sanity and to maintain some
sort of normality for our children we had to get out of
Eccleston and move somewhere more private. I'm sure, in
the same position, with barbs flying from all sides, some

people would have left the UK and moved abroad to somewhere detached and exclusive like Monaco, but I didn't want the kids growing up in an environment where money was everything and reality was nothing. We headed further north to the edge of the Forest of Bowland. I'd never wanted to be one of those people who lived behind a set of security gates but at that point we had no choice.

The unjustness of it all, the brutality of it, was overwhelming. I'd spent years being apart from my family, the biggest sacrifice that elite sport brings. In fact, part of my determination to secure the Tour win in 2012 was to quell the urge to keep on trying. I was very much a dad who liked being a dad. I loved nothing more than being at home messing about with Ben and Bella, being their mate as much as anything. During my career I actually had a 'B' tattooed on each thumb, one for Ben, one for Bella, so when I locked my hands together on the time trial bike I'd have my head right over their initials. It was a great way of distracting myself. I'd look at those two B's and tell myself I wasn't going to be a professional cyclist forever. Now, finally, I'd retired, only to find that my ability to be a family man, free of intrusion, free of negativity, had been hijacked. Gates can only protect you from so much. They kept unwelcome visitors at arm's length but were no barrier against the allegations constantly fired in my direction. Cath was the one whose support kept me going over the package. She always had my back on that issue. But in the long run the dismantling of both my reputation and me as a person created an all-pervading and overbearing pressure that went a long way to the eventual destruction of our family.

Was it all worth it? I must have asked myself that question a thousand times. I'd look at the mess I was in. This has only happened because I'm Sir Bradley Wiggins and I won the Tour de France and the Olympics in London. That's the only reason. No wonder I wished it had never happened at times. The minute I won the Tour de France I was nailed to the cross.

The controversy – in which I played no part – just wouldn't stop spiralling. I was interviewed by UKAD, chief executive Nicole Sapstead informing me they'd also visited British Cycling HQ as part of their investigation. I couldn't help thinking that if UKAD were poking round the offices of sports governing bodies based on articles in the *Daily Mail* then there was a problem. If there's a specific complaint or a widely held belief that a sport is crossing boundaries and doing something wrong, fair enough, but even then surely there's a formal procedure to go through. As with every other part of the package story, I felt that UKAD's investigation had all the hallmarks of an incompetent shambles. It ended up unable to establish if I'd received the over-the-counter legal decongestant Fluimucil or triamcinolone. Unsurprising really since I'd received neither. Their efforts, they said, had been hampered by a lack of accurate medical records being available from British Cycling, a convenient absence of data that saved some very big careers. You wouldn't get away with it in a GP's surgery, but British Cycling? Records were missing, drugs weren't logged. Utter chaos.

A separate investigation by the House of Commons Digital, Culture, Media and Sport (DCMS) select committee also concluded that it wasn't in a position to state what was in the Jiffy bag. By this time, Dave Brailsford and Richard Freeman had both claimed the package contained Fluimucil but naturally had zero evidence to back it up. Shane Sutton, meanwhile, told the committee that he didn't know what was in the package but that it was intended for me. The inquiry, as with UKAD, was a fiasco. Having no evidence that my TUEs were for performance enhancement didn't stop them deciding that was the case. Totally ignoring the real reason why I was taking that drug, the MPs declared that myself and Team Sky had 'crossed an ethical line'. But the problem with ethics in Team Sky didn't rest with the riders, it rested with the people who ran it. Success went to their heads.

Naturally, it was only a matter of time before Piers Morgan weighed in. 'Sir Bradley Wiggins is a flaming cheat,' he declared on *Good Morning Britain*. Journalist David Walsh, who'd spent a year embedded with Team Sky while writing a book on the team, all the time apparently noticing nothing amiss, was now happy to sit on the breakfast sofa opposite Piers and jump on the bandwagon. In the middle of a torrid period of my life, Piers' little display of supposed outrage did at least bring a smile to my face. I hadn't sung the national anthem on the Olympic podium in London and Piers – who else? – had laid into me on X. 'I was very disappointed Bradley Wiggins didn't sing the anthem either. Show some respect to our monarch. Please!' A reply, seeming to come from me but actually from a parody Bradley Wiggins account, was as brilliant as it was unflinching. 'I was very disappointed when you didn't go to jail for insider dealing or phone hacking,' it read, 'but, you know, each to his own.' It went viral. Piers has hated me ever since. It goes a long way to explaining his silly rant about me being a cheat. Clearly touched a nerve with old Piers there. I'm just sorry it wasn't me who wrote it, although I'll be honest there's been times when I've claimed it was me because it was that good!

Thankfully, there were other, far more respectable individuals, who raised their heads above the parapet in my defence. Steve Redgrave, an absolute hero of British sport, said the DCMS report was wrong to pinpoint me for crossing an ethical line. 'To me,' he told BBC Radio 5 Live, 'it's black and white. It's either a positive drug test and you are cheating or you're not cheating and everything's OK.' And away from the screeching headlines of the *Daily Mail*, other journalists took a more measured and professional view. After the release of the DCMS report in March 2018, I gave an interview to BBC sports editor Dan Roan. I was properly given the chance to explain what had happened. Dan asked all the searching questions that people wanted answering and I was able to respond in depth. It seemed like a turning point, the moment when I began to feel people started to believe I was telling the truth.

Of course, if those in the media had their sights set on me, they weren't looking elsewhere. And over time I came to wonder if that wasn't my true role in this whole pitiful affair. A handy diversion from something a lot more serious. My mind was drawn back to a set-to in a corridor at the velodrome in 2014. 'I'm gonna have the last laugh,' the person told me, 'but not yet. You watch!' Is that what he meant? Had he threatened that the situation with the Jiffy bag would happen to me two years before it did?

When I signed with Team Sky, they offered me a salary of €1.1 million. Dave Brailsford emailed me two weeks later. He wanted to up it to €1.3 million, but the extra two hundred grand wasn't for me, it was for Shane. At that time, Shane was performance director at British Cycling. He was on public money, with a cap on his earnings. When Dave and Shane set up Team Sky, they came up with the idea of doubling his salary through me paying him for 'coaching services' for the next four years. From the off there was, in my opinion, a muddying of the financial waters, a bending of the rules, that came from British Cycling and Team Sky being so intertwined.

But that was nothing compared with the financial scandal surrounding the package. Thing is, I'm not denying there was a Jiffy bag. I actually believe there was one. I also believe it *wasn't* meant for a rider at Team Sky. In my opinion, it contained testosterone patches and its ultimate destination was elsewhere. Afterwards, there was a lot of media discussion about testosterone being delivered to the velodrome in Manchester, although, naturally, records are lacking. If true, and public money had been spent to dope a rider, amid all Team Sky's and British Cycling's claims to be the ultimate in clean cycling, it would have been the scandal to end all scandals. A story that the package was meant for me at the Dauphiné would be a perfect smokescreen. My presence there fitted perfectly with the date and route of the package. But on closer inspection it was a tale that didn't make sense. After all, the package only ended up being handed over at the Dauphiné after Shane told Simon Cope to come to the race because he wanted a lift back to the airport. Simon was actually supposed to go straight to Sestriere in Italy where we were staying.

Clearly, only a select few people would ever have known about the parcel's true purpose. My opinion is they sat on it for five years until, with relationships creaking at Team Sky, one of them took that information, used it as a bullet, and told a journalist Dave Brailsford told the journalist the package was meant for me.

Something felt very strange to me. Before I went for the Hour record in 2015 a request for a TUE was submitted, and declined, without my knowledge. The Hour was indoors. Applying for a TUE contradicted the previously stated case that I needed triamcinolone for a general clinical purpose when racing outdoors at certain times of the year. In the context of what later happened, I can't help but wonder what the motivation was to make that application other than to heap further suspicion on me at a later date; to make it look like I was using TUEs very deliberately for performance gain. After all, while I was unaware what TUE applications had been put in, they were always going to sit there on my record. My guess is that my TUEs were always going to be leaked at some point, be it by Fancy Bears or someone else. The Jiffy bag story needed my TUEs to be in the public domain if it was to fly. It allowed insinuation to flood into the narrative. *If he was doing that, what else was he doing?*

Only now can I see how naïve I was. This was never about my medical records getting hacked and what was in that package, it was about something far greater. The last person in charge of Team Sky's medical supplies, the last person who would ever have known what was in that package, was me. And that made me the perfect fall guy. Who's the best person to pin a scandal on? The guy who's done nothing wrong! That way there can never be an outcome. It leaves people constantly trying to prove a negative. What a beautiful distraction. Except for the person who's left floundering in a quicksand of lies; the person who'll be destroyed by the whole hideous conspiracy. I was knifed in the back so others could save themselves.

I strongly felt a distinct lack of one-to-one support from Dave Brailsford. All I got was one phone call from him – 'I don't know what's going on here, Brad. Have you got any idea who could have done this?' I felt my reputation and all I'd achieved was trashed.

I'm sure nobody wanted me to be dragged through the dirt. I expect they saw it as unfortunate but felt I was big enough and strong enough to drag myself through the river of s**t and reach the other side. 'He'll get through it. It's just going to be a rough ride for a few years.' They were wrong about that. While other people got on with their lives, their careers, I was reduced to a shadow of my former self. It was like being trapped in a Netflix drama, at the centre of a plot I'd never known anything about. The viciousness of the assault, from people I'd trusted at Team Sky, and elements of the media, was unbelievable. Unless you've been in that situation, you'll never comprehend the feeling of utter hopelessness, and helplessness, it brings. It's like you've been stripped of a voice. I was always cautious of speaking out anyway. When the narrative is so set against you, anything you say in your defence just brings more disdain and criticism. Before you know it, you're just that nutcase with his conspiracy theories. 'Oh God! He's gone mental! He's lost the plot!' Eventually, I dealt with the pain, the invisibility, the degradation, in a different way. I took drugs. One of the biggest factors in my addiction was the repeated attempts to tarnish everything I'd achieved.

No one has ever been held accountable for the package. But when you ask yourself who's telling the truth and who isn't, bear in mind how incredible it is that no one has ever got to the bottom of something as simple as what was in a transportation of medical products by two respected and well-established organisations like British Cycling and Team Sky. Both prided themselves on efficiency and professionalism, and yet when it came to the contents of the medicine cupboard there was little in the way of clarity. They were both left floundering for excuses.

The affair is a stain on others, not me. I have no problem looking at myself in the bathroom mirror when I brush my teeth. Others, I expect, have to turn away. If they don't, they should.

Nor am I a cycling pariah. I do *An Audience With* theatre shows all across the country and repeatedly people tell me they believe me when I say I didn't do anything wrong; that the package had absolutely nothing to do with me. Even so, it's not nice feeling thrown under the bus.

The package was the worst period of my life. Every time I managed to put it out of my mind, something would happen to catapult it straight back in front of my eyes. The story, and all it implied, just never went away. It was a constant feature, like having four years with a stone in my shoe. All I could do was limp along helplessly as my reputation was deliberately and mercilessly trashed. No matter how many investigations or inquiries, there was never an outcome, and yet my name remained at the centre of it all. It's hard to forgive and forget, and when it comes to those so quick to put the boot in I have no intention of doing so. At the 2019 Tour de France, Matt Lawton came over to me trying to be friendly. 'Come on, Brad, I've always been a big fan.' The hypocrisy was incredible. After everything he'd written he wanted me to shake his hand and be mates? I told him in no uncertain terms what he could do. I wasn't going to be humiliated by journalists who I feel didn't know the difference between an investigation and a witch-hunt. I didn't need to take lessons in ethics and morality from the *Daily Mail*.

It's only now I'm in a good place that I have a full appreciation of how bad the package situation got, the full gravity of its effect on me. When you're in a mess like that, you can't see clearly. It takes distance to reflect. Ultimately, the only reason I've come out the other side upright is because I know I haven't done anything wrong. Throughout the whole horrendous nightmare, that's been my saving grace.

Despite those who tried to destroy me, I'm still Bradley Wiggins, winner of the Tour de France, winner of five Olympic gold medals, winner of eight World Championships. None of my achievements have been taken away from me. Why? Because there's no substance, no content, to anything that's been thrown at me. With the amount of scrutiny that was put on me, if I really had done something wrong, there'd have been an outcome by now.

I know what I did. Nothing. And that's why I'm still here today.

CHAPTER 13

ADDICT

'I can walk through walls on this!'

My Sports Personality of the Year trophy sits on the mantlepiece. Alongside it is my knighthood. Together they taunt me, endlessly reminding me how unworthy I am of the adulation I received in 2012. They symbolise the futility of what I achieved and everything that's gone wrong since.

I grab hold of them. 'These don't make me special,' I tell Ben and Bella. 'They don't elevate me in this house or anywhere else. They're just things. They don't define what someone's worth.'

I take them outside and throw them against the wall as hard as I can. I smash the trophy up until it's a mess of mangled metal. I stamp on the knighthood in its presentation box. I look at it crushed in the gravel. A knighthood? What's the point? It offers no protection from any of this s**t. It just brings more grief. Every day there are people calling for it to be taken off me. And for what? What have I done? No one can actually tell me what I've done wrong.

In July 2017, I was sitting in the shadow of Mont Ventoux. Next day was the 50th anniversary of Tom Simpson's death and I'd be riding up the mountain to pay my respects. It was a really unhappy period of my life, just before I started doing drugs, and as I stared into the distance I found myself trans-fixed by the swallows in the air. *What a life it would be, to be a swallow, not a human.* I'd have exchanged places in a heartbeat.

I'd never contemplated that retirement might be a problem. I'd only ever considered it an opportunity to try other things, like learning to swim properly or running a marathon. But once cycling had gone all I found were unanswered ques-tions. Everywhere unanswered questions. Be they from my childhood, such as my dad and Stan, or now, like the Jiffy bag, everywhere I looked I was faced with situations where I had no idea what had happened. There had been so many times during my career where I'd craved a normal life in the real world, and then when the chance finally came all I discovered was a mess. For so long I'd dreamed of being the polar opposite of a professional cyclist. Never for one minute did I stop to consider that, in my case, that might be complete and utter chaos. The 'real world' for me was destined to be a fast descent into oblivion.

Instead of finding the true me in retirement, I just started hating myself. I'd look at this person on something like Channel 4's celebrity winter sports show *The Jump* and think, *What am I doing here? What the f**k is this? This isn't what I wanted.* It was a feeling I recognised. I'd had exactly the same sensation after winning the Tour de France. The last thing I ever wanted was to be seen as a 'celebrity'. I've always had a healthy disdain of celebrity for celebrity's sake – those absolute nonentities who pop up on TV and in the newspapers all the time. At peak 'Wiggomania', when I was constantly being interviewed, or pictured in the papers out and about round London, I had a nagging fear that people's contempt for celebrity also applied to me. Part of being that silly person on the red carpet at SPOTY, of saying 'Susan' instead of 'Sue', was me mocking my own appearance in that celebrity gaze.

I hated everything about *The Jump* apart from one thing – the rowing machine in the hotel gym. That's when the idea of achieving in a sport other than cycling first arose. It was also the first sign that my entire identity was built on the back of being a professional athlete. Without that status, I had no self-esteem, no confidence. Could rowing allow me a stay of execution? Maybe I could make another Olympics, this time off the bike. Even if it was mere fantasy, there were three years before any decisions would be made on the Olympic team. In the meantime, if anyone asked what I was doing, being able to say 'I'm still a professional sportsman – I'm going for rowing in the next Olympics' felt like a comfortable fit. It was also a great and physically punishing distraction at a time when the witch-hunt and press-hounding around the Jiffy bag were at their most frenzied.

If I applied myself in the same way I'd done with cycling, I did actually believe I could become an Olympic rower. But there was an underlying element of unrealism. However good I got on a machine, rowing on water was a whole different skill. I always had way too much to do to make the starting line at Tokyo. That's without the fact I was starting out on my rowing journey aged 36 and lived up north while the national base was at Henley-on-Thames. I also began to see that my motivation was questionable. Did I really want to become a rower or was I searching, yet again, for an identity? Something that detracted from any last remnants of the old Wiggo 'rock star' persona and propped up my ego as an athlete.

I ditched rowing in 2018. The day I gave up was the day I started doing cocaine.

There's no process to drug addiction. It wasn't a matter of making a decision – *I've got a bit of time on my hands – I know, I'll do drugs!* I wasn't consciously thinking, *I'm desperate to try cocaine!* Someone put a line in front of me in a bar and I snorted it up my nose. End of story. I didn't stand there for ten minutes weighing up whether I should or I shouldn't. I didn't picture the depths to which drugs could take me or wonder if, after having had a starring role in one great Danny Boyle production, the Olympic Opening Ceremony, I was going to end up like an extra in another, *Trainspotting*. I just stood there feeling euphoric. It was like discovering something totally new, a feeling so far removed from my 'normal' that it was almost unworldly. A single thought dominated my mind. *I can walk through walls on this!* That's not to celebrate cocaine, it's just to explain how something so alien to me and the life I'd led to that point could get hold of me so incredibly quickly. Once I came out of the sporting world and saw just how accepted cocaine was in society, especially among creative and artistic figures I respected, its use became 100 per cent legitimised and validated. *This is what normal people do!* It wasn't like I was with a bunch of lowlifes crawling in the gutter, I was with people who I liked and valued. I was drawn to the narrative of drugs being a cultural touchstone, something cool. After 2012, I'd worn the skin of a rock star. Why not jump in all the way? Doing the odd line here and there made me feel better. It made my problems shrink into the distance. What's so wrong with that?

Whatever slight resistance there might have been was weakened by alcohol. I'd always enjoyed the occasional blow-out, but in retirement, as my problems piled up, it had become a crutch. Without alcohol, I felt I couldn't operate on a daily basis. I wasn't a roll-around drunk. There were never any photos of me spilling out of nightclubs and collapsing on the pavement. I didn't actually like being drunk. For me, drinking was about easing pain. Once you start using alcohol to block out reality, you've lost control. In my case, that loss of control opened the gateway for drugs. If I was a couple of drinks in and someone offered me coke, it was so much harder to say no. Before long, alcohol no longer felt enough. What began as a line every couple of days escalated into an everyday thing, then morning and night, then whenever I felt the need. Before I knew it, I was doing cocaine anytime, anywhere.

Cocaine was my little secret, but if you look closely there were clues to my mangled mental state in those early days. Occasionally in interviews I'd mention whole new career paths. 'I'm going to train to be a social worker,' I'd say, or 'I want to be a doctor.' I'm sure from the outside it must have sounded odd, but in terms of giving myself some purpose it was all I had. Bear in mind that while I was saying these things I was upping the drugs, my self-worth plummeting at speed in the opposite direction, and it makes sense that I'd try to elevate myself by thinking I could do something that no one would expect me to do, something positive for people who'd been through similar things to me. Maybe the fact I reached for helping professions should have given people a hint of where my head was.

None of those options were ever realistically going to happen. My future was drugs. I justified their presence in my life as a necessary coping mechanism for all the s**it I was going through. With cycling's protective arm no longer round my shoulder, and the legacy of everything I'd achieved on the bike so resolutely trashed by forces beyond my control, drugs walked through an already open door. What I hadn't understood is that they'd be accompanied by the ghosts of my past. For 25 years, seeking brilliance on two wheels had pushed the hurt away. All I had to do was focus on the next Olympics, the next season, the next training ride. Problem was, I never consciously understood that was how I operated, which meant when the cycling stopped I was exposed, naked. Initially, drugs felt like a comfort blanket I could wrap myself in. But actually they were a blanket made of wire wool. They scratched at my skin, opening old scars and allowing the pain to pour in.

For the first time in a long time I began thinking about Stan. High on drugs, sat outside a pub, I texted my mum. 'I struggled over the years with what Stan did to me.' My phone pinged. 'You didn't have to go through that on your own.' Her reply sent me into a spiral. It made me wonder what exactly was in that letter sent to her by British Cycling. I asked if she still had it. So many years on, unsurprisingly the answer was no. But I couldn't help thinking there must have been people who knew what Stan was like, only to have sat idly by while he'd abused me. They'd got on with their lives while I was left to compartmentalise the trauma of three years as the target of a paedophile. Living in the moment while parcelling up past suffering came to be a speciality of mine. I'd immerse myself in something to the exclusion of everything else. I did the same as an athlete, always moving forward, forever leaving disappointments behind. But just because you compartmentalise something doesn't mean it's gone away. It's avoidance, and any psychologist will tell you that's not healthy. I was never conscious that the compartment containing the abuse would one day explode. But when I retired and started doing drugs it became inevitable.

It wasn't just Stan. I'd think about my dad. I'd never resolved that relationship, and then he was murdered. As with the abuse, I'd buried that huge bundle of mental anguish. It was always going to resurface, but I was never conscious of that fact until it was too late.

There were times when I actually wondered if I was turning into my dad. I started to see a lot of myself in him when I was losing my way. After all, he was an addict, an alcoholic in his case, and, as had been rammed down my throat for years, genetics matter. Maybe I was predisposed to having these kinds of problems. In reality, the reasons I drifted into addiction were different, but even so my natural instinct was to bring my position back to my dad. In fact, sometimes when I was doing a line I'd ask myself, *What would Dad think?* I'd mull it over and conclude he'd probably do one with me. Although, to be fair, from what I understand, he never tampered with recreational drugs. Then another thought would pop up. *What would Grandad think?* No need to ponder this one. I knew he'd be horrified. *Those two men*, I'd think, *the bad one and the good one*. Simplistic, but that's where my head would go as I flitted constantly from one explanation to another for the person I'd become. I didn't seem able to separate any of it – Stan, my dad, his murder, success, fame, the package, the witch-hunt. Truth was, I'd had a lifetime of huge life events – some positive, some crushingly negative – happen to me in a very short space of time, and within that there was so much I'd never come near to dealing with. All the time I was becoming increasingly reliant on cocaine, never realising it was exacerbating my inability to get to the root cause of my issues. The more I took, the more I was stuck in a loop of confusion.

The drugs were both generating turmoil and feeding off it. I mean, who's ever found the answer to who they are in a wrap of coke? More than anything, it was the unjustness that got under my skin. What had I done to deserve any of it? Emotional hurt at a granular level. Abandonment at every turn. And then I abandoned myself.

At the same time I was still working, my most high-profile role being covering the Tour de France for Eurosport from the back of a motorbike. In a foreign country and constantly on the move, my supply chain was cut. You might think I'd be climbing the walls after three weeks off drugs but actually it was no problem. Being back at the Tour, doing a job I enjoyed, proved a great distraction. The problem came when I had to go home. Staring at four walls, the old thought patterns would re-emerge. It was inevitable I'd sink back into my old ways. Working at talkSPORT in London, for example, they'd put me up in a hotel and I'd spend the night drinking and doing drugs in my room. Eventually, I'd get an hour's sleep before getting up, going home and putting a brave face on.

Not that Cath and the kids were fooled. Nobody knows you better than your family. They can detect the slightest change in your mannerisms, your personality. I tried to hide my drug use from them but it was obvious. I'd always been this ultra-laid-back character round the house. Like I say, my home was my natural territory, a retreat where I could be the true me. But my addiction would display itself in a character who was slightly manic, fuelled by an underlying restlessness, an unease with myself. Addiction changed me from someone who was present to someone who was just there. I'd take Ben and Bella to school and then sit in the house all day taking drugs. There was a definite element of wallowing in self-pity. I remember the thought pattern in my mind clearly. *I've been put on this Earth to make other people happy. The sacrifice is that I'm not going to be happy myself. I've never been happy. I'm never going to be happy.* I'd blame the success of 2012 for everything that had happened, sitting there convinced that by winning the Tour and Olympics I'd brought everything crashing down on myself. I criticise myself for that now. Some might say I had reason to feel sorry for myself after all that had happened. But that can never be an excuse for what I'd become at that point. Life's tough. It's a struggle. Discipline is what I'd always been great at. Without it, you're nothing. You give up at the slightest struggle, and that's exactly what I did.

I wasn't fit to be a parent at that point, as evidenced by what happened with my knighthood and SPOTY trophy, not the actual prize they give you on the night I hasten to add, but a smaller replica given to every winner to keep. My daughter found that award not long ago, the old TV camera, an icon of British sport, all battered and bent. Now I'm in a different mental state and can truly appreciate what that accolade meant, I wish I could magic it back to how it once was. It's not like you can go on Amazon and order a new one. But at the time my mindset, exacerbated by the fact I was high on drugs, was very much that trophies, medals, anything like that, don't define anybody. So much did I hate my identity being wrapped up in my achievements of 2012 that I lost my mind over it. 'This stuff doesn't put Dad on a pedestal,' I raged as I smashed those things up. 'This isn't success.' I did that in front of my kids. No wonder there were times when they talked about trying to put me in rehab.

The desecration of my Olympic medal might have happened away from their gaze but it's equally sad to reflect on. Hundreds of thousands of people roaring me on, millions more watching at home. One of the great moments of London 2012, and there I am in a wardrobe, snorting cocaine, mocking my achievement, hating it for what I believed it had brought me. If someone else had done that to my medal I'd have been offended. 'How dare you treat it like that?' But me? That was OK. Because I could look at the person I'd become and ask, *What exactly did 2012 give me?* It was the equivalent of pissing on someone's grave, and in that moment I was pissing on my own. The gold medal, the Tour de France, all of it, was dead to me. The person I'd been in Paris and London was dead to me too. I actually Facetimed a fellow user during that depravity. 'Look how funny I am, doing coke off my London Olympic medal!' Forget the medal, what actually am I in that moment? I'm one of two drug-dependent people, each enabling the other's addiction.

No wonder that in the midst of this madness mine and Cath's marriage was collapsing. Cath is as big a casualty of the last 12 years as anyone. She paid the ultimate price for being my wife. She didn't know that ten years after she met me I was going to win the Tour de France, become the most famous man in the country, get carried away with hiding behind a veil and then have a massive amount of struggle. She didn't sign up to that. I moved out at the end of 2019. A year later, we announced our divorce.

Inevitably, the more family life disintegrated, the more extreme my drug habit became. Up all night on coke, just me and the dog, I'd put odd things on Instagram. I found one recently from 2019. It's me sat on the couch at four in the morning. All I wrote was 'Hope'. There's another I put on at 3.47 a.m. – 'The Smiths getting me through another night shift.' All those posts were a little bit cryptic in nature but you didn't need to be a crossword genius to work out what they were – cries for help. No different to when I texted Mum about Stan. Not really saying anything but at the same time saying everything. Except while that was a private message, now I was doing the social media equivalent of using a loudhailer.

High on drugs I was capable of all kinds of random acts. One time in the middle of the Covid lockdown I FaceTimed Shane. We hadn't spoken for years but something made me want to pick up the phone and make sure he was OK. He broke down in tears. 'Well, I never expected to hear from you!' The state I was in, I've no real idea what we talked about after that, but we haven't spoken since.

Around the same time I sent a WhatsApp video of myself at Disneyland to a fellow addict. I'm saying stupid stuff about Mickey Mouse and the way kids are behaving in the park. When I fell out with the person in question, they sent the clip to the *Daily Mail*, who naturally wasted no time in sticking a tale about my 'bizarre foul-mouthed rant' online. As much as I dislike the way certain newspapers behave, ultimately the life I was leading and the type of people I was befriending at that time meant it was a story waiting to happen. Of course, seeing an article like that would only add more fuel to my need to escape from the nightmare I was living. That fuel, of course, was drugs.

While I became highly skilled at hiding both my mental state and my addiction, clearly, as the Disneyland episode reveals, there were times when I took incredible risks, not least because, when it came to taking drugs, in my mind nowhere was out of bounds. I was listening to a radio station the other day, and then I remembered, on several occasions when I appeared, I'd nip into the toilets during ad breaks to do a line. In my head, coke was the only way I could function in that live environment. I look at that behaviour now and can't believe how reckless it was. If someone had caught me that would have been the end of it. I'd have leapt straight from toilet cubicle to front page.

But in some ways, risk was an addiction all of its own. If I was on a train, for example, I liked the fact there was only half an inch of toilet door between me, Bradley Wiggins, the (supposedly) celebrated cyclist, snorting coke, and people wandering past in the corridor. One time on a train I was really high. There were football fans on board and police were up and down the carriages making sure everyone was behaving. Straightaway, one of them recognised me. 'Can I shake your hand, Bradley?' I was chatting away to this copper, all the time thinking, *I've got three grams of coke on me here!*

Another time, on the day of my old mate Charlie's coronation, I was in a takeaway pizza place in Preston with the kids. There were people outside in the street waving flags, everyone having a really great day. Waiting alongside us were two traffic cops. 'It's Bradley Wiggins, isn't it? We used to pass you in the car when you were out training. Can we have a picture?' We gathered in close for the selfie, six grams of coke suddenly feeling very heavy in my pocket. In those kinds of situations I would use playing Bradley Wiggins – the Bradley Wiggins people thought I was – to my advantage. It's better that a police officer wants to talk to you because they like you rather than suspects you.

It's cringeworthy when I think about it, but I always got a huge kick out of being the only one who knew my little secret. In April 2022, I did a *BBC Breakfast* interview with Dan Walker about a charity bike ride for, ironically enough, men's mental health. The Beeb put me up in a hotel near MediaCityUK in Salford, the idea being I'd be fresh for an early appearance on the red sofa the next morning. I imagine for most guests it's an arrangement that works well. Except I stayed up all night doing drugs.

There's a word that always makes me smile when I hear it – 'seemingly'. It's the perfect word to describe how addicts slip under the radar. You appear to be one thing when in fact you're entirely another. That's how you hide it from people. That's how you function. That's how you go on breakfast television high.

My appearance came just before Dan left the BBC. It's still there on YouTube for everyone to see. Watch it and you'll see me messing about, swapping places with him on the sofa, reading the autocue, pretending to audition for his job. Everyone's laughing, and afterwards the production team told me I was great. Actually I'd been awake for 24 hours and was feeling totally manic. You'd never know. It just looks like a bit of fun. But that's because I'd learned to hide my addiction very, very well. I look at that footage, me on *BBC Breakfast* talking about how important it is for men to seek help for their mental health, and am left with one over-whelming thought: *For f**k's sake, Brad, nobody needed help more than you.*

As good as I was at throwing a smokescreen around the real me, there was no guarantee that interview wouldn't be a total car crash. While I recognised only too well what appearing on live TV high on drugs said about the person I'd become, the buzz of walking out of that studio thinking, *No one knew! No one f**king knew!* was amazing. It was like a game I'd invented. A new kind of competition where I'd win or lose on my ability to fool someone. I knew how mad it was. Lose, get caught in possession of a Class A drug, especially the quantities I was carrying with me, sometimes fifteen hundred quid's worth, and I was looking at a stretch in prison. Win, and the reward was the rush. I backed myself to win because I could hide my addiction in my personality. People knew I could be funny and so I'd make a couple of jokes as a way of diverting attention from what was happening underneath. Such a weird thrill to seek. What was to be gained from it? By making addiction a game, was my mind justifying it in some way? I don't know the answer. All I know is that each time I got away with it, the kick drew me to do it again and again.

It sounds incredible that someone with my profile, a five-times Olympic gold medallist, could be on drugs for six years without the media finding out but this wasn't a case of scouring back alleys for drug dealers. I wasn't hanging around in pub toilets asking if anyone had a wrap. I knew a few people who used cocaine and, having spent a fair bit of time with them down the years, trusted them 100 per cent not to tell anyone about my habit. It was more than a functional relationship based on drugs. I liked these characters and felt safe and secure, protected even, in their company. It's that 'big brother' thing again, knowing that someone's got your back, that they'll look out for you. Just because that feeling comes from an unorthodox place doesn't make it not real. If anything, it was the orthodox male protectors – Dad and Brendan in my family life, Dave Brailsford at work – who I felt had let me down. Now I'd found protectors in a different life. At that point, post-retirement, you might ask 'protectors from what?' But remember I was being attacked by elements of the press constantly. I was besieged by negativity. Everything I'd achieved was being discredited. Every day, I was seeing stuff about me that wasn't true. It felt like I was under a barrage of abuse.

I built up another network of suppliers who either didn't know or care who I was. I've deleted them all now, but for a good while I had a load of dealers' numbers on my phone. Occasionally messages still get through. I don't act on them but their sheer brazenness does make me smile, like this one from the end of last year: *It's Christmas! Celebrate with special offers! Buy three bags and get one free! Reply STOP to opt out!* Mad, isn't it? People don't realise just how easy it is. You literally reply to a message and a few minutes later your drugs arrive at your door like a pizza or a KFC. I knew one dealer who actually had a loyalty card, like you get at Costa. Every time you bought from him, he'd stamp it. After six purchases you got a free bag. Others would offer a discount if a user recommended them to someone new. Basically, they'd reward people for giving someone else a habit. You could even do bank transfers with them. The fact that dealers exist like that, offering deals and convenience like any other major commercial operation, shows what a massive part of society drugs have become. It's a crazy hidden world, but one that is prevalent everywhere. Politicians, police officers, business leaders, they're all doing it. It's become part of everyday life. A day at the races used to be about getting dressed up and having a glass of champagne. Now it's about getting dressed up and doing lines of coke off the baby changing mat in the toilets.

The deeper I got into addiction, the more drugs I'd be buying. The money I was spending was crazy. Once you become psychologically reliant on cocaine, believing you can't get through the day, the afternoon, the next hour, the next ten minutes, without a fix, it's got you in an iron grip. That's when it really starts affecting your behaviour, becoming destructive to yourself and those around you. One of the first things that vanishes is self-respect. Cocaine is seen as a party drug, edgy and glamorous, beloved of celebrities, musicians, models and all the rest, but the truth is it's a vile and dirty habit. Forget shindigs in the Hollywood Hills, the reality of cocaine is finding yourself hunched in a toilet cubicle, knees in someone else's piss, snorting a line off a lavatory seat. Glamorous it ain't. Every time I go into a public toilet now I think how hideous that whole cocaine scene is, the mess, the germs. And then you're sniffing it with a rolled-up £20 note. Where's that been? Who's touched it. And you're sticking it up your nose? It's appalling. And yet in the moment of doing it, you don't give a f**k. In Covid, people were wandering round with facemasks on and then taking them off to do coke in a toilet. What the hell? Not that I could detach myself from them. I was one of them. When the buzz wore off, I'd tell myself, *You bastard! You f**king horrible bastard.* I'd feel dirty, despicable. But then another voice would pipe up. 'Yes, Brad, but you need it. You know you do.' And so I'd do it again, and again, and again ...

Essentially, I was a functioning addict. I'd get up, wash, and go out and do whatever was in my diary for that day. I'll give you an example. In 2023, I went along to Herne Hill to record a documentary on impostor syndrome for the BBC. It's there on BBC iPlayer. Watch it now if you want. I can promise you won't notice a thing. If anything, you'll see a bloke who seems in a pretty good place, able to reflect on himself and his past in what would appear to be a healthy and self-composed way. And yet that's me at the height of my drug use. That's how well I could hide it. I'd do something like that, look at what I had on the rest of the day, and if it was nothing I'd think, *OK, I've got time to do more drugs.* The only time my two selves overlapped was in a follow-up documentary I made to *A Year in Yellow.* While there are times in that film where I'm able to unpack and contemplate the years post-2012, there's a darkness to my character, a noticeable undercurrent of unease, a barely hidden self-loathing. In some ways, it's the portrait of someone at the edge of sanity; someone who can no longer keep the volcano of emotional pain at bay. As ever, I'm reaching for personalities, disguises. At the start of the documentary I'm back at Hampton Court, scene of my triumph at London 2012, the Wiggo I displayed on the throne back then replaced by a bizarre, borderline deranged character in a huge overcoat à la Second World War submarine captain. In the end I decided the programme couldn't, and shouldn't, be shown. It was the right decision. I'm no longer that person, but I fear that version of myself, as shocking as it was extreme, would have come to define me.

I might have pushed back against one act of self-sabotage but there were others just as shocking. There was a time when I blamed cycling for everything that had happened to me, an entire two-year period where I never looked at a bike, let alone got on one. I'd tell anyone who'd listen, 'I can't stand cycling.' It was like meeting your best friend in the pub, punching them in the face and walking out saying nothing. Where those around me had failed to offer protection, the bike had always been there for me. It was the very last thing that should carry the can for the position I found myself in.

To further that separation from the person I used to be, I deliberately allowed my fitness to slide. I let everything go. My diet, which I'd looked after so religiously down the years, went out of the window, replaced by any old s**t. I became totally unrecognisable from the fit and healthy person I once was. By lockdown I hadn't trained for two years. I had a belly, the lot. I was smoking all the time, because it was rebellious. I liked the fact that people would see me doing it in public. I revelled in the thought of them looking at this one-time sporting hero and thinking, *F**k, what's happened to him?* I even once posted a picture of myself smoking on Instagram, a complete *F**k you!* to the world. *Just because I won something*, I was saying, *doesn't mean I can't do what I want with my body*. I looked at the comments. People were calling me out for not being a good role model. *So go get another f**king role model*, I'd think. *I don't want to be a role model. When was it written that I had to do that for the rest of my life?* I was full of anger, projecting everything at cycling and fitness, and all at the expense of nobody but me.

Because truth is when I saw pictures of myself with fat round my waist and a fag in my mouth I'd be ashamed of what I'd become, how I'd let myself go. I feel sad now when I look back on that time. There's a realisation of just how disassociated from myself I must have been to have done that. I'm glad to say Bella persuaded me to stop smoking. Filthy habit.

The irony is, of course, that while the tabloids were papping me outside pubs in Soho, drinking and smoking, they were missing the real story – I was actually there to pick up five hundred quid's worth of coke. Forget booze and fags in the street, what was going on in the toilet? I thank God they didn't know because I'm sure they'd have treated my addiction with about as much sensitivity as a pack of dogs on a lump of meat. Let's face it, back at the office they weren't looking at those pictures pondering whether a bloke who's won five Olympic golds and the Tour de France only to end up propping up a wall, fag in hand, a shadow of his former self, might not mentally be in a very good place. I was always conscious, and scared, of what the papers would say if they found out. We've seen it so many times. Someone in the public eye, a *Blue Peter* presenter or whoever, is caught doing a line of coke and the tabloids have a field day. I couldn't help thinking that, with me especially, they'd go to town, sure to insinuate that if I was doing drugs in retirement then surely I'd have done so as a rider.

The fact the papers never did find out is due to the isolation in which, for the most part, I indulged the addictive side of my personality. I'd always sought isolation in times of misery and dejection. Take my little corner of the bedroom, for example, as a kid. I'm happy in my own space. But with drugs it was damaging. After I moved out of the house I'd find some anonymous hotel, stick the 'Do Not Disturb' sign on the door, and that would be the end of it. Stocked up with drugs, I'd literally not leave the room for five days. I'd have the curtains closed the whole time. It reminded me of something Elton John said about his own addiction – 'At some point you get sick and tired of opening the curtains at night and shutting them in the morning.' In that gloom, I'd stay up for hour after hour. I'd do cocaine morning, noon and night. I wouldn't ring anyone, speak to anyone, nothing. I'd be wearing the same pair of joggers, would barely eat (cocaine kills your appetite), wouldn't look after myself in any way. I'd exist in my own seedy little world. No one to bother me. No one to ask what I was doing. Just me. Five days might sound a long time to be doing that, but time passes very quickly when you're under the influence. Before you know it, 10 or 12 hours has gone by. Between snorts of cocaine, I'd find myself watching old videos of the good times, partly reminiscing, partly wallowing in 'poor old me', but mostly, again, convincing myself that my success was responsible for the state I was in.

Sleep would come sporadically. I'd get to a point where I'd just collapse. Waking up a few hours later, I'd reach for the drugs and start all over again. It was an endless cycle. Shame – self-hatred – pain – cocaine – shame – self-hatred – pain – cocaine. Spinning out of control, faster and faster.

Self-destruction on an epic scale. With every hour that passed I'd feel dirtier. Physically and mentally dirtier. Every now and again I'd look at myself in the mirror and think, *What have you become?* Anyone who's been a closet alcoholic will know what I'm talking about. Addiction doesn't stop you despising yourself. Every time you do your drug of choice you throw another log of revulsion on the fire. And there's nothing – or so it seems – to stop you fanning those flames higher and higher. You simply cannot stop yourself. And so there I'd be, on my own, in a dingy hotel room, snorting drugs. A few years earlier, I'd been one of the most famous people in the country, mobbed wherever I went. That's what happens when you're an addict. You end up cut off. Humiliation your only companion.

Even before I started dipping in and out of hotels, I could go for extended periods without sleep. I'd think about getting my head down and then get a text from a user. 'Why don't you come round tonight?' Before I knew it, I'd be carrying on. The longest I went was four days. I was hallucinating by the end. The thought of staying awake for that long now is hellish, but at the time, in this weird cocaine-induced mindset, I saw it as a challenge. *I haven't slept for three nights now – wonder if I can do four?* I finally crashed at five in the morning. Another time I was up north at a friend's house. I stayed up for two nights, having already been up for 24 hours before going to see him. After three nights high, I then drove back down the motorway to London. Every now and again I'd park up at the services, doing a line in the car to keep me going. So, so reckless. Beyond-belief reckless. Forget the consequences for myself if I was caught, much worse was the fact I was putting other people's lives at risk. It feels almost unimaginable that I could do that now, but that's where drugs take you. Your morals go out the window. You become a dreadful person. Self-centred, self-absorbed. You think it's OK to do things that you would never ever do otherwise. For a long time, I was deeply selfish. *This is my vice. I want it, and I'm going to do it.*

From the outside I guess it's hard to understand why I never saw the damage I was doing myself; why, at all times, I wasn't doing everything in my power to stop. But you have to understand, the way I was seeing it I had every justification for my little vice. I had all the motivation I could ever need to carry on, because, in the moment, the drugs pushed away the negative thoughts, they knocked down the walls of my mental prison. When you're not functioning properly, drugs offer an easy escape. That cocaine in your pocket isn't a bad thing, it's a key to freedom. You depend on it so much emotionally that you carry it round like a toddler with a favourite teddy. And, like that toddler, if it was taken away you'd be bereft. That's how, and why, you reach a point where you've no intention of stopping using. What begins as a drug you take occasionally to make yourself feel better becomes your absolute lifeblood. In search of support, peace, release, it's the one thing you can rely on. Drugs don't judge. They don't ask what the f**k you think you're doing. They just let you get on with it. Which in itself makes your reliance on them even stronger. In the end, something that started out as an occasional vice grips you and takes your soul away.

Today, I have an understanding of how better to deal with my past. For a long time, relief – or what I saw as relief – came in the form of a wrap of cocaine in my pocket. As time went on and I pushed the threshold, pushed the risk element, constantly seeking some different type of escape, that extended to ketamine, essentially an anaesthetic, and MDMA, also known as ecstasy, both of which also delivered temporary highs. 'Temporary' being the operative word. Soon enough I'd be back down in that pit of despair.

Scrabbling around in the blackness, I'd reach for my self-destruct button and push it again and again.

CHAPTER 14

LOW

'Stuck constantly on this wheel.
This f**king wheel.'

I'm in my hotel room unwrapping cocaine. Reaching into my pocket, I find my phone. I choose the camera option and look into the screen, that black mirror. My face is hollow and drawn. I've stopped eating. There's nothing of me. I press 'Video' and start speaking.

'I'm recording this,' I say, 'because I haven't been so good the past week, doing too much coke, and I'm worried about myself. If I'm found dead in a room in the next few weeks, and they find this video, I want to say that it's not a selfish act. I don't do this for selfish reasons. Self-sabotage, yes. Self-hurt. Self-harm.'

I carry on sifting, chopping the drugs.

'It feels so unfair,' I continue, 'I've come off the worst. Yes, I've made mistakes, like doing too much of this, but I've been taken advantage of for many years on every level. Since dot.'

My head is whirring, overwhelmed with the impossibility of facing down my demons, of fighting the world, of standing up for myself. My only companion is my own despair.

'I don't have a father, I don't have grandparents. The only thing I've got is two amazing kids who look out for me, and Cath of course, she's always had my back.'

I pause. 'I'm 44 next year. I don't have a home. I don't have any money because of the bankruptcy. People tell me I've saved their lives at the [theatre] shows. They turned their lives around because they watched me do that [win the Tour]. What happened the other way, when I did it? For all the people it inspired, I bore the brunt at the opposite end.'

The drugs are prepared now. Ready to go. 'Anyway,' I say with a resolution built on quicksand, 'I'll come back. It's more of a case of not being found dead in the next few weeks.'

I'm so alone. All hope, all self-respect, lost. But I have to make this video. I want it to be there on my phone, just in case. In fact, more than just in case. I really do feel like I'm near the end.

I found myself in a crack den.

Earlier I'd done a theatre show. Talking about myself on stage, answering questions, made me feel happy, comfortable, and people were always generous in thanking me for the enjoyment I'd given them as a sportsperson and, frequently, for being the catalyst for their own journey to better mental health. Back in my hotel room, however, the only voices were those of the demons in my head. Only one way to drown them out. Desperate for drugs, in a town I didn't know, I reached for my phone. A contact directed me to an address. 'There's a guy selling.'

At first I thought I'd wandered into somebody's living room. People were just sitting around. Then I realised – they were all off their faces. I saw pipes being handed round. Any naïvety I had about drugs had long gone by this point. I knew straightaway it was crack cocaine. As I waited for the dealer to sort my drugs, someone turned to me. 'You want some?' No one had any idea who I was. Why should they? In that moment, I was exactly the same as them. Just another lonely drug addict passing through, getting their fix. They handed me the pipe. And I did it. I lifted that pipe to my lips and smoked crack cocaine. The high punched into my brain and that was it. I took my place with the rest of them. I say 'the rest of them' with no measure of disrespect. I was in no way above them. I was one of them. An addict lost in their vice.

Something strange happened that night. There was a point where I felt like I was looking at myself from the outside, a tiny pinprick of self-awareness which allowed me to see the depth to which I'd sunk. *How the f**k have you ended up here? You won the Tour de France. Now look at you. In a crack den. A f**king crack den! Smoking drugs. What happened to you? What the f**k happened to you?* Just hours before I'd been on stage, *An Audience with Bradley Wiggins*. I looked around. This was my 'audience' now, ten people, eight blokes and two women, both of whom were chain-smoking crack all night. With their heads shaved they reminded me of Sinéad O'Connor, two lost souls, their addiction being fed so some bastard could make some easy money.

I stumbled out of the house at eight in the morning. I could barely speak. Smoking crack all night had wrecked my voice. I felt disgusting. Doing drugs makes you feel soiled, squalid. It's seedy. It involves grubbing around in toilets, dealing with dodgy characters, sneaking around behind people's backs. But smoking crack in that house was different level. I was revolted by what I'd done. In my head, cocaine could be justified. It's prevalent, all sorts of people do it, it's pretty much part of everyday life. But now I'd had a crack pipe in my hand, and that frightened the life out of me. I knew I didn't want to be like that. I couldn't be like that. I was at my lowest point.

Thing is, as a drug addict, while a moment like the crack den might make you realise you've got a problem, it doesn't necessarily mean you'll address that problem. What needs to happen is that you get help. But you're not going to do that because you know underneath that you've got no intention of stopping. You just won't do *that* again – crack cocaine – because that's really s**t. Coke in a toilet, on the other hand, that's fine. These are the conversations you have with yourself, rather than the one you should be having, which is, *I'm going to get to the root of all this and turn my life around.*

Anyone who's been addicted to drugs will recognise this vicious circle. In fact, not so much a circle as a wheel, spinning out of control. At one point on that wheel I'd be high as a kite. And then slowly I'd sink lower and lower, overcome by emotion as a storm of thoughts burst into my head about the state I was in with the drugs and the weight of issues I was dealing with. A desperation would start. A need to escape those depths as fast as I could. And so I'd get more drugs. And so on and so on. Sleep offered some respite, but on waking I'd be overcome by the most awful comedown, as if someone had thrown a cloak of bleakness over me while I was out of it. In this twilight world maybe I'd recognise the trap I'd set for myself and force myself to stay off the drugs for a day or two. Classic cold turkey. In withdrawal, I'd crash but never sleep properly. I'd be in a permanent state of sleep deprivation, crying all the time, overcome by emotion, thinking about why I turned to drugs in the first place. Which is all the stuff I can't get out of my head. And because I can't get it out of my head I quit the cold turkey and take more drugs. Stuck constantly on this wheel. This f**king wheel. And the crushing realisation that, with no hope on the horizon, there's no way, or reason, to get off it.

Leaving home, being anchorless, had simply allowed that wheel to spin further out of control. In 2021, I had a daughter with a woman I met while I was living in London. Ava is a beautiful little girl and I couldn't be happier to be part of her life, but clearly being a father again wasn't a path I'd planned to go down. Before she was born, a tabloid newspaper found out about the pregnancy. They wanted to run the story on the front page, using photos snatched while we were out in public. You didn't need much imagination to see the headline they were after – 'Wiggo's Lovechild!' – twisting something they knew nothing about into a scandal they could use to sell papers and make money. I was visiting the kids back up north at the time. Stewing, drinking a bottle of beer, it felt like the world was closing in on me from all sides. It was the nearest I ever came to losing my mind. The more I thought about it, the more wound up I'd become. *Right*, I thought, *I'll give them a story. I'll kill myself.* I smashed the beer bottle over my head. Blood everywhere. In my eyes, pouring down my face. Ben and Bella were in the house. They'd seen me blow up before – the knighthood and Sports Personality trophy being a case in point – but this was different level. I'd just committed a deliberate act of self-harm.

I could hardly walk into A&E at the local hospital with blood streaming down my face. It would be all over social media in no time. And so Cath did her best to mop me up, eventually managing to stem the bleeding. Unbelievable that I could do that. Not only careless for my own life but no thought for Cath and the kids. The news I was to be a father again was shock enough for everyone, without then inflicting an act of violence on myself. Looking back now, there were times during my addiction where in all honesty I should have been sectioned.

And yet, weirdly, within this mental maelstrom there were moments of absolute lucidity; moments where I spoke with real openness and clarity about my troubles. *Geraint*

Thomas Cycling Club podcast is a case in point. Geraint has been a fixture in my life for 20 years. He's someone I love and respect immensely. A picture popped up on my phone the other day of me and him riding alongside each other during his first appearance at the Tour in 2007 when, aged just 21, he was the youngest cyclist in the race. Maybe that's why, in my head, I wasn't so much taking part in Geraint's podcast as speaking directly to him, effectively unloading on him because I wanted him to know where my head had been at certain points in the past. I talked unbroken for a really long time, taking in everything from the fallout with Chris Froome to my struggles dealing with fame after 2012. It was important to me that I was straight with Geraint. There were times when my identity battles, and the effect they had on those around me, had impacted our friendship, in particular when I didn't turn up to his wedding in 2015. Understandably he was upset – to him it must have looked like I just hadn't been arsed – and he didn't talk to me for a while. In the end, Ed Clancy, who along with Paul Manning had won gold in the team pursuit at Beijing with me and Geraint, told him why I hadn't made it; a desperate and inescapable need to be at home with my family. I'm pleased to say it was a relationship that was repaired. I messaged Geraint when he was on the way to winning the Tour in 2018. 'F**king hell, Geraint, what you're doing is amazing!' 'Thanks,' he replied, 'that means a lot to me.' Geraint really is a true gentleman and that's why I poured my heart out to him on his podcast that day.

There was one thing I didn't mention to Geraint – Stan. But then a year later I was asked to talk to Alastair Campbell for *Men's Health* magazine. It was the first time in a long while that I'd done an interview not specifically about cycling. Not only that, but Alastair understands what it's like to live with mental health problems. If ever I was going to talk in depth about why I was the way I was, this was going to be it. I only needed to look at the drug addict I'd become, to understand that burying the abuse deep in my mind, pretending it never happened, wasn't going to work anymore.

There were other factors pushing me towards openness. Working for Eurosport meant regularly driving over to Ealing Studios. Ealing was where Stan had lived. He'd died in 2003 but that changed nothing – the abuse doesn't die with the abuser – and passing his old house was a catalyst. I began thinking about what he'd done. *Jesus, that really did happen.* I thought about the 13-year-old me, that kid who just wanted to be a cyclist, to get on his bike and achieve. I thought about how much I'd wanted someone to believe in me and help me succeed. And I thought about how that person had abused my trust and violated me. Stan groomed children. In my case, he'd identified two overwhelming character traits on which to prey – an all-consuming desire to succeed and an overarching vulnerability that came from an inherent lack of self-esteem. He'd used those traits to satisfy his own perversions.

At weekends during stints with Eurosport the kids would come with me to the studios. At precisely the same time I was thinking back to the teenage me, there, in the passenger seat, was Ben, my teenage son. Ben's not me, but clearly having your own son two feet away is a pretty stark reminder of the person you once were, your own dreams, your own innocence. It also prompted thoughts of how, with no father figure in my life, I was abandoned to my fate.

No doubt about it, having children of my own, children who were growing up, considering their own futures, finding their own independence, was a direct reason why I began to consider the idea of opening up about the abuse I'd suffered. If I was to do so, then it would have to be in a place of reassurance and security. Alastair offered precisely that. His reaction to my mentioning sexual abuse wasn't going to be one of tabloid sensationalism or jaw-dropping incredulity, it was going to be appropriate and sensitive. Anyone who's opened up about something that sits so deeply within them will know how important it is to feel safe and believed. Even so, right up until the interview started I'd still not made any firm decision whether to say anything to Alastair. It just happened organically. The conversation turned to mental health and, knowing how big a part the abuse had played in my struggle, it just felt right to tell him. Instead of the constant internalising I'd been doing for years, I did it, I said it out loud. 'I was groomed by a coach when I was younger.' That was pretty much it. I didn't go into any detail but the relief felt like shouting from a mountaintop.

It was still a huge step, however, to go from chatting with Alastair to the whole world knowing what had happened to me. It was that uncertainty which, with the interview done, led me to panic and ask Alastair if he'd mind not including the sexual abuse in the article. His reaction knocked me back a little. He told me it was the bravest thing any of his interviewees had ever done. His view was that it was absolutely vital, both for me and others out there in a similar position, to leave it in.

Speaking out that day was groundbreaking for me. Saying those few simple words released an avalanche of pent-up hurt, anger and frustration. It was only then that I realised just how much I'd been bottling up. The abuse, and repressing it, had left me a mental wreck. Vocalising my pain felt like laying a foundation on which to rebuild.

That is, until the magazine was published. At that point journalists with a lot less sensitivity than Alastair began demanding more detail. They started asking questions. 'Why has he never said anything up to now?' But that's not always how it works when you've got something so huge and mentally damaging in your past. Because it's not your past. It's your now. It's your always. Some articles used the word 'accusations'. I found the suggestion I'd somehow invented the years of abuse particularly hurtful. At a time when I should have found strength and empowerment, I was left retreating, belittled, scolded, into my corner. My go-to cure for my wounds was – no surprise – more drugs. Prolonged cocaine use brings on anxiety and paranoia. In a state of drug-induced psychosis you can't see the wood for the trees. It just feels like everyone is against you. There were times when even I started to wonder if I'd made the whole thing up.

It seemed like I was destined forever to be crushed into the dirt. Every time I felt the pressure couldn't get any greater, something else would come crashing down on top of me. My career might have been trashed by forces beyond my control, but at least no one could take away the financial reward. At least that's what I thought, but slowly I came to realise that safety net had been hacked away too, a legacy of mismanagement hidden from me for years. Back in 2012, my image rights company had been set up in such a way that it would take the hit if two other companies linked to me, one which dealt with endorsements, and another which was effectively Team Wiggins, suffered problems. To mitigate any such issues, all three should have existed independently. The minute they were linked I was f**ked. The image rights company ran up a debt of almost £1.5 million which was passed on to me without my knowledge. At no point did anyone say to me, 'If this carries on you're not going to have enough money.' All this was happening while I was still riding. It was only several years into retirement, with the situation at crisis point, that I was made aware.

When the full state of my financial affairs became apparent, no one was more shocked than me.

Earning 350 grand a month, like I was at my peak, you think it's going to last forever. But then you take your eye off the ball, the situation with companies and investments becomes more complex and harder to decipher, and before you know it there's nothing left. You're left staring into a financial black hole and thinking, *F**k, how's this happened?* You've paid professionals, assuming they've got it all in order, only to find out the whole thing's a monumental mess. I felt massively let down. These 'experts' were supposed to be looking after me, protecting me, but had in fact left me open to ruination. After a long and successful career, I thought I was going to be made for life. Every assumption I'd had about my financial future had been well and truly shattered.

As if that wasn't bad enough, HMRC were also on my back. I was deemed self-employed while at Team Sky, something that wasn't unusual among professional cyclists. HMRC, however, argued that I, and others at Team Sky, were actually employed. Sky challenged the ruling and I acted as a witness, throwing in an enormous amount of my own money towards the legal fees, because if my employment status was changed I'd be faced with a tax bill dating back years. Then, at the last minute, Sky pulled the plug on the fight, accepting that I was employed. Not only had I spent the money fighting the case, I'd now have to pay the tax as well.

The situation was untenable. I just didn't have the hundreds of thousands of pounds that were owed, the result being that in 2022 I entered into an Individual Voluntary Arrangement (IVA), a financial agreement designed to help people pay off creditors and avoid bankruptcy. But still the threat of insolvency bore down on me constantly. Such were the sums involved, it felt like there was no way out. Same as there was no way out of the doping allegations, the drugs, any of it. It was another dark and lonely time in my life. Occasionally I'd peek through the curtains of whatever hotel room I found myself in. But there were never any flashes of sunlight.

As the days drew shorter towards the end of 2023, I'd imagine a world without me. As with that New Year's Eve in Morzine 11 years previously, it wasn't that I was actively suicidal, it was just that I couldn't see beyond the despondency of my own existence. Equally, my behaviour with drugs was pushing the envelope into a space where I could have killed myself anyway. I was doing more and more coke in shorter and shorter periods, the risks getting greater all the time. I'd put my body under immense stress by barely sleeping for days, then even more stress by going in completely the opposite direction and, in an attempt to get myself functioning normally, heading to the gym for flat-out training sessions. Exercise would offset the urge to do drugs, but inevitably any stability would be short-lived and I'd fall back into my usual ways. I absolutely felt my own mortality. It was far from the realms of imagination that I'd be found dead. Maybe I'd fall down a staircase, or off a balcony, even have a cocaine-induced heart attack. My musical hero John Entwistle died in exactly that way. I wondered what the tabloids would say. My guess was they'd revel in it. 'Look at him. We knew this would happen. Look at how he behaved after London 2012. That's what he was like.' There'd have been no context, no attempt to understand what drives someone to such depths.

It was in this state, genuinely fearful for my life, that one night I sent Ben a video. It was late, I'd run out of drugs and was wandering the streets looking for a cashpoint to get money for more. I spoke as I stumbled along.

'I don't know what to do. My life's so empty. I can't get out of my head how worthless my life has been. I can't stop thinking about Stan and what he did to me. I don't want to be here anymore.'

The full video is about four minutes long. I'm a husk at that point. I haven't slept for days, have no stability, no real work. I'm just existing, feeling sorrier and sorrier for myself.

And yet somewhere within that swirl there was a clarity to what I was saying. I look at that video now and can see I'm reaching for something, conscious that my story, my time, is only going to end one way if I don't turn myself around. I wasn't saying, 'I don't want to be here anymore,' as in I wish I was dead. I was saying, 'I don't want to be here anymore,' as in I can't keep on being an addict. There's something else in that mix – the realisation I've brought a lot of this on myself. *How had I got to this point from 2012?* I'd asked myself that question a thousand times. My instinct had always been to blame other people. But it was me alone in those hotel rooms. It was me taking those drugs. I had to take some responsibility for my actions.

When it came to my addiction, as weird as it might sound, that video – that mad, rambling video – was actually the beginning of the end.

CHAPTER 15

THE COMEBACK

'We will get through this together.'

It's 10 p.m. when my phone pings. It's a picture. Ben. He's hooked up to a machine. 'I've been in a car crash,' he tells me. 'I've been taken to hospital.'

My son has nearly died in a motorway accident. It's every parent's worst nightmare. And I'm high.

Ben is at the Royal Preston Hospital. I'm in a hotel room in London. This can't be happening. My son needs me and here I am in a hotel high on cocaine. The first train to Preston is 5 a.m. I try to get some sleep. It's impossible. I'm frightened out of my mind. I need to see my son, to be at his side.

I arrive at the hospital at 8 a.m. I can still feel the drugs in my system. Nobody notices – I'm on the way down – but there's no escaping the fact I'm still high. I look at Ben. He's 18 years old. But I look at him and see him aged two, twelve, five, nine. Everything, everyone, he's ever been.

For the next two days I don't leave the hospital and for the next ten I sit at his bedside and start to plan. Notes fill my phone. I go back to what always worked for me as a cyclist.

Process. I sit there and work out training regimes. I think about how to build routine and with it, stability. I even work out how much money I'll save if I kick my habit. I vow that the coming year, 2024, is going to be the best of my life.

As Ben's hospital stay comes to an end, I look at my phone and write four final words – 'Can I do it?'

There are countless videos of me on YouTube. All the landmark moments – the Tour de France win, London 2012, Rio 2016, the lot. But for me, there's no bigger video than the one I sent Ben that night in 2023. Afterwards he, Bella and Cath essentially staged an intervention. They drove down to London, got me out of my hotel room and took me back up north. Between them they helped me get back on my feet. They gave me a reason to live, allowed me to see a bit of hope. It wasn't an overnight rejection of cocaine. There were relapses, especially when I was back in London and temptation would get hold of me – hence the situation I found myself in when Ben had his car accident – but I was able to maintain good long periods without cocaine. Slowly, steadily, I started to regain control. For the first time in years I began to look beyond my next wrap of cocaine. My thought process was clear. *Addiction is not going to be the end of me. I'm going to come back from this. I'm going to start again from zero.*

Re-establishing discipline was a huge part of my recovery. I'd let go of my preoccupation with training and diet, as if it wasn't normal to exist like that anymore, as if I was denying myself a chance to loosen the shackles. But that obsessiveness was all I'd ever known, and actually, without it, and without a goal, I'd drifted into other areas – dangerous areas. With my vision less clouded by drugs, it became apparent to me that the times when process was front and centre were the most stable of my life. To dismiss it completely had been damaging. Cycling, and the routine that came with it, had never been the enemy. They had kept me on the straight and narrow. On the bike there was one thing I always understood – it doesn't matter if you suffer a setback or a disappointment, you don't stop riding, don't stop training, you get back up and go again. Always go again. What made me good on the bike wasn't rising to the level of my goals, it was falling to the level of my daily habits. Look after those and the goals take care of themselves. I fell down in retirement because I jettisoned that attitude. In craving normality, I forgot what I was good at. I left my cycling principles at the door.

Slowly but surely I found myself improving. Training gave me positivity, it gave me purpose, and eventually I added to it by embracing my competitive side again, another core part of my personality I'd ditched overnight without ever considering the consequences. Some people say being an extreme athlete isn't a healthy and balanced way to live. But there is no healthy balance in me. I'm either on drugs or I'm doing everything possible to be the best athlete I can be. There's no happy medium. Some people are predisposed to be a certain way, and I'm one of them. And so I train and weigh myself every day and compete in HYROX, a combination of running and fitness challenges that's gone viral in popularity. If you think thrashing yourself in a gym isn't fun, then try being an addict. There's no fun in that, believe me. No having two glasses of wine and going home. Not when you could have four glasses of wine and a bag of coke. That's who I am. I've seen both sides of the coin and I'll tell you what, being like this is a lot better for me and everyone around me.

These days it's not unusual for me to go training at five in the morning and then again at six in the evening. In between I'll be getting on with my life, be it dropping my daughter off at nursery, delivering talks on high performance, meeting new and interesting people, making plans or whatever. Two years ago, if I was supposed to meet someone at nine, I'd have texted at ten, 'Can we start at 12?' I'd have then interrupted that meeting to nip out and do a line, before finishing early and buying more drugs on the way home. Up all night, I'd have cancelled everything the next day. That was what I was like. Unpredictable. Unreliable. No one ever knew if Bradley Wiggins would turn up, and, if he did, which Bradley Wiggins it would be. Being normal, whatever that is, didn't work, but I'm productive as a fitness freak. The difference is that I'm no longer using exercise and competition to stifle negative thoughts in my head. I'm using them because they're good for me.

Something else was huge in my recovery – being believed. For an entire year after the *Men's Health* article I felt like I was fighting a losing battle and no one thought I was telling the truth about Stan. I couldn't prove it. Therefore, I must be lying. In all the time I was doing drugs nothing made me feel more alone. Then, more than a year later, I gave an interview to Polly Vernon from *The Times*. I went into detail about the years of abuse. I didn't know what to expect when it was published. More opprobrium probably. But barely had it hit the streets than four other people came forward to say that they too had suffered at Stan's hands. I couldn't process what I was hearing. I broke down crying for about ten hours. Hysterically breaking down. After all those years damming up the pain and emotion, here, finally, was validation. No one could doubt me now. Stan was a paedophile. It happened. And I wasn't the only one.

For all of us affected by Stan, the knowledge of one another's existence was a huge step forward in coming to terms with the experiences of our past. Where once all we had was our own fear, anxiety and helplessness, now we had each other to corroborate our memories. Among those who got in touch was the other lad who'd been at the hostel in Devon. We hadn't seen one another since those dormitory days. He too believed our food had been drugged. He too had woken with no pyjamas on. And he too had internalised his experiences. We both knew what the other had been through. It didn't need saying. And we both knew the mental toll it had taken in the decades since. Another former Archer Road cyclist explained how he and his brother had been abused by Stan. Until now, neither had been aware of the other's predicament.

The flipside of discovering there were others out there was the realisation of just how widespread Stan's activities must have been. What he did to me really did mess me up. Multiply that by the years he was coaching and the number of children he came into contact with and he damaged a lot of lives. I've heard stories about him offering to 'wank riders off' before races 'to release the pressure'. I've heard reports of kids being abused while staying at his house. These aren't situations that people have dreamed up, they actually happened and, I believe, were known about. One former clubmate who contacted me reflected that, with hindsight, older riders such as himself should have done more to help. He mentioned an incident where a fellow cyclist had told him how Stan had offered to masturbate him before a race. 'I can remember thinking at the time that he wasn't a paedophile, he was just a bit odd,' he told me. It's obvious he was a paedophile but back then attitudes were different. People turned the other cheek, no questions asked, which is precisely how people like Stan got away with it for so long. It hurts me that there might have been those who knew what was going on, had the power to act and did nothing. If other riders knew, then who else? Other coaches? Other people in positions of responsibility? No child should ever be left to suffer alone. Abusers rely on isolation to implement control. In my case, add in the absence of a dad, the fact that Stan was well thought of as a coach and that I was lauded as 'Wiggo's boy', the club's star of the future, and you begin to see the cliff face that was in front of me in terms of telling anyone. Who was I to speak up? Who was I to shatter illusions, to wreck the fairytale?

Children must be encouraged to report any and every sign of abuse. No half measures, no muddying the waters with 'he's a bit odd but he's all right'. Abuse is abuse, and children have to know that they will be taken seriously and listened to if they're to find it within themselves to speak up. One of the things I toyed with in my head, as both child and adult, and which I used to block the abuse out and determine that it be something I'd take to the grave, was the suspicion that only if I could say I was anally penetrated, raped in that manner, would people have direct sympathy for what I'd been through. It was a feeling I recalled sharply when I did start talking about Stan. I felt, particularly with the tabloids, that without rape in the mix, the headlines would be unsympathetic. That thought process would make me question whether what Stan did was rape or not. Was what he did bad enough to say that? How much more did I have to say to validate what he did to me? I felt I had to explain more and more to be believed, as if there were key words I needed to say. Sometimes people don't understand that 'What happened?' isn't always the right question. There's so much more to living with abuse than 'What happened?' It misunderstands completely the complexity of what someone who's been abused is going through.

Ultimately, myself and the others who Stan preyed on were badly let down. British Cycling should have had systems in place to prevent paedophiles being able to operate in clubs. It's obvious to me from the letter they sent to Mum's house in 2003 that they knew Stan was a problem. I asked British Cycling if they could find a copy in their archives. 'There's no copy,' they told me. So where does that leave me? From where I'm sitting it feels distinctly like I, and others, have been very firmly swept under the carpet. Who by? Maybe we'll never know, but with a bid for the London Olympics very much on the horizon in 2003, I expect the last thing anyone at the top of cycling, or sport in general, wanted was a very public case of a catastrophic breakdown in safeguarding, especially one involving an Olympic athlete. Stan had clearly seen the opportunity to inveigle himself in a sport where there were lots of kids around. With no challenge forthcoming, he'd then spent years doing what the hell he wanted. Whichever way you look at it, that's clearly a massive failure of a duty of protection. Even more so if, for years, what he was doing was known about and then covered up.

More positively, the NSPCC got in touch to ask if I'd help with a campaign to prevent child abuse in sport. After spending so much time in retirement doing things like *The Jump*, it was nice to be asked to contribute to something meaningful. I found it fulfilling to talk about creating safer sporting environments for children. I hoped I was going some way to helping others avoid what happened to me, at the same time boosting my own self-esteem, a definite building block to getting to where I am today. I never wanted my success to turn me into a celebrity, something which, in my eyes, has no value, but every now and again I was pushed down that route. I'd much rather use whatever renown I have to help and inspire people who've been through similar things to me, whether that's sexual abuse, abandonment, addiction, growing up in a difficult environment, or whatever. I'm not the fount of all knowledge on these topics, far from it, but experience counts for something and speaking up gives me my worth.

I can add bankruptcy to that list of unfortunate subjects I know a bit about. Ultimately, and unsurprisingly, the IVA failed and in June 2024 I was officially declared insolvent. I'll be honest, at first I was frightened. Your initial thought when you're made bankrupt is, *F**k, I'm not going to be able to live. I'm not going to have a pot to piss in.* And actually everyone else thinks that as well. When I attended that year's Sports Personality of the Year, a contributor to the comments section on one newspaper website asked, 'How did he get there if he hasn't got any money?', as if when the judgement was made I was quite literally kicked into the street in the clothes I was in. Thankfully, while bankruptcy does sound apocalyptic, it's not quite that bad. In reality, an agreement is reached with a court-appointed receiver which allows you to keep enough of your earnings to get by. Bankruptcy happens to lots of people. I just happened to be one of the more high-profile. It didn't mean I was living in the gutter, scraping around for fag butts in bins, not that it stopped sections of the media from portraying it that way. Every story seemed to describe me as homeless and couch-surfing. There was even some bullshit about me being loaned a campervan and it ending up trashed in car park. I laugh at that kind of nonsense now, but when you're in a bad place that almost gleeful narrative about your downfall only adds to the sense of desperation. Throughout the bankruptcy proceedings, newspapers were throwing large amounts of money at me to give a big interview, but I never did. I couldn't forgive the lies and insinuations. Bankruptcy was a lesson learned the hard way. Today I'm back on two feet and earning a living again. I wasn't a businessman, but I am now! I'm right across everything. I know for sure it will never happen again.

It was during the bankruptcy period that my old poster hero Lance Armstrong reached out. No stranger to losing pretty much everything after his admission of drug-taking, he was worried that insolvency would tip me over the edge. Lance booked me a flight out to his home in Aspen, Colorado, but has since admitted he had no idea whether I was actually going to get on the thing. He was entirely justified to think like that, because while I was definitely making strides towards full recovery, I was still prone to the occasional relapse. The day before the flight I'd done a talk in Leeds and given out awards at a school. I was then up all night drinking in the hotel. The idea was I'd leave at 5 a.m. to make an 11 o'clock flight at Heathrow. I actually left at six, blind drunk still as I got in the taxi to the station. Naturally, I missed the train, which meant I missed the plane. Thankfully, the airline put me on the next flight three hours later. At that point,

Lance knew that, OK I was late, but at least I was in the air. Once in Aspen, I was actually supposed to have my own accommodation, but when finally I got there Lance was adamant – 'Right, you're staying with me all week.' He wasn't going to let me laze around for a single minute. 'We're going in the gym tomorrow,' he'd say, or 'Get yourself out for a run.'

Exercise is liberating, but it was talking that made the big difference. Lance told me how he'd given up alcohol six months previously and how being free of it had allowed him to reflect and change. Right there and then I vowed to do the same. It's the sort of thing people say all the time and then two days later they're propping up the bar again. But Lance's actions really did inspire me. This was a guy speaking from a place of authority. Been there, done that. But he wasn't bullish. He came at me and my situation with a lot of empathy. And it wasn't just Lance. I found myself surrounded by all sorts of amazing people living happily in sobriety. It made me see that not only was existing without alcohol possible but there was something great to be found on the other side. I'd only ever been around people who saw drinking as an integral part of life. 'Go on, have another!' And so I would, and then, in addiction, I'd end up in a toilet cubicle doing a line. I was constantly in this washing machine of f**ked-up-ness. Churning around in there I'd never felt able to refuse alcohol. But after meeting Lance and his friends, I was equipped to come back to Britain and tell myself, 'I can do it, and I will do it.' There was no doubt in my mind. I truly believed it.

And that's what happened. When I came home I stopped drinking completely. That had to be the way. There's no in between with me. Whatever it is, trying to win the Tour de France, drinking, drugs, I'll take it as far as it will go. I take everything to an extreme level. The thing with not drinking is that people always want to know why. It's the same if someone orders a soft drink. 'Oh you're so boring.' I bypass all that stuff. If someone asks me why I'm not drinking, I say, 'Because I do drugs if I drink and if I carry on I'm going to die.' Either that or 'Because I'll be found in a hotel room dead.' Amazing how a little bit of bluntness tends to put an end to that particular topic of conversation.

I'm not going to get all evangelical about ditching alcohol, but as someone who's had a dependency on both drink and drugs, it's incredible how socially accepted one is compared to the other. Drink kills more people than any drug but because it's so resolutely intertwined into our society nobody bats an eyelid. At Christmas it's all mulled wine and carol singing. Can you imagine if someone offered cocaine and carol singing? But what's the difference? One's taboo and the other isn't, and that's about it. If you worked in an office and at four o'clock on a Friday the boss produced a bottle of wine and said, 'Come on! Let's have a drink!' everyone would be laughing and smiling. If that same boss started doing lines off their desk, people would be totally shocked. Cocaine is everywhere but has to remain hidden. It's happening in every pub, every restaurant, on trains, buses, more likely than not down your local cop shop. But nobody can admit to doing it. In the meantime, people get smashed on alcohol and that's totally fine. That was why it was so important that I got on that plane to Colorado. It gave me an avenue of escape from a culture so heavily soaked in booze.

I confided in Lance about my drug use too. One thing he said struck me in particular – 'We will get through this together.' He had the realisation that there was something serious in me that needed addressing quickly. I'm sure also that he saw the bike as part of the remedy. Lance and his old Tour de France lieutenant George Hincapie were heading out riding one day and asked if I wanted to go along. 'I haven't got a bike!' I replied, but it made me think. I really did want to get out and ride again. Instead of blaming the bike for what happened with Stan, the difficult relationship with my dad and the fallout from 2012, I wanted to reconnect and make it part of my life again. *Just go out and do the thing you love doing!* It was in Aspen that I fell back in love with cycling. In the months since I've done public events where people can ride with me, and again, chatting to them about cycling, hearing their stories about how much it has contributed to their lives, has reaffirmed my own love of the sport. It would have been so sad to lose that forever and I know now that I'll never let that happen. In fact, as I write this today I'm actually waiting for my new bike to arrive. Life's come full circle. Like the kid I once was, I'm excited about cycling. I bought a load of cycling books the other day, feeding my renewed passion for its history.

Having regained control, the next step is to maintain it, which is why I go to meetings of Cocaine Anonymous (CA). Initially I was scared of physically going to a support group. In my head I could see someone piping up, 'Hang on, you're Bradley Wiggins, aren't you?' The drugs, and the paranoia they bring, built that fear in me. Increasingly, though, I saw how ridiculous that was. I'd be sat on my own, ruminating on my life, and think, *For f**k's sake, Brad, go and get help. You can't turn your back on it because someone might recognise you're Bradley f**king Wiggins. You can't be destined to live like this forever. Just get over this Bradley Wiggins complex you've got!* Even so, some wariness did remain, and initially I did online sessions where I could melt into the background. But over time I tested the water and found I much preferred the human element of being around a bunch of people all trying to pull in the same direction. I soon realised everyone else was far too involved in their own journey to be sat there going, 'There's Bradley Wiggins!' It doesn't matter who we are, the point for all of us sat there is that we've reached a point where we need to be at that meeting.

Cocaine Anonymous is essentially the same idea as Alcoholics Anonymous, a 12-step programme to overcome addiction. At meetings, everybody sits in a circle. We can speak if we want to or we can just sit and listen. If we do speak, we start off with, 'Hello, I'm an addict.' I try to go to CA as often as possible, at least once a week, hearing stories of people from all walks of life. One person might be 25 years clean, another just two days. Some come into there meetings utterly broken, unable to hold back the tears as they reveal what has brought them here, others are more composed, but whatever people's circumstances it's always incredibly humbling to hear such honest reflection on what is often the worst time in somebody's life. Pain is at the root of so many addiction problems and we allow each other to talk openly about our scars. Then there's the shame. Addiction feeds on shame, so it's incredibly liberating not to be hiding it anymore. You're no longer alone.

It's so hard to break free from drugs when all you have is yourself. Try to stop and you're bombarded with messages from dealers with this week's deals. Say you've got no money and they'll give it you on the tick. Suddenly, you owe five hundred quid to a drug dealer. They've got a hold over you, and that's never a good place to be. At CA, I know the person next to me understands exactly how I feel, exactly the pressure bearing down on me to get back into using. I'm white-knuckling at the moment. I'm not using, not drinking. But if something awful happened tomorrow I'd find it very hard not to seek some kind of escape. Addiction doesn't exist in isolation. It exists alongside everyday life, which is why organisations like CA are there to give you a host of ways to deal with the challenges that will inevitably arise along the way. I always feel invigorated after meetings, often finding myself thinking of people's situations and words long after a session has ended. CA is international so I can attend wherever I am in the world. On New Year's Day 2025, for instance, I found myself sitting in a little church in Aspen for just that reason. Aspen's a bit of a hangout for the rich and famous. The week before, Robert F. Kennedy Jr, a recovering heroin addict, was sat in exactly the same place. His addiction began aged 15. Drugs are no respecter of age, status, anything. Whoever they afflict, we should never judge. I don't sit here in guilt. And I don't look down on anybody who has found themselves in a similar predicament.

The next step is, inevitably, therapy, something I've resisted for years. My instinct has always been to sort my problems out myself. As you can see, that's not always worked out particularly well! Now, though, I feel ready to listen to someone else. I'll never take it for granted that the addiction side of my personality has gone and therapy will better equip me to deal with unhealthy thought patterns. I'm still fully computing what happened to me and I need help unpacking the million and one thoughts in my head. Reflecting for this book has made me realise just how deeply into my past my addiction was anchored. It would be so easy to think I was just filling the void left by the end of my cycling career. Yes, that acted as a spark, but the fuel it fed on was the experiences I had growing up. It's something I need professional help to address, a realisation that's grown the more I've come to understand how low my baseline for being OK has been throughout my life, how normalised I am to pain. Cocaine felt like an answer. But drugs can never be the answer. Drugs are dirty and horrible and make you a dreadful person. They make you selfish, thoughtless and unreliable – and those are the better characteristics. Over time you end up falling out with the very people who care about you the most, and so deeply ingrained is the hurt that it's incredibly hard to heal those scars. I remember David Bowie talking about his own sobriety and how he'd never consider having a drink again because it would jeopardise the relationships he'd so painstakingly rebuilt with friends and family. Addiction takes everything from you. The biggest fight you'll ever have is getting some of that back. It's a fight that needs to stay won. That's a very good reason never to use again. There can never be a justification that overrides that basic fact. There can never be a justification for me using drugs again full-stop. The only way to deal with my pain is to get strong and sort myself out. I see therapy as a huge part of that.

Of course, it wouldn't be me if there wasn't a contradiction. While the drugs became a hindrance not a help, and I'm sure it would have been a lot cheaper to go to therapy from the start, they did give me something in terms of addressing who I was. Drugs for me were never about being a party boy, they were about escapism. There was something going on deep inside of me and, strangely, when I started doing cocaine, it opened up a passageway to understanding, releasing thoughts about all the different traumas within. In seeking an escape through drugs, I was actually drawn to a desire to find answers. The distraction of cycling had gone and I needed to get to the bottom of what was amiss. I realised the void in my life didn't come from the absence of the bike, it emanated from something that had been there much longer, something which, again, my intense relationship with sport had hidden. It was an understanding of who I was. My own children knew who they were because they'd grown up with two parents who were open and honest and going in the same direction. My dad wasn't there. My mum was present but, when it came to any meaningful information, wasn't forthcoming. I didn't expect that to be resolved, but I could still search for my own answers.

I need to emphasise that I'm in no way saying drugs can be a positive presence in people's lives. Drugs took me into another world, one of self-pity and zero self-worth. They were a huge part of my downfall. I wouldn't think of doing them now, because my life's great. I'm just recognising that my time as an addict was part of the journey to where I am now. An ugly, horrific part of the journey, but one I cannot deny.

My journey as an addict will end only when I die. Writing this now, I'm six months clean. No alcohol, no drugs. I can't say I'll never go back, because the truth of addiction is that people relapse, but every day clean is, in its own way, an achievement. Nor am I saying it's easy. I'm an addict and so sometimes there are cravings. But I've got the support to keep me upright. I've got a house again, which means stability, and I train every day, which means routine. I always make sure I've got a plan, and I stick to it. It's not a case of keeping myself busy so I don't fall off the wagon, it's about knowing my pathway, same as I did in the run-up to the Olympics when I had goals, structure and knew what each day entailed.

I wake every day now, not in fear of myself, not in hatred, but with a growing sense of pride. My name is Bradley Wiggins and I'm an addict.

I also have a purpose.

EPILOGUE

In 2024 I got up on stage at Sports Personality of the Year. I didn't have sideburns, didn't wear an eccentric suit and didn't call Sue Barker 'Susan'. Well, to be fair, I couldn't. Sue quit SPOTY after 2012. Apologies, Sue, if I was the final straw.

I was there to present Mark Cavendish with a lifetime achievement award. This time I was gracious and sincere. Then again, back in 2012 I was receiving an award, now I was giving one out. Can I be totally sure how I'd have reacted if it had been the other way round? If it had been me once again in the spotlight? I can't be 100 per cent confident but I'd like to think I'd have dealt with the situation as my true self rather than the attention-diverting, praise-avoidant person I was in 2012. After all, I was still messing about backstage, having a laugh with Cav, but when the moment came to behave a certain way I was able to do so. The 2012 me, on the other hand, wouldn't have been able to distinguish between the two scenarios. I don't suppose I'll ever find out how I'd react if the shoe was on the other foot, but what I do know for certain is how good it felt to be there that night. Posing for the cameras, happy and proud, with my two amazing grown-up children, I thought back to the person I was the year before, walking around forlornly, lost in despair, in the middle of the night, pouring my hopelessness into videos on my phone. I may not have always known who I am, but the person I was in December 2024 bore no resemblance to the one I'd been a year earlier.

It wasn't just me on stage to give Cav his award. I was standing alongside Chris Hoy and Laura and Jason Kenny. With Cav there too it was like the Mount Rushmore of cycling! To be part of that generation was amazing. More than that, I couldn't help thinking how sportspeople can connect in ways far beyond just what they do for a living. Chris Hoy has been a beacon of hope for many thousands of people who, like him, have received the devastating diagnosis of cancer, Laura has talked about miscarriage and ectopic pregnancy, and Cav has opened up about his experiences with depression. And then there's me. I transcended our sport in a manner unparalleled by any other cyclist. People related to me in so many different ways. As much as an avalanche of middle-aged men in Lycra suddenly appeared on the roads, I was also on the radar of those who liked a certain type of music or who had a couple of Fred Perry T-shirts in the wardrobe. Sportspeople do occasionally step out of their lane but the place they end up isn't generally on stage with Paul Weller.

There were times when I rued that transcendence, blamed it for so much that went wrong after 2012. Now I'm thankful for it, because it gives me a platform where hopefully I can connect in a different way. Sadly, there's a whole host of men who've had similar issues to me, whether that be an absent parent, sexual abuse, addiction, or whatever. Many such men have told me how what I did on the bike was the catalyst for them to take up cycling themselves, and the tremendous mental boost it gave them. Now, rather than inspiring men to get on a bike, I hope to help them address the reason why they found cycling such an incredible escape in the first place. What was it in their life that was causing such turmoil in their head?

For me, the chance of a second wave of inspiration has been a huge catalyst for regrowth. Feeling like my own openness can have an effect on others means I want to shout my experiences as loud as I possibly can. There was a time, as a recovering addict, when I worried that if I went public I'd be destroyed by the tabloids. But why shouldn't I share my experience? It's precisely that stigma which pushes people into corners, which leaves them with no escape, which ends up with them being found dead in hotel rooms. I'm proud to be able to talk. Proud that the person who hid in his shell throughout his childhood and racing career has not only emerged but is flourishing, unrecognisable from his former self. I'm articulate, I've educated myself, I'm confident. I'll probably look back in ten years' time and think, *God, when I was 45 I thought I was it!* But I know growth is constant.

There's no such thing as the finished product. In the meantime I'll allow myself to be happy that the narrative surrounding me now isn't one of shallow celebrity. It's not about pictures of me in the paper having a fag outside a pub. It's about things that matter; things that we must address if we are to live a contented life.

I'm incredibly lucky to have two children who have carried not only me but themselves through to the other side. It was hard for them growing up and I'm so proud of the amazing young adults they've become. They've seen close-up the price of success. They've seen the before and after. They had those years where mum and dad were normal people getting on with day-to-day life like everyone else, and then they had the aftermath. While they understand why all that happened, it meant they had to grow up quickly, something which ended up with them reverse-parenting their own dad. The fact they could care for me and help me through addiction says so much about their emotional intelligence. I'm lucky that when they realised I was an addict they felt for me because they knew I was capable of being anything but that. I wasn't some deadbeat. I was someone who'd achieved in life, who'd won the Tour de France and had always been a big part of their lives growing up. They came at my problem from one place only – wanting to help. They'd seen the decline and understood why it happened.

That's not to diminish those nightmarish times. Both freely admit there were periods during my addiction when they'd say goodbye and not know if they'd see me again alive. They had to watch me change from this dad who was very present, totally invested in family life, to someone on drugs who they barely recognised. Bella remembers one time heading down to London to visit me, only to receive a message. 'Don't come. I don't want to see you. Just go home.' She ignored it and found me high on drugs in my car, which I'd actually been sleeping in for a short while, near Battersea Power Station. 'I'm so grateful you came,' she recalls me telling her, 'because I don't know what would have happened.' That's an incredible responsibility to put on someone at a young age. Ben, meanwhile, became a confidant. In the later stages especially he lived through the addiction with me. He says there were times, in particular when the extent of my financial worries became clear, when he felt I couldn't see a way out; that I almost gave up. He saw me reach a point where I didn't know who I was anymore. If I didn't recognise myself, how were those around me, him and Bella especially, supposed to recognise me either?

The video I sent to Ben while staggering to the cashpoint that night in 2023 is a case in point. But it was by no means the first, same as I'd often text long and rambling messages to Bella along a similar theme. Together, Ben, with his positivity, his encouragement to re-engage with my athletic side, and Bella, with her forensic approach to problem-solving, have played a huge role in pulling me from the wreckage of the person I was then and rebuilding me as the person I am now. Two different perspectives, two different mindsets, acting as one. As with my daughter Ava, both Ben and Bella have been a huge part of the motivation and inspiration to make sure I turn up in life now, for myself and for them. A few months ago, I was in London with Ben for the day. He told me later that when the time came to say goodbye it was the first time in years that he'd felt at peace with watching me walk into the distance. At last he knew I was in a good place. At last he knew I was going to be all right.

Having grown up with me as a dad, you could definitely read something into my daughter studying psychology A-Level, same as you could my son being a professional cyclist. It would be understandable had the scales fallen from Ben's eyes with regards to the sport. But I'm glad to say he doesn't see the negative elements, he just has the love of it. His drive to succeed comes from a different place to mine, but he's the same in that he's had to carry the weight of a cycling father. He's proud that his dad won the Tour but has also had to live with the pressure of people telling him, 'You're going to be as good as your old man.' It takes a lot of mental strength to deal with people putting that kind of expectation on you. In any area of life, having a dad who's achieved the ultimate in the field is always going to be a burden. Constant comparisons, constant questions, soon become a frustration. He's proud to carry the Wiggins name now, but in his younger years it was difficult.

Watching Ben progress as a cyclist would shine a light on my trauma. His early years' racing inevitably brought memories of Stan flooding back, while as he developed more and more I was reminded of my own dad's words – 'You'll never be as good as your old man.' I've been staunch in saying Ben will be better than me. I've been a constant driver of that narrative and have said it again and again in his earshot. While I genuinely believe he surpasses me as a person and a bike rider, I know also that I'm saying the words I really wanted my dad to say to me. It's stark that Ben's the same age now as I was when I was in contact with my dad. Those father–son relationships couldn't be more different. Yes, I'm Ben's hero, like my dad's my hero, but as characters me and Gary are poles apart compared with me and Ben, although there were times on drugs when I felt differently. Once, reaching out in desperation, I messaged a picture of myself to my mum. It had been two years since she'd seen me. I was rundown, haggard, a mess. 'Look!' I texted, 'I'm in a bad way.' Her reply came straight back. 'Oh, God, you look like Gary.'

Her reply gnawed at me. Did she just mean, 'God, you don't half look like your dad.' Or was there more behind the message? As in, 'You've ended up just like your dad. Drunk, lonely and your life falling apart.'

Free from drink and drugs, I don't feel the need to torture myself about such things. It's been a long and often painful journey, but I've reached the point where I can say honestly and unequivocally that I'm proud Gary's my dad. There was a side of him as a person that didn't work, but then again there's been times when *I* haven't worked as a person. I know how easy it is for that to happen.

I sometimes wonder what it would be like to meet Dad again as the person I am now. I've got a thousand things I'd like to ask. Equally, I know I'd never have reached my own place of peace had he been around. It needed his complete absence for me to work through my problems. I find comfort now in being able to forge my own relationship with him in my own way.

I wouldn't change anything about my relationship with my dad. There's not a day goes past when I don't think about him. When recently I moved into my new house, immediately I put out loads of pictures of the kids. But then I realised I'd done something else. Without even thinking about it, I'd put photos of my dad everywhere. On one shelf he'd be there in his racing gear, on another he'd be holding me as a baby. It occurred to me how, despite the dysfunctionality of the relationship, and the depth of my childhood desperation and craving, the person I am now receives a huge amount of comfort from just knowing that, while it might not have been the perfect relationship, I did have a dad once.

In one of those pictures I really do look like Dad. As an eight-year-old I went to Paddington Recreation Ground, where he met my mum, and watched the last event before it was demolished. I'm the spit of him, and I like that. It makes me feel close to him. If I could speak to Dad now, I'd tell him the little boy in that photo owes him everything. But maybe he knows that anyway. Maybe that's what happened when he appeared on my shoulder in my final race, at the velodrome in Ghent that played such a role in defining both of us.

My real partner in the madison that day was Cav, appropriate enough since he's basically flesh and blood too. We've always seen each other as brothers. Whatever's happened down the years we've had each other's backs. Like Ben says, 'Think of Brad, you think of Cav; think of Cav, you think of Brad.' After I retired, Cav was one of the few people who kept asking how I was. If he couldn't get hold of me, he'd be ringing Ben. He knew I was struggling and was constantly making an effort, messaging and asking if I was OK. Cav's one of the great cyclists. He's also one of the great human beings. Winning the madison with him, first at the World Championships, then at Ghent, was a beautiful way to finish a career which bit by bit I'm coming to appreciate all over again. There was a time where I held so much bitterness about cycling that to look back fondly on my time in the saddle felt almost alien to me. I've come to see how wrong that was. Winning the Tour de France was my lifetime's ambition. It was a landmark not just in British cycling but in British sport full-stop. Chris Hoy, no less, called it the 'greatest individual achievement in the history of British sport'. I blamed it and the London Olympics for everything that happened afterwards but what came my way after 2012 was never the fault of the bike. If anything, the bike was a place of purity. Man and machine working together to create something magnificent. I'm proud of everything I achieved on the bike, and will never again deviate from that point of view.

It would be wrong, though, to ignore the sport of cycling's propensity to mess people up. The number of professional cyclists I raced with who are no longer with us is as startling as it is depressing. I think back to those times when everyone's ego was flaring, everyone was racing to be first over the line, to the top of the climb, and then, in a flash, it seems so many of those same people are gone. I hear it way too much – 'Did you hear such-and-such died the other week?' Same when I'm looking at a photo from my career. All too commonly, alongside me, or in the background, will be someone who has died, often in tragic circumstances. I saw just such a picture the other day. In it was the French cyclist Robert Sassone, who won the madison at the 2001 Track World Championships. Robert took his own life aged just 37 having been diagnosed with cancer. In another photo I spotted Walter Bénéteau, also from France, who I rode the Tour de France with in 2006, found dead in a hotel room in Bali aged 50. Then there was Dimitri De Fauw, a Belgian lad I knew from the Junior Worlds in Cape Town, who I encountered again in my first few Ghent Six Days. He took his own life aged 28, said to be haunted by a crash at the 2006 Ghent Six Day when, during the madison, he collided with the Spanish cyclist Isaac Gálvez, who died of his injuries on the way to hospital. Stephen Wooldridge, an Australian Olympic and four-time world track champion, a familiar face to the Great Britain boys who regularly came up against his incredible talent, was 39 when he took his own life.

Perhaps best known of all those taken too soon is Marco Pantani, found dead after suffering heart failure from acute cocaine poisoning having isolated himself in a hotel room in Italy. He was just 34. Pantani won the Tour de France in

1998, and, as my story shows, isn't alone in struggling in the aftermath. I don't get the sense that the other British victors, Chris Froome and Geraint Thomas, will have the same problems as me in retirement, but Jan Ullrich, who won in 1997, had issues with alcohol and cocaine, and Lance also struggled with drink. It would be interesting to assemble a group of Tour winners and see what life was like for them. Just what was the price of success? There are people who dismiss sportspeople who've suffered addiction issues in retirement as weak and self-indulgent. They think they brought it on themselves and that's that. But that's not how life works. It's oversimplifying complex situations. Sportspeople carry the same psychological scars as everyone else. It's just that the intensity of sport means they're compartmentalised. Retirement is the flashpoint. With sport absent, repressed issues are released from the cannon. Effectively, in elite sport, we're institutionalised. My narrative from childhood onwards was that I was a cyclist and nothing else. 'You're that cyclist, aren't you?' people would say. 'That cyclist' – I couldn't have put it better myself. But what was I when I wasn't 'that cyclist'? Only when I stopped did I find out.

I realise, now more than ever, there's only so much that someone can take. And I used to take a lot – because I was accustomed to taking a lot. The weight of the world was normal to me. After all the childhood stuff, I went into a relentless regime of training and competing, became an Olympic champion, a husband, father, then more racing, more Olympic gold, my dad gets murdered, my grandad dies, more racing, Tour de France win, London 2012, Hour record, another Olympics. My son summed it up succinctly when he said whatever was happening in my life I never had time to compute it. It was always onto the next thing, and the next. Hearing that come from Ben, who knows me so well, was eye-opening. As a cyclist it was helpful to me that I didn't have time to compute anything. I was never diverted from my path to more and more success. As a person, however, it was disastrous. I was constantly avoiding the emotional reflection I so vitally needed. They say a vacuum will always be filled. Into mine eventually came cocaine. What started as a 'harmless' part of a night out, and then a coping mechanism, soon got me in a seemingly inescapable stranglehold – 'seemingly' being the operative word because one of the driving reasons for writing this book was to re-assure anyone with an addiction issue that they can actually escape its clutches. It is possible to kick a habit and rebuild from your lowest point. It's why I've kept those videos I recorded when I felt all was lost. I look at them now as a reminder of who I was and a marker of how far I've come.

These days I'm an addict to sobriety, but there are still areas for me to work on. Acceptance of praise is one of them. See me in the street and tell me you liked this book and I'll struggle. Chances are I'll use deflection. It's something I need to address, but at least the deflection no longer comes from a dislike of myself. There was a time when people would ask, 'Are you Bradley Wiggins?' and I'd say, 'I used to be.' I'd make it sound self-deprecating, hiding the underlying level of self-hatred. I assumed when they said 'Bradley Wiggins' they meant the version they'd seen on TV in 2012, and so being asked if I was him was like someone pressing a big red button marked 'Self-worth and Insecurity Issues'. After all, what was I if Bradley Wiggins, the bloke from 2012, wasn't there? These days, it's different. I'll still say 'I used to be' but in a comedic way, a modest way. It's deflection minus self-flagellation. But I've still got a really low baseline of what I think is worthy of adulation. If someone came up to me now and said what I'd done on the bike was amazing I'd be completely all right with it, appreciate what they were saying and accept it, but there'd still be part of me that thought that by winning the Tour de France I was just doing my job. It's like what Roy Keane says about praising the postman for delivering the mail. I'm the same if someone tells me I'm a nice person. 'Yes, but I'm supposed to be.' I think some of it is a reaction to being overpraised, for being called a hero and a legend. I also know that somewhere there has to be a balance. I need to accept praise rather than instinctively rebuff it.

I know a lot of my ingrained psychological issues aren't my fault. But I try not to see myself as a victim. It's odd, for example, to see myself described as a 'victim of abuse'. I've never thought of it in that way. Yes, I was abused, but that doesn't mean I'm a victim. I try to refrain from using that word. Easy to fall into a bad state of mind if you see yourself as a victim. The things that happen in our lives form who we are today. We can't change them. But is that the same as being a victim? I don't think so, same as I don't think it's a particularly helpful word when we're trying to look forward rather than dwell on the past.

I see my life in more positive terms. I can look at all the s**t that happened around the package and the TUEs, for instance, and know that, actually, my legacy hasn't been damaged. People tell me all the time how great it was that I won the Tour de France, that those golden days in the summer of 2012 will always be a treasured memory. Sometimes when I'd do a theatre show I'd focus on the bad stuff, to the extent that Ben and Bella pulled me up on it – 'This isn't what people have come to see you for.' It took me a while but over time I've come to see that they were right, and now I'm more than happy to reminisce about all things 2012 and every other highlight of my career. I can speak with confidence and purpose about myself and what I achieved.

I've reconnected with my knighthood in the same way. It will always feel odd to see 'Sir Bradley Wiggins' embossed on a bankcard or printed on a plane ticket, but that doesn't mean I don't respect and value the honour. I hold the memory of being knighted dear. 'You did remarkably well, didn't you,' the Queen reflected, 'all of you cyclists? Me and Philip [actually she probably said, 'Philip and I'] watched the cycling intensely.' After London 2012, the Manchester tattoo artist Louis Molloy got in touch to say he'd just inked a picture of me on the back of someone's leg. He added that he'd love to work on me. Which is why, if I pull my shirt up, you'll get a glimpse of Henry V, a fellow knight who also just so happened to conquer France, albeit six hundred years before I did. It's a work in progress and will eventually extend to a battle scene from Agincourt. I have a lot of tattoos, basically a pictorial version of this autobiography. No prizes for guessing in which period of my life I added the Greek god Atlas, who carried the weight of the world on his shoulders. Back then I could only dream of feeling free, like the swallows I saw at Mont Ventoux. Now I can look at those birds, captured in ink on my arms and hands, with empathy, not envy, along with several butterflies which every day remind me that something ugly can eventually blossom. The tattoo that's missing is the one that recognises my dad. My plan is to have a proper old-style pirate dagger with 'Dad' emblazoned on it. I think somehow it suits his character.

While multiple identities have accompanied me through life, tattoos have never been a disguise. If anything, through all the extremes of personality that followed 2012, they've been a visible reminder of who I really am; the part of me that remained untouched; the part that enabled me to survive. But there's one imprint on me invisible to all eyes except mine. Throughout everything that happened to me, in childhood especially, but also beyond, Grandad, with his dignity and humour, his common decency and sense of what was right, was a source of inspiration and strength. It's a huge sadness that he never lived to see me win the Tour de France, and not just because he could have cashed his winning betting slip at the bookies. But something happened on the day I secured victory that makes me wonder if he did know I'd won it after all. As I powered head-down to the finishing line in Chartres, I genuinely felt Grandad was with me. Exactly as with my dad in my last ever race, his presence made me feel unbeatable. He gave me another gear. In some ways, Grandad being there meant more than the triumph itself. If it hadn't been for him, no way would I have been in that position. Only because of Grandad did I have anything even resembling the tools to survive the various stages of my life, including the storm that hit post-2012.

I never considered how my life would be affected by reaching the pinnacle of cycling. I was essentially a famous person who wasn't interested in fame. Not easy for someone who from that point on would rarely be out of the tabloids. Winning the Tour was precisely what I'd wanted my whole life and then when it happened I was hit with an awful realisation – it wasn't what I signed up for. I wanted the success but hated what came afterwards, to the extent that I spent many years actively wishing it hadn't happened. While the mod personality I plumped for at that point is still in me to some extent, no way would I reach for it again as a disguise, or any other mask for that matter. I watched an interview with Johnny Depp a few years ago where he was talking about his obsession with Marlon Brando. When Depp finally met his hero, Brando asked him how many films he did in a year. 'I don't know,' replied Depp, 'three or four.' 'Too many,' Brando told him. 'We only have so many faces in our pocket, so many faces we can put on.'

That struck a chord with me. I can, though, forgive myself for 'Wiggo'. It's not uncommon for people to lack the confidence to be themselves in front of others. My mistake was to take that to an extreme that was unhealthy both for me and those around me, a dislike of my true self that lingered and lingered until I became normalised to it and had no sense of the person I'd become. Only recently have I been able to look back and see that actually I was in a really bad way. But it's not something I beat myself up about. Same goes for the clothes I used to wear, a visual reminder of the person I'd created. Rather than live in denial, there's a part of me that would like to keep those suits and put them on show one day in an exhibition. Let's face it, none of them fit me anymore! Back then I was 30 kg lighter.

I'm a different person now, in so many ways. Beneath my life are layers of tectonic plates that have been constantly rubbing against each other. With a better understanding of who I am, hopefully that seismic activity has now abated. The plates have settled. I might not have all the answers, but I've changed my relationship with my history to the point where I don't need all the answers. I've accepted that some things have to exist in the past; that the future is where my focus needs to be. British Cycling is a case in point. When I retired they wanted to put a statue of me in the Manchester Velodrome. I refused. I was pissed off with them about the Jiffy bag situation, but more than that I felt rejected and unappreciated. British Cycling had been my safe space at so many tumultuous times in my life, but towards the end it felt like they'd hung me out to dry. Yet something else to add to the hopelessness I felt as I slid into drug addiction.

More recently, however, that relationship has changed. My son's own cycling journey has taken me back to the velodrome to watch him race. Seeing the place through his eyes has gone a long way to repairing the hurt and damage. I've seen a lot of the old staff from back when I was racing. The people at the top of the organisation, meanwhile, have gone out of their way to make me feel part of something, a reminder of the stability and purpose that was so precious to me. In 2024, my pain was further eased when British Cycling inducted me into its Hall of Fame, something I can't imagine ever accepting just a short few years ago.

I'm enjoying rediscovering my relationship with cycling. Last summer, I rode around the Serpentine in Hyde Park. *Bloody hell*, I thought, *in 2007 the Tour de France came down here!* It feels sometimes like the magnitude of such events is only just starting to dawn on me. At the time, I took so much in my stride, and then later I was overwhelmed by a whole host of other thoughts and memories, most of them far less positive. Nowadays, people would say everything I achieved in my career I did with post-traumatic stress disorder, and who's to say they're not right? But it doesn't really matter what labels are attached to me. What matters is that I'm here, a new person, a different person, to the me I was in those darker days. There were times when I was clinging on to anything vaguely resembling reality. It would have been so easy to release my grasp; to have accepted defeat and plunged into the abyss. But I didn't. I live in the sunlight, testament to those around me who, through everything, held me close. And testament to myself for finding it within me to reach for a new beginning.

I wouldn't change anything now. Every moment of the past 45 years, good or bad, has made me the person I am. Hence *The Chain*. We all have a chain. The question is how we deal with its presence. I hope my story goes some way to show that none of us should feel shackled to our past, that there is always hope, a pathway forward. I want to live in a world where people feel encouraged to deal with the issues they carry in their head. Life isn't about ploughing on regardless, it's about being honest with ourselves, asking for help. Only then can we hope to make progress. Only then can we fulfil our potential. Only then can we deal with the chain.

There was a time when I never saw my chain. I never understood how, slowly, silently, it was dragging me closer and closer to oblivion. How, unchecked, it would have destroyed me and so much precious to me. Writing this book has flicked a switch. I see now that it exists. And I see that I will always carry it. But I don't see it as a burden, something to fear, something I wish to break and consign to history. I see it as something that makes me; something that explains me. Now I know the chain exists I can use it to strengthen the bridges I have yet to cross. I can take those steps in the knowledge of who I really am.

I hope by writing this book that those who have suffered similar experiences to my own will find hope in knowing they are not alone. I have been honest in my writing because I hope my honesty will help others. I can guarantee there are a lot of people out there keeping a secret of one kind or another. I want them to know that sharing is the key to moving forward. There are situations that seem impossible to deal with, as if they can never be escaped, but I know from experience, not least how cathartic it's been to write this book, that emotional openness is the only way to find release.

I'm back looking at that little boy, feeding the ducks in the park with his dad. I was him. I am him. I will always be him.

Free.

ACKNOWLEDGEMENTS

More than anyone I'd like to thank my incredible children, Ben, Bella and Ava. I would never have made it to this point without you. Thank you.

Ben O'Connor, thank you. I simply would not be where I am today without your loyalty, friendship and drive to do the best for me.

Mark Cavendish, you are a brother to me and always will be. Thanks to you and your beautiful family. You always care.

There are many others whose kindness and support has carried me through difficult times. I am hugely grateful to have friends who never fail to check in on me and have been there for me when I needed them.

Jed Stoneman, Dave Broadbent, Andy Palmer, Colin Sturgess, Jamie Alberts, Jon Cammegh – I can't thank you enough.

Ryan Pickard, you'll never know how much you inspired me to pick myself up. You are a true friend.

Alan Sellers and Scott Cosgrove, you have done so much for me. A sincere thank you.

Thank you to Darren Winter, my Australian brother, for always reaching out.

The same goes to all who offered a hand.

My beautiful little sister Madison! Love you.

Lance Armstrong, what can I say? You saw someone in pain and went out of your way to help them – thank you. I needed it, and it helped.

Thank you to my cousins Lois and Adam for always reaching out and never failing to bring a smile to my face.

Dia and Audrey Noir, thank you.

Lou Molloy – love you, mate.

Maurice Burton – thank you. You have always been an ally, always looked out for me and provided a precious link with my dad.

Polly Vernon – thank you for listening. Your understanding was very important for me at a difficult and vulnerable time.

Jonathan Taylor at HarperCollins, thank you for giving me the opportunity to write so freely about my life. Also, for putting my mind at rest in those moments when, inevitably, I'd wonder what the reaction would be to opening up in such an emotionally honest way.

Thank you also to John Woodhouse for your understanding and empathy; for knowing what this book needed to be and helping to put my thoughts into words.

It's inevitable in sport that you never get to thank 99.99% of the people who believe in you. So I'll take this opportunity to say to anyone and everyone who has supported me on the bike, who has stood at the side of the road and shouted my name, who has willed me on to victory in front of the telly, a big, big thank you. I say that from the heart. My cycling journey is dear to me. That it is to other people too is as heartwarming as it is humbling. I'm glad, and grateful, that you were there along the way.

I want also to thank you, the reader. By taking in my words you have given me reason to carry on as the person I am now. In your own way, each and every one of you is a lifesaver. You will always have my gratitude.

Finally, from my heart, I'd like to say a deep thank you to Courtney for everything you've done for me. You are without doubt one of the of the biggest reasons for where I am today. There isn't a moment where I ever forget it.